A MEDITATION ON GOING HOME

A Meditation on Going Home

DELBERT L. WIENS

Introduction by Alvin C. Dueck

RESOURCE *Publications* · Eugene, Oregon

A MEDITATION ON GOING HOME

Copyright © 2024 Delbert L. Wiens. All rights reserved. Except for brief quotations in critical publications or reviews, no part of this book may be reproduced in any manner without prior written permission from the publisher. Write: Permissions, Wipf and Stock Publishers, 199 W. 8th Ave., Suite 3, Eugene, OR 97401.

Resource Publications
An Imprint of Wipf and Stock Publishers
199 W. 8th Ave., Suite 3
Eugene, OR 97401

www.wipfandstock.com

PAPERBACK ISBN: 979-8-3852-0048-1
HARDCOVER ISBN: 979-8-3852-0049-8
EBOOK ISBN: 979-8-3852-0050-4

VERSION NUMBER 01/24/25

Unless otherwise noted, Scripture quotations are from New Revised Standard Version Bible, copyright © 1989 National Council of the Churches of Christ in the United States of America. Used by permission. All rights reserved worldwide.

Scripture quotations marked KJV are from The Authorized (King James) Version. Rights in the Authorized Version in the United Kingdom are vested in the Crown. Reproduced by permission of the Crown's patentee, Cambridge University Press.

Dedicated to my wife (1966–2023)
Marjorie Gerbrandt Wiens
Who edited many earlier versions of this book

Contents

Introduction by Alvin C. Dueck | ix

Preface | xv

Chapter 1　The Writer, His Motives, and His Mentors | 1

　　　　　　Excursus A: *Korn* versus Corn | 16

Chapter 2　Gratitude for Canonic Texts and Heritages Shaped by These Texts | 21

Chapter 3　The Images, Metaphors, and Stories That Shape This Meditation | 37

　　　　　　Excursus B: On Learning from *Korn*: Misplaced Idealism? | 56

Chapter 4　The Places and Times of *Korn* | 61

Chapter 5　The Work of *Halig* | 78

　　　　　　Excursus C: Treasures from the Past | 103

Chapter 6　Reflections on Mutual Aid | 105

　　　　　　Excursus D: The Strange Rarity of *Sacred* in the English Translations of the Bible | 122

Chapter 7　Mutual Nurture of *Halig* | 128

Chapter 8　The City as a Kaleidoscope of Peer Groups | 150

Chapter 9　The City and Its Congregations | 167

Chapter 10　Faith, Time, and Science | 183

Chapter 11   The Need to Question Our Readings of Canonic Texts | 206

Chapter 12   My Haphazard Pilgrimage Home | 220

A Glossary of Words for Which I Stipulate "Technical" Meanings | 235

Bibliography | 243

Introduction

THESE MEDITATIONS BY DELBERT WIENS recount his years growing up in a village named *Korn* and his reflections after periodic returns to his natal community. This is no mere anecdotal chronology. Rather, it is a narrative told by a consummate storyteller with the wisdom of an ancient philosopher and a fearless traveler. He scaffolds his reflections on the mythic *Korn*'s transformation into the modern Corn with insights garnered from his research in cultural history, his immersion in biblical literature, and his memory of ancient mythology.

Prof. Wiens's attachments to *Korn*, Oklahoma, run deep. He views his own story as profoundly shaped by its ethos, its leaders, and its spirituality. His reflections are honed by his education in a village school, his voluntary service in Vietnam, his theological training at Yale Divinity School (YDS), and his immersion in ancient history at the University of Chicago. In the end, he believes the village elders possess a wisdom still worth recovering. But he does not romanticize the church; he knows its weaknesses.

The book begins by articulating a conceptual framework through which Prof. Wiens interprets rural America in the first half of the last century. He does so in ways reminiscent of Martin Buber, Alasdair MacIntyre, Michael Walzer, and James Davidson Hunter. Borrowing from Martin Buber, a Jewish philosopher and theologian, Prof. Wiens makes a distinction between what is a sacred "Thou" and a neutral "it" as he traces the church's struggle with secularity. Hunter emphasizes the importance of a morality of everyday life. Beginning with his father, Delbert grew up with real life models who embodied in their life the values of the community. Scholars such as James Davison Hunter and Alasdair MacIntyre have lamented the absence of a coherent moral narrative. Hunter attributes this loss to the "denial of the moral as a category of lived experience."[1] According to Walzer, the result is the thinning out of a thick moral vocabulary unable to steer our public and private lives. What remains are abstract moral principles unmoored from

---

1. Hunter, "Denial of the Moral."

a thick morality. Moral character is reduced to the language of personality and spiritual inclinations. However, *Korn* provided a sacred canopy to cover all of life.

This book is about Prof. Wiens's moral formation as a Mennonite, philosopher, and leader. He was shaped not only by the ideas and vision of the Mennonite tradition but by the practiced morality of elders and members of the concrete Mennonite community (some two thousand people) living in and around Corn, Oklahoma, in the first half of the twentieth century. It is about a person whose faith was profoundly shaped by a community like Korn whose parts were organically connected. The concrete community honored common sense, observed community rituals, and revered accumulated wisdom. At its best the village was intimate, caring for its own, and keeping the common good in mind.

In contrast, abstract, urban institutions are communities with specific objectives such as education, tax collection, and international charity. Each institution focuses on one aspect of village life, and often with little communication between the parts. The individual is viewed as the vortex of abstract "laws" and when separated from the communal whole, are interpreted in terms of rational principles. The latter are communities of city dwellers who have left the premodern world behind and are now bereft of an older narrative.

After sketching the outlines of this theory in the first three chapters, Wiens applies his model in the next six chapters to service in the world, family structures, medicine, education and spirituality. The first nine chapters are largely narrative accounts before the book closes with several chapters that address complex philosophical issues that Prof. Wiens encountered repeatedly. Chapter 10 focuses on the conflicts between faith and science, and he explores how recent research can move toward greater reconciliation as suggested by Ilya Prigogine's view of science. A penultimate chapter focuses on what it means to speak of Scripture as mythopoetic and also as a record of real history. In the final chapter, Delbert recounts his harrowing journey from Vietnam to Oklahoma. Interspersed between chapters are excurses which expand on some theme in the chapter.

In the book Delbert tells us he knows who he is; he is from *Korn*. But he then quickly adds: "But who am I?" Well, there are actually many "Delberts." For me, the most prominent Delbert is the one who loves the church and who does not think piety is outmoded. A thread running through his many writings is the health of a congregation that mirrors the values of earlier villages and the reign of God.

Some may think Delbert's love of the church is actually romanticizing premodernism. This book is not a hagiographic account of the Mennonite

Brethren church. He is deeply pained by its errant wanderings. This Delbert worries about how the church and its leaders have sold out to modernism and forfeited the gifts of premodernism. He critiques programs that hoped to double church membership such as the "Decade of Enlargement." He shares how his own congregation was asked to leave the Mennonite Brethren family over the issue of affirming persons with differing sexual orientations. He is critical of those who don't take scientific research seriously. This doesn't sound like romanticizing to me.

Some divide being a scholar into two categories. There is the quiet, persistent scholar whose personal mascot is the hedgehog. On the other hand, there are scholars who, like the fox, find much pleasure in chasing rabbits. Delbert is both hedgehog and fox. The latter is a delight to watch as he follows a trail further and further away from the topic under discussion. Delbert the hedgehog shows up in the depth of the philosophical material he reads and digests (see chapters 10 and 11 in this volume).

Then there is the Delbert who is a lover of words: their sounds, their etymologies, their unique histories and meanings, and the emotions they evoke. All intrigue him. This book abounds with well-crafted, elegant sentences and word combinations. There is the Delbert who is an old soul with a curious mind. This Delbert is open to critique and ecstatic about a new idea or way of reading a text.

However, you may not know Delbert the humorist. The following story reveals this version of Delbert. He writes:

> Many years ago, a student asked how I had remained acceptable to Mennonites. I decided to try to keep a "straight face" and a matter-of-fact tone while inventing a response sufficiently absurd that his stereotype might be challenged. "Every generation or so, our elders send out a bright youth to learn as much as he can about the world and then return to report if there is any reason for us to rejoin it. They hope that we can return to reassure them that, yes, the world remains so absurd and bad that we are entirely right to retain our separation from it. I was one of those and, of course, I reassured them that we should continue to remain separate." I remember only that I was sure the student was intelligent enough to be amused by my response. I have, however, forgotten how that conversation ended.

There is also the Delbert who is transparent, confessional, and self-deprecating. Pondering the controversy that surrounded the publication of his essay "New Wineskins for Old Wine," he comments that he wished he had written more warmly rather than so analytically. After decades of teaching abstract philosophy, he wonders about his inconsistency in honoring concrete communities while abstractly interpreting them. All these "Delberts" have been a gift to me as I have grown to know them.

It was in the mid-1960s when, in my third year of my college education, Delbert's essay titled "New Wineskins for Old Wine" was published. I devoured it. For a young scholar living in a Mennonite community and studying to be a psychologist, this was heady stuff. For Delbert, the self is embedded in a community, rather than an isolated, autonomous individual as in the psychology of the day. Rural and urban cultures shape the contours of one's spirituality, one's emotions, and one's convictions.

I recently found my copy of the article with its multiple underlinings and comments in the margins. As I reread it, I again became aware of Delbert's impact on my scholarship and faith. I too critiqued excessive professionalism as an attempt to recover the experience of earlier, concrete communities. I realized that healthy communities can be a source of healing, not only the skilled therapist. In his book titled *Tribes*, Sebastian Junger argues that the suicide rate of returning veterans is so high because vets do not have a healing community to enter upon return. Those who did have close-knit communities, such as First Nation peoples, recovered much more quickly from post-traumatic stress disorder than those who did not.

As I read "Wineskins" I was in the early stages of leaving my concrete Mennonite Brethren community in Winnipeg, Manitoba, Canada, and entering graduate school (Appalachian State University) in Boone, North Carolina. There, we were invited to live with the African American Mennonite community, lead the young people's program, and run the camp program while I was studying counseling at the university. I experienced firsthand the organic, thick, rural, Black community. Over the years I saw the younger generation attend the university and move away to large cities, never to return.

For decades Chaim Potok's book *My Name Is Asher Lev* was required reading for my courses. It traced the tension between an artist caught between the ethos of his Jewish community and a modernist artistic sensibility. I used the novel to illustrate the shift in values and perspectives when living in villages, towns, and then cities.

My mother had lived in a village but I grew up in a suburb of Winnipeg where I studied modern psychology first at a Bible school in a town and later at the University of Winnipeg. I lived in a city where abstractions were well honed and valued. We lived our lives in a time when advanced education, the church, and family were separated from each other, and in my graduate studies I struggled with how to integrate them. I traveled with students to Guatemala, China, and Africa to learn how healers relate their faith to healing in their unique cultural settings. Much of my scholarship revolved around how faith and psychology could engage in conversation and how the church could be a source of healing.

Thank you, Delbert, for your encouragement along the way.

ALVIN DUECK

Preface

IN ADDITION TO INTRODUCING themselves and their intentions, prefaces are the place for writers to thank those who have informed their message and assisted their efforts. I begin mine by thanking the great "cloud of witnesses" who built the cities that shaped lives and identities. The quoted phrases come from the last chapters of the Epistle to the Hebrews where the writer compares the builders of earthly cities with pilgrims seeking a "lasting city . . . the city that is to come."[2]

We translate *city* from *polis*, a Greek word from which we also derive *politics*. It named the walled centers of originally independent city-states that reshaped patterns of behavior and the identities of their citizens. These city-states were soon subordinated to empires that again reshaped institutions and identities. We are creatures who must be nurtured into our humanity within a nexus of communities, and since the earliest communities were small groups of collectors and hunters that learned to domesticate plants and animals, it became possible for them to settle in *camps* that became *villages*, each with its surrounding fields and pastures.

Many early modern biologists had claimed that "ontogeny recapitulates phylogeny," asserting that in important ways the lives of individuals repeat stages of the development of the species to which they belong. Later scientific evidence did not support this unnecessary version of evolutionary theory. For example, that the bundle of cells expanding in a female's womb briefly has a vaguely scaly appearance was taken to be a consequence of fish having preceded humans. My playful observation that after birth infants "hunt" for a mother's breast to "gather" their nourishment also "recapitulates" the stage of hunting and gathering that preceded agricultural settlements may also be amusingly trivial.

But it at least points to my conviction that patterns and attitudes developed in premodern rural communities that I still encountered in *Korn* helped me to survive culture shock. Since postmodern humans confront

2. Heb 12:1; 13:14 (NRSV).

strange others and startling economic and cultural challenges, I am convinced that we must build into present communities the kinds of rituals and practices that relevantly "recapitulate" for postmodern youth what will enable them to thrive in constantly evolving ecologies.

I will show in chapter 10 that in my lifetime some of the certainties enshrined in classical "laws of nature" have had to be reformulated. I will show that some of the assumptions that supported incomplete and inadequate "laws of nature" also distorted our modern reading of canonic texts. That, too, must be corrected so that more of us can more clearly interpret canonic texts and the deeper wisdom revealed in them.

I think of myself as a cultural historian, one who tries to clarify the worldviews—the fundamental assumptions—about what is real, true, and good that underlie the intentions of those who built the villages, towns, and cities that shape us and our ecologies. Having discovered this as one of my "callings," I rejoiced that my own life began in a small rural village and that I also experienced the life of small towns on the way into large and larger cities.

The early formation of the people of Israel emerging through the Red Sea and experiencing their formation during forty years of wilderness wanderings loosely applies this mantra to a social organism. Americans identify themselves with pilgrims disembarking from the *Mayflower*. I use this image to express the profound sense of gratitude that I have developed for those who made it possible for me to relive what original and more recent "elders" experienced.

Since all infants are natural hunters and gatherers, I too had "dipped into" the earliest adventures of those who emerged from savannas and forests to build civilizations. I, therefore, begin by expressing gratitude for having been the child of Heinrich (Henry) Reinhart ("HR") and Barbara Kleinsasser Wiens. Several years after his birth, my father's parents moved to a rural community in western Oklahoma that, less than twenty years earlier, had been settled by those allowed to run when a gun was fired from a fixed point to claim a quarter section (160 acres) of virgin sod.

Though my father was perhaps halfway through high school when he had to drop out of school for the second time to help support his family, he was so "promising" that, at age nineteen, his small, rural congregation called him to become a pastor, one "apprenticed" to a senior lay pastor and respected farmer, though less educated than he. The pastor of the larger Mennonite Brethren (MB) church in the village of Corn, Oklahoma, mentored him. That one had become an "elder" whose leadership was acknowledged by many MBs who had settled in Midwestern states.

Though having perhaps only three or four years of education, this elder had read so widely that he carried on scientific experiments on his own farm. My father told me of having been taken on dark nights into the fields while Elder H. H. Flaming pointed out the constellations and told him the myths, explaining the functions and meanings of astral divinities. Elder Flaming's insights into human nature and his readings of scriptures were so respected that he was deemed a wise one who best voiced wisdom not yet clearly articulated by most.

After age twenty, my father was able to attend Tabor Academy in Hillsboro, Kansas. There he met Barbara Kleinsasser, a "Prairie Hutter" from central South Dakota whose father had been taken from a Hutterite colony by an uncle who had left the colony to become a developer of unbroken sod. She had been sent to Hillsboro to attend Tabor Academy. I had been given a wonderful heritage and loving, intelligent, progressive parents. I will continue to speak of that heritage and to honor its leaders.

HR brought Barbara to Corn, Oklahoma, a village so remote that the nearest paved road was six miles south of us. After my first year in its parochial high school, my parents moved to the town in California's San Joaquin Valley named Reedley. After graduating from college, I was subject to being drafted into the army or into the "alternative service" then possible for "conscientious objectors" to military service. I volunteered to enter the Mennonite Central Committee's program for community services or international relief efforts.

After one year in their home office, I was sent to Saigon, Vietnam (VN), to offer the proverbial "cup of cold water in the name of Christ" to those from north of the fourteenth parallel who were already disembarking from mostly USA naval ships in Saigon and other harbors. I arrived there in August 1954, about two months after the division of Vietnam into a "communist" north and a "democratic" south.

After being given the advice and assistance I gladly received from Vietnamese officials, American diplomats, and military officers, I soon realized that I was being drafted to help win the "hearts and minds" of Vietnamese who were forced to choose between very different worldviews. Would the ideology of Marxist Communism better secure freedom from colonialism and the prosperity the Vietnamese desired or would Western democratic ideals and a capitalist economy best serve them?

Though still a Mennonite idealist with "straw behind my ears," I was caught within cross-cultural and cold-and-sometimes-hot-war conflicts. Along with culture shock (I had not yet heard of that liminal condition) my "simplistic" religious ideals had to navigate between conflicting ideological "crusades." Several wonderful Mennonite Central Committee volunteers helped shape our program and did the "real work in the fields" while I struggled with logistics and officials in Saigon. I knew that blundering was inevitable and hoped that boldly blundering forward was better than spinning in circles.

After years of wondering how I had survived, I learned to be grateful that the disciplines and training I received in *Korn* had given me almost adequate strength and resilience. When that might not have sufficed, I was accepted into a wonderful family in Saigon. I have often marveled that a Mennonite conscientious objector to military service was "adopted" by an officer in the French Army in Indo-China. He was chaplain to Protestants in its regular army and those in its Foreign Legion and was pastor of the French Reformed congregation in Saigon.

He and his charming wife had a handful of young children and took care of rooms full of orphans in the servant quarters alongside their parsonage. Thank you, Bertrand and Daisy DeLuze, for having been better Christians, and sometimes even better "Anabaptist Mennonites," than I had been. From them and many Vietnamese I was beginning to learn that I should not judge strange *others*.

Their heritage included the French Huguenots and when my wife and I much later toured with them in Provence, France, we experienced the similar forest hideouts used for worship and the kind of torture chambers featured on a Mennonite tour we had much earlier taken of early Anabaptist and Mennonite sites. In Saigon I did not know enough about similar Reformation heritages to understand the similarities and differences of our Reformed heritages.

In the early sixteenth century, some of the educated youth who gathered around Ulrich Zwingli, a Reformer in Zurich, Switzerland, decided to reject the infant baptism that Christendom and major reformers continued to accept. Infant baptism had implied citizenship in both the kingdom of heaven and into the civic states of their homelands. The radicals who insisted on their right to follow what they understood to be the truth were called "Anabaptists" (re-baptizers) and that title persisted despite their objection that what they had not responsibly chosen had not been a valid baptism in the first place.

The Peace of Augsburg in 1555 ratified what the religious wars of the early Reformation had achieved. It essentially decreed that the religion of the citizens of a given territory must be that of its prince. This political compromise disrespected liberty of conscience, but it did contain a stipulation that citizens could sell what could not be removed and then emigrate peacefully. It also ruled that if one of Christendom's ecclesiastical principalities was ruled by a reformed prince, he would have to abdicate.

PREFACE

After three years in Vietnam and seven months of wandering "west," I enrolled at Yale Divinity School because my visit there told me that it might be the kind of monastery I needed to continue to recover. A week before, I had realized that my tears of gratitude while sailing past the Statue of Liberty had been genuine and that I was "coming home."

Mentors like Paul Minear, H. Richard Niebuhr, and Hans Frei, at Yale, taught me that in addition to demanding courses and brilliant lectures, the opportunity to experience the *presence* of a master who interacts with students remains priceless. After four years of teaching in Corn Bible Academy and in Tabor College, I attended the University of Chicago, under the supervision of the interdepartmental Committee on the History of Culture who equally earned my gratitude. After approving my request to study the philosophy and religion of the Greco-Roman Hellenistic Age, that program appointed Prof. Karl Weintraub to my committee. Weintraub was an eminent historian who was chairman of the Committee of the History of Culture. Prof. Robert Grant, another member, a notable historian of early Christianity, became my thesis advisor.

I remembered that Prof. Paul Minear at YDS had told me that reading a first-century epistle was like listening to one end of a telephone conversation that becomes clearer if one learns about the one you cannot see or hear. I told a few old friends that I was trying to learn to think like a pagan so that I could better read the New Testament and other ancient texts.

I am enormously grateful for students during the three years I taught at Tabor College and at Fresno Pacific College, which became Fresno Pacific University. Their abilities and interests inspired the courage and energy I needed to try to live up to their expectations. Colleagues like Paul Toews, Devon Wiens, Dalton Reimer, Richard Wiebe, Robert Enns, and many others modeled good teaching and helped shape the curriculum and vision that guided our efforts.

Prof. Elias Wiebe, who had been chairman of the Department of Education and who supervised a required course in educational values for master's degree candidates, invited several FPU colleagues to make presentations. For a number of years Prof. Adina Janzen and, then, Prof. Robert Enns taught that course. Much of the material in this memoir was stimulated by my lectures and subsequent discussions with teachers in surrounding schools who enrolled in that course.

Gordon Wiens was a former student at Fresno Pacific College who became an aeronautics engineer until deciding to teach science in a Fresno high school. He organized a study group that included our former pastor Bill Braun, Silas Langley (a scholar of medieval philosophy and theology), Stan Friesen (whose dissertation traced the contributions of early nineteenth-century missionaries in Africa to the development of comparative anthropology), Marshall Johnston (a scholar of ancient Greek and Latin writers at Fresno Pacific University), and others. For a year or so, they critically responded to what I was writing and encouraged me.

I end this preface by returning to what I experienced while growing up in a rural village still in living contact with medieval and even primeval traditions. Even technologically sophisticated postmodern civilizations may need to help every new generation to *recapitulate* early stages of human life to realize their potential—and even to survive. Now, many years later, this is the book I am readying for publication.

In addition to my gratitude to my elders, to students, and to colleagues, I am profoundly grateful to my spouse who died June 4, 2023. Marjorie Gerbrandt Wiens, MD, has literally enabled me to live and to thrive. She was the only cardiologist "on call" and in the hospital during my first heart attack. We were married during the summer after my first year at the University of Chicago. She has edited an almost endless number of the revisions of what I have been writing. More importantly, the two of us had become the "one" who has sustained our identities while enriching our common life.

Linda and John, our children, with their spouses, Steven Pauls and Carmen Pauls were cousins who have supported our senior years and whose larger "clan" has graciously included us. Linda and Steve's children, Rowan, Nolan, and Daniel Pauls and John and Carmen's children, Jacob, Nina, and Simon Wiens helped Marj and me to retain our youth while respecting our age. To these and to the entire "cloud of witnesses," I dedicate this book.

Since Marj's death, Prof. Alvin Dueck assisted me in preparing this manuscript for publication. He was another cherished colleague at Fresno Pacific University, where he taught psychology and helped found our affiliated Mennonite Brethren Biblical Seminary's Marriage and Family Therapy program. There he trained pastors and students to become more effective counselors until Fuller Theological Seminary in Pasadena, California, invited him to guide their students to more closely integrate theology and psychology. While there, his writings at the intersection of these sensibilities led to John Templeton grants to collaborate with Chinese psychiatrists and psychologists in exploring indigenous forms of spirituality in their psychology of religion research.

His critical insights and supportive instincts have been so appreciated that I can only hint of his contributions. I have depended on him to guide me through the computerized complexities of compiling the volume that is being published. More importantly, his shared religious and ethnic heritage and our long friendship have shaped our careers and our intentions. His scholarship in cultural psychology and mine in cultural historiography have so closely complemented each other that he has helped me clarify to those of my heritage, and to others, the subtle dangers of modern and postmodern technological assumptions and attitudes that subvert traditional classical and Christian worldviews.

Delbert Wiens,
2024

CHAPTER I

The Writer, His Motives, and His Mentors

IN THE FIRST PART of this introductory chapter, I tell stories to convince readers that beyond the normal bonding of children with their parents and with those who are a living part of their "larger family," I took for granted that I had experienced odd relationships to those with whom I had grown up. The birth of my sister Judith followed mine within two years, but her interests were so different from mine that, despite her admirable qualities and my respect for her devotion to others, our lives were quite different.

Another sister and a brother were born while I was in high school. During my junior year at Fresno State College, I lived at home with them while commuting to Fresno. In Vietnam I had missed them the most. After returning, I enjoyed Kathy and Douglas for several summers, but they belonged to a different generation. I grew up wanting to become a peer of my elders.

Robert Vogt, a student at Corn Grade School three years older than I and who, in its high school, had become one of their best athletes. Much later he confessed, "I didn't like you while growing up. You were the one my aunts mentioned when scolding me, 'Why can't you be more like that nice little Wiens boy?'"

Another story illustrates my early reputation. After graduating from Yale Divinity School, I had returned to teach English because for one year they had not been able to hire an English teacher for Corn Bible Academy (CBA). I had been invited to entertain a Sunday evening audience with adventure stories, and was accompanied by two Corn couples. One of the wives was a second cousin with whom I had enjoyed clan picnics and home visits. On the drive back to Corn from Gotebo, we noticed that she was quietly giggling while sitting between her husband and me. Her quiet laughter exploded into almost hysterical shrieks until she became a bit abashed and was able to gasp, "To think . . . to think . . . that Delbert Wiens . . . would ever do anything exciting."

There was silence while the rest of us stared ahead and smiled. Though Robert Vogt had not yet summed up my early reputation for me as "that nice little Wiens boy," all would have agreed with him. Indeed, his older brother had been the driver who was returning us from Gotebo. That brother had recently become the superintendent of Corn Bible Academy.

The sister born a bit less than two years later than I had come home from Corn Public Grade School crying because boys had mocked her for having a brother who "read the dictionary," and I indignantly started to protest that canard. Then I realized that a bookish vocabulary and eager attention to the *Reader's Digest* "Increase Your Word Power" features had made me guilty as charged, even if I did not often use dictionaries.[1]

THE HERITAGE THAT HELPED TO SHAPE MY PARENTS AND *KORN* ELDERS

My father's Uncle Henry joined central Kansas Mennonites seeking cheap farmland or business opportunities. Their parents or grandparents had come to Kansas from Ukraine, Crimea, and Poland for the same reason. Those who came to what later became the eastern part of Washita County, Oklahoma, where what had been a tiny part of a Cheyenne-Arapahoe Indian reservation had been opened to homesteaders and settling along eastern and western sides of the Washita River. Probably less than a fourth of it lay on its western "Bessie" side of the river.[2]

The village later called Corn was situated nearer the eastern border of Washita County. It was *Korn*'s acknowledged center.[3] Our western border was along a road from Clinton past Bessie, where I was born, to Cordell, where I lived during half of my first ten years. Perhaps a dozen Mennonite families had lived on this border. When my father became the principal of *Korn*'s parochial high school, we moved into the center of our own ethos. Though at last at home, I was an outsider in its grade school. I became aware of oddities in cultural history long before I heard that phrase.

---

1. See Excursus A for a more detailed history of the two names: *Korn* and Corn.
2. Penner, *Mennonites on the Washita*, 112–113.
3. Penner, *Mennonites on the Washita*, 88, 205–207; Wiebe, *Let Us Stand United*, 25–33.

The two thousand or so of *us* considered by *Englisha* neighbors to be an ethnic *them* was more complex than I had imagined. The *Korn* church was larger than the four country congregations north and/or west of it combined, and three of these belonged to a different Mennonite denomination. There had originally been a small rural fifth church belonging to a third closely related group of Mennonites. All of the early settlers had come intending to remain loyal to our religious and cultural ideals and patterns of life. Our mother tongue was German.

We agreed with our neighbors, whom we called the *Englisha*, that we were significantly *other* to *them*. We were ethnics, and *ta ethnē* was the New Testament word for *gentiles, nations, "them."* (When I can, I avoid capitalizing *gentiles*, a common name for *others* not belonging to a chosen *"us."*) Premodern rural villagers did not organize their lives around systematic theologies or by equally abstract scientific or political ideologies.

Contemporary readers may be puzzled when I express gratitude that I had experienced life in a rural village in western Oklahoma that was still strongly linked to an earlier worldview and to the treasures that could be learned from a disappearing generation of respected elders. I have agreed that the nostalgia of senior citizens must not distract any of us from addressing the good and the bad of our "progress" and I repeat my conviction that those who do not understand the past stumble into unfortunate consequences.

Years after leaving Corn, I realized that *Korn*, the early name that expressed my *mythos* of Corn and those who lived on its surrounding farms, had extended my post-graduate education. While many were still living in sod houses, its founders realized that the young with little to do during long winter days were spending long periods with each other and sometimes staying overnight in the homes of their girlfriends.

When one of the boys got a finger shot off while hunting, the adults decided a school was needed and found Prof. Duerksen. He was a Mennonite Brethren (MB) emigrant who had attended a German university and had become a German teacher in a non-Mennonite Kansas College that was closing that program. They invited him to start a school, helped him to secure a farm adjoining the village, and Corn Bible Academy (CBA) was created. Soon older teenagers were reading German university textbooks that included Goethe, Schilling, Kant and other literati. Those acquainted with the Bible schools and Bible institutes of the Bible Belt will guess that neighbors might distrust *Korn*'s old but complex ethos.[4]

---

4. Penner, *Mennonites on the Washita*, 278–99.

THEY HAD TO LEARN HOW TO REBUILD TRADITIONAL COMMUNITIES

I had listened to my elders. Despite the questions I learned to ask during my college years, I still aspired to inherit the promise of things modern in a way that would express what it meant to be an Anabaptist disciple of Christ Jesus. I graduated from college and enlisted for a Voluntary Service assignment with the Mennonite Central Committee (MCC) through which almost all North American Mennonites channel their relief and other charitable efforts.

A year later I was in Vietnam helping to resettle some of the hundreds of thousands of refugees that were leaving the North Vietnam of Ho Chi Minh who was the heroic liberator who helped deliver his fellow citizens from "white Western colonizers." John Foster Dulles, then secretary of state, had picked a former mandarin, Ngo Dinh Diem, who had been in the court of a recent Vietnamese emperor, to become the president of a "free Vietnam" as defined by Western "Cold Warriors."

President Ngo was a Christian who had sworn fidelity to the Virgin Mary and was then in a New Jersey monastery. Despite his good intentions, he did not control large sections of South Vietnam, nor his own canny brother, whose glamorous wife, I thought, matched fabled oriental "dragon ladies." I went to Vietnam perhaps two months after he did in mid-1954.

I met an English contractor in a Chinese village in Cambodia while returning overland from Singapore to Bangkok. The next morning I crossed the Mekong River to return to Saigon. He invited me to accompany him to his local agent. Well "into his cups," he asked me whether I knew why an American military base he had contracted to build hadn't yet been finished. No, I hadn't, and he raved on, "I'll bribe any yellow face in Asia to do business here. I gave the president's sister-in-law her 20 percent, but I have my principles. I will not bribe an American officer demanding 5 percent." I decided that I now had evidence for what many in Saigon insisted was her usual take. There were more reasons why a great many South Vietnamese patriots were happy to be "liberated" from Western and American domination by Ho Chi Minh.

Here, with others in our unit, I offered the biblical cup of cold water in the name of Christ. "We envy you, Delbert, we really do," said a wonderful, charming young lady in the education office of the official US aid mission in Vietnam. She had grown up in a suburb of New York City and her father was an oil company vice-president. How could she envy me? Unlike her, I was not a sophisticated center of the young adults in one of Saigon's elite international sets. She sensed my stunned incomprehension and finished lamely, "You seem to know where you come from."

I did know; I came from *Korn*, Oklahoma. I was also becoming aware that I was not who I wanted to be. It was not that I had failed in the tasks I had been sent to do. The problem was in myself. I had been taught the ideal of incarnating the Sermon on the Mount, but how could I "give to those who asked" after learning that those who asked might not be the neediest and often had ulterior motives? And while regularly saying no, was I learning the empathy their suffering deserved and remaining capable of acting? Toward the end of my stay in Vietnam I had become spiritually, psychically, and physically drained. I understood the apostle Paul's words about going to save others and becoming the castaway. I knew where I came from, but who was I?

I KNEW I WAS THE SON OF HEINRICH REINHART ("HR") AND BARBARA (KLEINSASSER) WIENS

My father had been kept at home to take care of his ailing mother, to clean the house, and to cook his family's meals the year he should have completed grade school. He had later been asked to drop out of high school to help save a failing family farm. Our ethnic ethos had taken for granted that daughters would do that and even work as maids in nearby towns, but his parents chose to allow them to complete high school. One of them then married a young man from Corn who attended Tabor College, and when HR was past twenty years of age they invited the younger brother, who had been deprived of the education he had wanted, and to live in Hillsboro, Kansas, with them so that he could finish its academy and two years at Tabor, our MB college.

After marriage to a fellow Academy student from South Dakota, HR and his bride moved to Corn after the first year of the Great Depression. This included the era of the Dust Bowl. He had been hired to teach the upper four grades of a country school northwest of Corn. My mother was hired to teach the lower four grades, but though students could all watch the mating and birth of farm animals, observing the progress of a teacher's pregnancy was unthinkable. And so, she could not teach. My father had resumed his unpaid lay pastor position in the Bessie country church. In spite of the food often found in our Model A Ford after a church service, it became obvious that my father had to find a better paying job to survive the loss of my mother's job.

A year or two earlier, I had discovered the flash cards my mother had used while teaching in a one-room school in South Dakota before marrying

HR. Lining them up on the floor against the wall, I would ask *"Mama, wass sagt das?"* (Mother, what does that say?). She would say, *"Dass sagt"* (that says) and say the English word. That was when they began to speak English with me. Perhaps before attending grade school, I was able to take my turn reading from the German Bible during Bible study sessions on Wednesday-night prayer meetings in our country church.

When I was five years old, our family moved to the county seat on the western border of our ethnic turf where my father had been hired to manage the only auto parts store in the county and do the accounting for its attached repair shop. Its owners were also members of the Bessie MB country church. I attended the first four years of grade school in Cordell, after which, though my father had finished only two years at Tabor College, his abilities and relational skills had been recognized, and he agreed to move to Corn to become its Bible Academy principal.

MY MORE INTIMATE RETURN TO *KORN*

Since the three classes I was asked to teach at CBA after my return from Vietnam and my graduation from Yale Divinity School (YDS) was not a full-time assignment, I was asked to assist the former full-time English teacher who was serving the large MB church while they sought a "suitable" pastor. Like my father, his admirable skills had been learned from the traditional patterns in a rural southern Minnesota Mennonite community, and I happily agreed. Though not using the German word, he soon asked me to conduct an *Andacht*, a devotional service, with a retired farmer in their old people's home. I asked the old man to tell me about his life, and he told me of crop failures, the illnesses that had troubled his family, and his apparent failure to be a successful farmer. Of course, he had suffered the Great Depression and the years of the Dust Bowl era before experiencing post-World War II prosperity. He told me that he had become convinced that God had abandoned him. Though he could not clearly express the resolution of his despair, it was clear that he had eventually experienced God's healing *Presence*.

I had not taken the practical theology courses YDS had offered. Nor had I received the mentoring of a lay elder, and I sought for a suitable response. I dared to tell him that my own travail had been different from his but the *pattern* of doubts and their resolution had been the same. I doubted that he would quickly understand the distinction I was making, but he responded with such joy that despite the differences between our lives, I suspected that he might also be rejoicing that those awkward *words* revealed the treasures we shared.

I don't know how my father would have responded, but eight years later, while he was preparing to die, he expressed regret that though his country Mennonite church asked him to become a lay pastor at age nineteen, he had never been able to attend a seminary. I dared to tell him that I thought that the mentoring given him by one of the last of our lay pastors—who had been designated an elder and mentored other pastors—had better prepared him for ministry than the 'Bible Schools' or 'Institutes,' then considered acceptable by 'Bible Belt' churches, could have. I had earlier known of his despair at being robbed of the education he had eagerly wanted.

MY RETURN TO HR AND OTHER MENTORS

By then my father understood that, beneath my brash rhetoric, I had learned to honor his heritage and that he had become a mentor to me. He had modeled how to be pastoral and how to confront those angry at him. The year I taught at CBA, several adults to whom I was introduced as "HR's son" grasped my hand and stared into space while tears welled into their eyes. I assumed that those responding openly to me were remembering HR and I have supposed that the use of initials made them both a title of honor and an icon of their deeply bonded lives.

While passing in the hall shortly after school began, the superintendent asked me whether I wondered why I had been asked to come. "Constantly," I replied. After graduation from seminary, I returned home, waiting for a "call." As the weeks passed, I realized that my mother was getting impatient. Finally, she burst out, "I don't know why you are sticking around. You know good and well that no MB church will ever have you." For me, a call didn't have to be from a church, but I said only that I was at peace with waiting a bit longer. About three weeks before the 1961 fall school terms began, the phone rang and an apologetic CBA board member asked if I could accept a one-year, part-time assignment to teach three English courses. They had been unable to replace a teacher and were desperate.

The superintendent took me into his office and showed me a letter of recommendation no one had requested. A much-admired minister who had also grown up in Corn had written, "Dear Brethren in Corn, Delbert Wiens has just graduated from Yale Divinity School and we don't know whether he is worth a hill of beans anymore. *But he is HR's son, and we have to find out. Hire him.* I had reasons to admire a still partly premodern culture willing to welcome home prodigals—or even give a possible heretic—a chance. The sentence I highlighted in one of the most effective letters of recommendation I have ever received was more about our heritage than about me. Maybe, just maybe, ethnic blood could be at least temporarily thicker than baptismal water. I said I would come.

It is true that in ethnic communities the duplication of given names and surnames may require the use of one or more initials, plus perhaps an added middle name. But since practical reasons do not formally contradict an honorific use, I cite the influence of J. B. Toews, J. A. Toews, John E. Toews, and John B. Toews. The first three had the same given name, had distinguished churchly and academic careers, and had become college presidents. I will cite the third (John E.) most often in following chapters as the commentator on Romans whom I have most closely followed. The fourth (John B.) wrote important historical studies on MB origins and other topics, as had J. B. and J. A. Toews. Though as distinguished, Paul (whom I will also continue to cite) and James Toews were not named *John* and did not need an initial. They were the youngest of the six I choose to mention. Paul taught American history, was given startling access to Russian archives on Mennonites in Russia, and edited studies of MB academic institutions and denominational developments. James became a consultant in welfare and health policies in Oregon and later in Washington, DC. None of these came from *Korn*. Surely my experience of a small sample of such excellence among a small segment of my heritage is less odd than I had thought.

As among Native American peoples, immigrant Jews, and more recent immigrant religious traditions, rural enclaves of Anglican, Catholic, and Protestant ethnic communities often retained the presence of enlightened sages and of sanctified saints, and contact with first-rate scholars. Ignorance or rejection of these old-fashioned traditions may account for many of the sad consequences now afflicting our villages, towns, and cities. In this book I hope to encourage many to recapitulate our experience of richer heritages that can help to rebuild our cultural health and holiness.

Shortly before the start of World War II, some local "patriots" had met to sit in chairs provided in the space along the auto parts store's front windows to chat with each other. On one of those days they chose to taunt my father working behind the counter by loudly praising Joseph Stalin, "America's greatest friend and ally" in the coming war against Germany. After a while my father quietly responded that they needed to learn that Stalin was as evil as Hitler.

He was vividly aware of Stalin's brutalities against those of our ethnic clan members who had been sufficiently prosperous to remain in Ukraine and of the far greater number of murders of Russian citizens who resisted communism than the murders committed by German armies and Hitler's attempts to destroy Europe's Jews. He knew that those taunting him did not agree with doctrinal traditions that our elders had taught us, and he did not confront them with biblical passages they had not well enough understood to interpret differently or how to counter with other passages.

Another "patriot" confronted my father by demanding, "Wiens, what if *all* believed and acted as you do?" My father waited until his accuser "heard" the irony of his accusation and hastily departed. All who knew HR knew also that if everyone were like "this Wiens," there would be no wars.

Nor did he confront those taunting him in the auto parts store with a biblical text accepted by our elders that

> our struggle is not against enemies of blood and flesh, but against the rulers, against the authorities, against the cosmic powers of the forces of evil in the heavenly places. Therefore take up the whole armor of God, so that you may be able to withstand on that evil day, and having done everything, to stand firm. Stand therefore, and fasten the belt of truth around your waist, and put on the breastplate of righteousness. As shoes for your feet . . . proclaim the gospel of peace.[5]

I was proud that his *presence* and repute had enabled him on the next day to brush past a group that confronted him on his way from the bank to the store. They threatened to beat him up for not being a patriotic American. We were ethnic Germans and many of our young men were conscientious objectors to bearing arms. Can any of us stand aside when innocent and even not-so-innocent victims face brutal violence? It is as necessary for us to rethink the resort to force as it is for others of us to rethink whether their refusal to resort to force masks more subtle weapons that are equally non-spiritual.

Because my father may have been the only minister in the larger *Korn* community who understood the issues and who also had the legal smarts to manage the constant rejection of appeals for recognition of the right of those drafted to agree to accept alternative service to their country's welfare that did not entail bearing arms, our family suffered "official" abuse.

Each time appeals up the bureaucratic ladder denied their appropriate classification, FBI agents had to be sent to verify their sincerity. These agents had learned that coming first to our home in Corn had most efficiently aided their unwanted task, and they had appreciated HR's transparent candor and cooperation.

One day the knock on our door announced the chief FBI director of its agents in several surrounding states. On the drive to the young man being

---

5. Eph 6:12–20.

interviewed, he told HR that, before joining the FBI, he had been a Methodist minister and they warmly responded to each other. He also invited my father to accompany him to Cordell to visit the county draft board office. While he strode to the desk, my father quietly slipped into a chair near the door. Perhaps the only member of the board who did not know my father by sight was present that day.

When the reason for his visit was announced, the board member interrupted with explosive insistence that a *Wiens* in Corn was the source of their problem and was the worst traitor in the area. After he subsided, the chief gestured behind him, "There he is," and began *his* tirade. He wanted to know how they couldn't understand that Congress had granted sincere objectors to bearing guns the right to substitute work in the national interest instead of military service. His agents had to waste time investigating conscientious objectors rather than importantly hunting Nazi spies. And if previous appeals failed, the final appeal to the president assured that justice would prevail. Couldn't they understand what best served the country?

I don't use quotation marks because I remember best the emotions of the report he gave us when he got home and I trust my memories of the themes the FBI chief expressed. I later appreciated that my father may have wondered whether he had too much enjoyed hearing what that Washita draft board member heard. I don't think their attitudes and practices changed, and I add only that when he was driven back to Corn, he saw a field that had young tender ears of corn. He took an armful knowing that the owner of that corn-on-the-cob would be happy that the chief's family would enjoy them.

And I know that I was learning to appreciate the wisdom of sage elders and not to reject old traditions while some of my church comrades overhearing the speculations of their still-young parents were learning to reject "old fogies." Since the home and "street" south German dialect spoken by my Hutterite mother was unintelligible to those in *Korn*, whose Low German evolved from the flat lowlands of Holland and North Germany, my parents spoke High German and English to each other. Until between age four and five, I spoke only the academic and churchly High German that marked me a pious and academic "preacher boy." Fortunately, my church friends also had to learn English before or while attending grade school.

Like many of my peers, I should have been tempted by the "grass" beyond our ethnic "fences." But I had begun to admire my father's wisdom and relational skills. Even students he had to discipline mostly respected his fairness and appreciated his genuine concern for their welfare. The year I returned to teach English, a former CBA student confided that another student's aggressive attempts to win the affection of a girl he desired had so frightened her that my father had to intervene. The man telling me about this incident told me that, for a while, he and other boys had taken turns guarding our home at night lest that angry boy deliver on his muttered threats to assault him.

I could have reminded my father that one of the summers I was home from studies at Tabor College, the National Association of Evangelicals was holding a West Coast assembly in our large Reedley church. He was then the assistant pastor and he and my mother were hosts to several Evangelical national officials. HR's parents had inherited a small house from its bachelor owner in return for caring for him. When we moved to Reedley, my grandfather and a cognitively disabled older son had moved into the deceased bachelor's home, and we occupied the larger one so that my parents could feed and care for them. After the NAE officials left, I chided my father for having allowed our guests to assume that we were awed yokels in the presence of greatness when they too eagerly recited what they took to have been brilliant responses in debates with liberals. My father smiled and told me that he had decided it was time for me to learn that even the great of this world have feet of clay. I later told him he had misjudged and that I had decided to look elsewhere for the great of this world. I did not then admit that my "elsewhere" should not automatically exclude evangelical leaders and that to cling to scornful judgments revealed my feet of clay as much as their ripostes had done.

I had learned to admire Dad's courage and strength. While a student at Tabor's academy or college, he had climbed the brick wall of its large administration and classroom building and into an open classroom window on the third floor. Awed students awaited his reappearance on the ledge that hid its mostly flat roof. He rejoined them after walking around the building on a narrow ledge.

A few years later, when directing and teaching at the two-room grade school, he was accosted by three large teenage sons of out-of-state families of itinerant cotton pickers. They gave up their assault when he quickly tossed each of them to the ground. Even into his early middle-age years and overweight, he could easily flip onto his hands to walk and almost *run* down the street with his legs stretched above him.

During the first or second year of his superintendence of Immanuel Academy in Reedley, California, some money had been stolen from a student's clothes hanging in the men's shower room during a physical education session. I suppose my father had talked with the one accused of having taken the money and had realized that real evidence was nonexistent. He also knew that this one was a loner who had been widely disliked, and he decided to teach those who shunned him a lesson.

It was early in the second semester and a substantial sum of tuition money had been deposited in the office safe. He filled a money sack and walked into a study room where the accused and a number of others were doing their homework assignments. He gave him the bag of money and our car's keys and asked if he would please take it downtown to have the bank deposit it. On the way out of the room, he turned and warned him that his old car's brakes weren't entirely reliable and to be careful. The others sat in stunned amazement while the accused took the money and left.

The money was deposited in the bank, but my father had to deal with the consequences of his action. Whether or not he had suspected that the accused was homosexually oriented, it seemed likely that he was when he developed a crush on my father and began to haunt the alley behind our house. After graduating, he moved to a different part of California and became a trusted bank officer. Since my father normally followed up after disciplinary actions in his teaching and later pastorates, I am sure that he continued to take an interest in his welfare. Those he disciplined often became close friends.

ELDER H. H. FLAMING, MY FATHER'S MENTOR

Later in life, I wished I had asked my father to tell me more about his "master mentor." I think he was the one who told me that though this elder had received only about four years of grade school education during a limited number of winter months, he had read so widely in nearby libraries that he had carried on scientific experiments on his own small farm. At greater length, HR talked about accompanying him through the fields on dark nights while the elder pointed out the constellations and explained the stories, the *mythoi*, expressing what I later learned in universities about the classical worldview, theology, and understanding of the natural and human sciences.

When he became the principal of CBA, my father attended the state college at Weatherford, about sixteen miles from Corn, while I was completing grade school. He received a bachelor of science degree so that the school would have a teacher capable of teaching biology and agriculture courses. Another Corn boy, who was a classmate at CBA, became a professor at Oklahoma State University in Stillwater and was a nationally recognized expert on the science of the growing of corn and other crops. A few at Corn may have planted their gardens and perhaps larger crops according to the lore of the phases of the moon and of the conjunctions of the planets, though I never heard gossip about it, and I doubt that the *Farmer's Almanac* they followed relayed astrological lore.

The year I taught English at CBA, members of the MB Church Council decided to bring its constitution and bylaws up-to-date, and asked me to be their secretary. Its sentences elicited memories of the context and of those who wrote these documents (the constitutional bylaws referenced above). I had stumbled into a postgraduate seminar in cultural history and was learning to look for sages among farmers who might not have finished grade school.

I have excused my two or three eavesdropping episodes on youthful curiosity. I confess what ironically illustrates my growing respect for some church leaders and for the importance of taking traditional elders seriously. Our home was so small that guests slept in my bedroom. I was placed on the couch in the front room if a visiting church leader was placed in my bedroom when several would come for meetings of an important district commission on which my father was a member. If, after a few minutes, I turned my back to the table where they sat, changed my breathing, and appeared to relax, their conversation would get interesting.

I remember a session that dealt with a serious moral issue. When able, later, to act responsibly, I realized that I had never talked to anyone about what I heard. Curiously, I could not, later, remember any of the details about these problems. I had remembered only the earnest efforts district church officials made to bring healing to those implicated and to restore reconciliation and grace. Those whom I could respect as the great in this world were not only brilliant and gracious teachers I had later known, they included also those who humbly and lovingly rebuilt the small communities for which they were responsible.

I close this part of my meditation on the influence of saintly elders in our tradition with my father's description of Elder Flaming's ability to guide its most important deliberations. At regularly scheduled district or larger gatherings of ministerial and lay delegates to discern and to order the faith and the life of their scattered communities, many hours over several days could be devoted to earnest debates about difficult theological and moral issues.

HR told me that H. H. intently listened. When he rose to speak, a hush of respectful attention followed and he would say, "Brethren, I have been listening, and here is what I have heard." My father told me that it quickly became their consensus.

I later wondered whether this brief account of his influence could have been adequate. I also reflect on my father's respect for his saintly intelligence. I now wonder whether the "hearing" of Elder H. H. had also gone beyond what other delegates had said. What else had he heard or read? Yes, it would become their consensus, but would it have also been an enlightenment they had received—and have felt like a revelation?

I remember only a brief accidental meeting on the street of Corn the year I taught there. We greeted each other and I remember that though no larger than I, his erect spare figure and serene countenance expressed an aura, a *presence*. I have wished that a careful account of his life and influence had been compiled while those who had known him still lived.

WHAT HAD THE ELDERS BEEN TALKING ABOUT?

Beyond the usual issues of daily life, they told us about the inherited virtues and practices they continued to cherish. Because these were neither problems nor projects, I suspect that they mostly took for granted the good things that had been built into them. They had absorbed them by osmosis in growing up.

Since they wanted us to be both modern and godly, they transformed their talk about the traditional ethos into the modern ways of stressing the principles—and the dos and don'ts of right and wrong behavior. I think it was the most conservative communities as far north as Canada who were the last to create age-graded Sunday schools for the young that systematically transformed biblical stories into lessons about morality. A significant number of our parents talked about those features of the old ways that were barriers to entering fully into the brave new world. Some parents, like my own, muted this kind of critical speaking when children were present. Others enlisted our support in dismantling "mere tradition."

Even if they doubted that they could themselves fully escape aspects of the old-world ethos many were trying to outgrow, they wanted the young to become what they wished to be. Since few of us had the wit to be suspicious of their attempts to create us in the image of their waking dreams, these negative ways of talking were as exciting as the positive ways.

They talked about new ways to farm and about the kinds of education that could deliver them from their rural spaces when they could not be farmers. Since our rural spaces were rapidly filling up, many of those who wanted to farm knew that they would have to prepare for jobs and careers that were not about planting wheat and milking cows. This kind of talking opened up our world and fired our youthful imaginations. We listened and we were ready to fully become the dreams our parents had for us and for themselves.

Since I wanted to become like the elders I had oddly learned to admire and had, apparently accidentally, stumbled into teaching ambitious and able modern youth in Corn Academy and in Tabor College, I knew that I needed competent mentors to become legitimate. So far, I had also, apparently accidentally, stumbled from one major field to another. As a freshman at Tabor, I had repeated what two premeds ahead of me had declared at the desk confronting enrolling students. Apparently, I had known only that I loved books and intended to become educated. Knowing that no medical school would accept my Tabor grades in science and mathematics, I returned to California. After scanning the many pages of Fresno State College's catalog twice, I decided to study English literature since I liked to read.

While in Asia, a leading churchman and a missionary I admired had recommended Yale Divinity School and, after completing a long journey around the world, I chose it because its serene landscape had vaguely felt monastic. When enrolling, I selected "Teaching and Research in Religion" since that seemed to offer the greatest latitude in selecting the courses I would enjoy. I taught English at CBA and reluctantly became a philosophy instructor at Tabor College.[6] To combine my newly-awakened interest in the history of my heritage with what I had taught at Tabor, I enrolled in the interdepartmental History of Culture program at the University of Chicago and defined my field to be the philosophy and religion of the Hellenistic Era of Greco-Roman culture. They would have understood had I confessed wanting to learn how to think like a pagan somehow encountering a New Testament text. At thirty-four years of age, I had found my calling. I had decided in Vietnam that since I had regularly stumbled into unexpected challenges, I should at least dare to stumble forward.

---

6. After teaching one year at CBA, I was asked to teach required "English Comp." courses and do some of the chores of a departing staff member. Several weeks before fall classes began, a professor of English, who for one year served as President of Tabor College to replace the one who had retired, told me that the head of the Bible Department had died in an automobile accident and used more diplomatic rhetoric to tell me that, as the loosest body around, I would teach the Introduction to Philosophy course he taught. "I can't," I responded. "I've never taken a class like that." He smiled and told me that theologians and philosophers had similar thought patterns. I burned a lot of midnight oil keeping a chapter ahead of students. More courses were added, and by the third year I commuted to Bethel College in North Newton, Kansas, to teach varied classes in the afternoon so that their "legitimate" philosopher could take his scheduled sabbatical year researching and studying elsewhere.

Excursus A
Korn *versus* Corn

How and when Corn got its name cannot straightforwardly be answered from Prof. Penner's account at the end of his sixth chapter. In fact, the first appearance of that name is a heading on unnumbered pages of pictures.[1] I count ten uses of "Corn" and eight uses of "*Korn*" in five pages that concentrate on the time, place, and composition of that village. His usage of the name seems arbitrary. I mythically use *Korn* to name the ethnic community in and around the village of Corn.

For that matter, the question of the name of the community that first nurtured me is less revelatory than asking why Lloyd Penner's effort to characterize *The Mennonites on the Washita River* required ninety-two pages to tell the story of their heritage from the early sixteenth century through most of the nineteenth. Of his three hundred pages, two-thirds concentrate on the larger heritage from which the Washita River Mennonites and into which most of their heirs moved. The *story* of their journey through time and space most truly points to their character.

Prof. Penner links both names to his brief history of the three post offices in this area.[2] An unnamed government agent came to this part of the Cheyenne-Arapahoe reservation that had just been opened to homesteaders to select a site for a post office. Penner suggests that no thought had been given to its name. That agent saw a corn field near the store of a non-Mennonite settler living five miles north of what would become Corn. He suggested to a distant postal official that it be named "Corn."

Lloyd Penner said that the postal department "evidently made a mistake in signing the official papers, and the name was *Korn* until some years

---

1. Penner, *Mennonites on the Washita*, 102.
2. Penner, *Mennonites on the Washita*, 113–14.

later—in 1918—when its name was changed again to what should have been the original spelling, 'Corn.'"³ Acknowledging that the German word *Korn* could not survive World War I antagonisms, he concluded his account with, "Actually, as far as can be determined, there was no connection between the spelling and the language of the community."⁴ Even if Penner is technically correct about the officials, his account is so incomplete that it has led to confusion.

The story of Corn's name requires a more detailed account, which comes in a book by Prof. Vernon R. Wiebe, *Come Let Us Stand United: A History of Corn Bible Academy 1902–1977*.⁵ This seventeen-page text had two columns on each large page. It began with an Author's Note and ended with two hand-drawn maps he and J. W. Vogt sketched. I cite and supplement his information. Unfortunately, the puzzle about the name remains, and he also does not distinguish the different meanings I specify.

In 1867, what would become six counties when Oklahoma became a state in 1907 was "given" to a few more than three thousand nomadic Cheyenne and Arapahoe Indians roaming on more than four million acres of western prairies. By August 3, 1874, all were ordered to report to their respective agencies. Only about five hundred Indians then agreed to so limited an area.

Those who agreed temporarily gathered near a War Department's fort in western Oklahoma Territory. In early 1882, some were persuaded to move west onto 160 acres they could choose. An Indian agent they could trust was asked to take a few of this group to check out the land assigned to them. Rivers and canyons made the trip difficult for horse-drawn wagons, but they did come to a small portion of the larger site on Cobb Creek to a place called Colony. Four years later, in February 1886, that agent convinced about one hundred still-reluctant Indians to make the difficult trip to Colony, from which each family could search for its homestead.

In 1889, General Conference Mennonites in Kansas had received a quarter section of land to open a mission station at Shelly, and this helped to bring this part of Oklahoma to the attention of Kansas Mennonites. Since Indians chose land on well-watered sites and Shelly bordered the Washita river, a substantial number of Cheyenne-Arapahoe had chosen nearby sites. Several other Mennonites came to assist the mission and Shelly quickly became a center for stores and other businesses serving nearby homesteaders arriving later. My father's uncle, Henry Wiens, with another Mennonite,

---

3. Penner, *Mennonites on the Washita*, 114.
4. Penner, *Mennonites on the Washita*, 114.
5. Wiebe, *Corn Is Born*, 1–22.

established one of its two general stores. Shelly was a bit less than seven miles southwest of what became Corn.

On April 19, 1892, the shot was fired that allowed twenty-five thousand white homesteaders to run from a fixed spot to claim a 160-acre plot, but many plots remained unclaimed and a number of MB men living near Buhler, Kansas, visited leftover claims and chose lots that lay several miles or more west of Colony. On the way back to Kansas they stopped at the state's first capitol and "were given patents to their quarter sections for two dollars an acre. This amount was forgiven if the homesteader lived on the land a minimum of three days each six months."[6] Then they returned to Kansas, waited for spring to come, and thirteen families came to Oklahoma in March 1893, to plant gardens and a summer crop. In August 1893, sixteen Kansas Mennonite families arrived. Now "quarter sections without creeks were being filed."[7]

Post offices were quickly established, the one at Cloud Chief, perhaps less than ten miles south of what would, in 1918, be named Corn. Its post office had been opened twenty days before the gun sounded on April 19, 1892. Cloud Chief was the county seat of Washita County—until a gang from Cordell one night put the county's small building on a wagon and hauled it to their town.

The first post office serving a few Mennonite homesteaders was located in Henry Kendall's store, five miles directly north of Corn's later post office. Seger's post office, near Colony, was located in Crawford's store, four miles southeast of what would be the site of Corn. Earlier I opened my discussion of confusions about naming the Mennonite settlement by mentioning the one in Kendall's store. I now add that after having been robbed several times by outlaws, he got a six-shooter to keep them away. To get closer to the MB church site that was rapidly replacing Shelly as the center of the eastern segment of *Korn*, the one at Kendall's was moved to a farm house two miles farther south and, shortly thereafter, to Corn.[8]

After shelters for families on producing farmsteads, churches and schools had to be built. Vernon Wiebe in *Corn Is Born*, reports that the first MB church was a twenty-by-forty-foot sod dugout. "It was four feet in the ground and four feet above the ground. The outside walls were of earth."[9]

The long walls, which had a few small windows, ran from the east to the west, and it had a door on the west end from which the men entered

---

6. Wiebe, *Corn Is Born*, 4.
7. Wiebe, *Corn Is Born*, 6.
8. Penner, *Mennonites on the Washita*, 113.
9. Wiebe, *Corn Is Born*, 7.

and one on the east end for the women, with a platform in the middle of the south wall against which the preacher stood and looked north to the choir facing him. The seats were in east-west rows with the women seated east of the platform and the men, west of the platform. The choir was seated facing south where the preacher was standing. Swiveling his head to the right, he could see the women. The men sat to his left. "The meeting house was dedicated on Thanksgiving Day in November 1894."[10]

Streams of settlers kept coming and, soon, services were held once a month at the small church at Shelly and in school houses. This would not do! Lumber for a much larger-frame-church was hauled seventy miles in horse-drawn wagons and the church was dedicated on Easter Sunday, April 10, 1898.[11]

Though names of post offices and local public school districts could be adjusted to fit the settlers, or features of their ecologies, etc., they became official when registered by an appropriate governmental agency. As noted above, the Indian agent had seen either a corn field or, if Vernon Wiebe's source was more accurate, a single corn stalk. That detail would have been irrelevant to the nearest federal post office postmaster. Lloyd Penner's source had apparently supposed that an original "Corn" had mistakenly (and arbitrarily) been written *"Korn."* But why would an American postal official make a mistake? I assume that he had respected the *Korn* that the settlers actually used among themselves and that mail from elsewhere had been addressed using the German word.

Just north of Kendall's store was a settlement called Missouri Valley. As Vernon Wiebe had learned, most of the country public school districts surrounding the village's public school had been established in the winter of 1892–1893: Pleasant View, Sparta, Greenfield, Shelley, and Corn Valley. Wiebe said the public school on the quadrant just north of what eventually became Corn was named "Corn Valley."[12] The other local public schools all had English names. Until speaking of Corn Bible Academy after 1918, he had also arbitrarily used "Corn" and *"Korn"* to speak of the village and its institutions.

Both Lloyd Penner, Vernon R. Wiebe, and their immediate ethnic readers understood instinctively what they were talking about. Later readers worrying about mostly unimportant factual details discover the confusions. I do not have the evidence that produces certainty, but I surmise that until 1918, *Korn* was that village's official and normally used name. I assume

10. Wiebe, *Corn Is Born*, 7.
11. Wiebe, *Corn Is Born*, 7.
12. Wiebe, *Corn Is Born*, 6.

that Penner accurately reported at least the detail that "Valley" had been separated from the Indian agent's suggested name for its post office. Indeed, I suspect that he had written "*Korn* Valley." Had the postmaster at *Korn* later gotten that German spelling officially changed for his post office? It would have been likely that soon after 1893, its public school's name had also been anglicized.

CHAPTER 2

Gratitude for Canonic Texts and Heritages Shaped by These Texts

Having expressed gratitude for an odd early life, I admit that to contribute to the heritage given us by our elders, we must go beyond them by wrestling with the good and the bad of their lives and of our own to rebuild our disordered communities. I have insisted that heirs of a healthy culture who have not known and not, at least partly, relived aspects of their older heritage suffer sad consequences. The stories I continue to tell suggest the nature of some of those consequences for those coping with the conundrums of contemporary life. I interpret them in the light of our culture's oldest stories that many dismissively think to be only fairy tales.

I recognize that the oldest traditions of some cultures led to worldviews whose moralities, theologies, and life styles clashed with that of others. All of them cherished their values and truths. To take all of them seriously cannot mean taking any of them to have fully reflected the truth, the beauty, and the goodness that all should continue to seek. At least it is important to understand why peoples and cultures differ and to live peacefully with them. What would be best is to work at discovering together which of our disagreements are real and which are only apparent and then to continue reinterpreting our stories and even our *mythoi* so that we can live graciously and lovingly with each other even while disagreeing with each other.

The Greek word *mythos* (stories) clarified important truths about relationships with the supernatural, natural, human, and subhuman *presences* that shape lives and histories. Later enlightened Greek sages and philosophers understood that the stories chanted by bards like Homer pointed *truthfully* to what had been experienced from the primordial age when properly interpreted.

Later Hebrew prophets and scribes took for granted that their earliest memories of Abraham and Moses pointed truthfully to God's *Presence* with Israel when properly interpreted and that later eras and circumstances need adequate reinterpretations. Exegetes of foundational stories know that all continuing interpretations must be interpreted in the light of the worldviews and expectations of the living hearers and readers who in different eras cherish foundational *mythoi*. When cultural historians write histories, they use current images, metaphors, and stories that relate past *mythoi* to their consequences. Sages among them suggest what might help to repair cultures and civilizations experiencing disorder. We who live in the third decade of the twenty-first century must also wrestle with the good and with the much bad news we live with daily.

When theologians and literary interpreters describe the theopoetic rhetoric of ancient *mythoi*, they recognize that they were intended to point truthfully to what was really experienced using linguistic or other media that cannot literally express what was most deeply felt. The systematically logical formulations of ideologies that demythologized ancient polytheisms and the systematic theologies that protected monotheists from misinterpretations were enlightening and necessary to guide the behaviors of the individuals who dedicated themselves to the beliefs, hopes, and loves called for by the *Presence* and *presences* they worshiped and honored. But they followed the foundational interactions that made communities, cultures, and civilizations possible.

The images, metaphors, and stories that emerged from the human experience of many levels of relationships that underlay this process coalesced in worldviews that continued to be modified by the consequences of ensuing events and the influence of subsequent ideologies. Eventually tacit and later written constitutions shaped what, for better or worse, expressed the secondary *presences* that the writers of the New Testament called "principalities and powers." Modern secular democracies or deliberately atheistic tyrannies also demanded loyalty to their quasi-sacred principalities and powers.

WHY PRIMARY SPEECH MUST BE MYTHOPOETIC

I assume that when the disciples asked Jesus why he insisted upon using parables, they were asking for what we call "the truth, the whole truth, and nothing but the truth." The meaning of the Greek word for *parable* is "a placing beside," as in the brief explanation given in *Cruden's Complete Concordance*. It adds that in the Bible it is especially used "for the illustration of spiritual things by familiar earthly objects or incidents," adding also that in the Bible it is "applied even to short proverbs."[1]

Cruden's third paragraph of his entry on "parable" cites Matt 13,[2] where Jesus explains to his disciples that he uses parables to explain to those who have eyes and ears open to see and hear and a heart that understands "the secrets of the kingdom of heaven." Those who shut their eyes and close their ears and with a heart so dull that they will not repent will also not be healed. The word for *turn* in v. 13 was used in a religious or moral sense. It implies a change of mind or of a course of action. A turn in one's relation to God, as from darkness to light, makes it a synonym for *conversion*.

Cruden concluded that "those who really desired to know would not rest till they had found out the meaning."[3] I like this phrasing because the stories, analogies, images, and allegories that constitute the rhetoric of theopoetic meditations and of poetry is attributed also to prophets by Ezekiel, "Then I said, 'Ah Lord God!' They are saying of me, 'Is he not a maker of allegories?'"[4] This rhetoric is also enjoyed by the childlike whom Jesus said inherit the kingdom of heaven.[5] It is also appropriate for those with deaf ears and closed eyes since rhetoric that addresses the *heart* points to the heartfelt tenor of the relationships of *presences* that transcend the flatness of mere objective facts or supposed abstract certainties. The all-grown-together connotations of parables and poetics is, paradoxically, the natural and *truthful* way to evoke faith, hope, love, and to speak of an ideal *shalom*.

Although it remains true that some become at least temporarily and/or partially "tone-deaf," it seems likely that since hard hearts were once childlike that parables and other *mythoi* that require meditation and interpretation have also the power to enlighten eyes, open ears, and soften hearts, especially when crises or death shatter supposed certainties.

The apostle Paul, who proclaimed good news to the gentiles, also understood that to compare the good news and to counter the bad news of competing cultures, he had to take seriously the messages revealed by the most ancient texts of the Mesopotamians, Egyptians, Semites, and Indo-European poets, sages, prophets, and scribes.

In seminary I had learned that the New Testament had required an Old Testament from which to clarify and to fulfill its good news. Paul's message of good news was a fulfillment of his Hebrew Scriptures and that

1. Cruden, *Concordance*, 480.
2. Matt 13:10–17.
3. Cruden, *Concordance*, 480.
4. Ezek 20:49.
5. Matt 19:14.

Israelites had known from the framing of the story that Jacob received the name *Yisra-El* after wrestling all night with a mysterious opponent.[6] For Hebrews that name literally meant *to wrestle with the creator God named El.*

I also inferred from Roman-gentile and Hebrew Christ-followers that all later written testaments presuppose earlier collections of *mythoi*. All earlier collections whether or not written, I refer to as Ur Testaments. For example, stories (in Greek, the mythoi) of Jacob's flight from Laban and the story of Esau with an army—the twin brother from whom he had stolen a birthright—preceded the formation of what later Christians called the Old Testament.

My next chapter will describe important images and metaphors that I use to explain the story of my *Korn* heritage. The rest of this book compares the heritage I oddly learned to cherish with that of my heirs who, along with their modern or postmodern contemporaries, experience the confusions that inevitably accompany the mixed blessings of *progress*.

I ask readers to take seriously their foundational "Ur," "Old," and "New" Testaments in order to be able to live with the *them* who do not belong to *us*. Beyond living peacefully, we can share with them the dialogues that compare the mixed good and bad news of our histories with the open childlikeness that Jesus said is required of those who learn from others how to enter the kingdom of heaven which is the kingdom of truth.[7]

WHAT I WANTED TO CONTRIBUTE TO FELLOW PILGRIMS

A seminary exegetical assignment on a text in Matt 14 and a sermon based on it, frames a mantra that helped to center my life as a teacher. A baccalaureate sermon delivered to seniors of Tabor College and their friends and families in May 1965, and a long analysis of some MB practices printed later that year in *The Christian Leader*, form the context for the motives and content of my message to those who shared the heritage I cherish. That analysis was titled "New Wineskins for Old Wine."[8] In this chapter I describe what I

---

6. Gen 31–33.
7. Matt 18:1–5; John 18:33–40.
8. The Matt 14 sermon was preached at Ebenfeld Mennonite Brethren Church, southeast of Hillsboro, Kansas, during the 1963–1964 or the 1964–1965 school years. The summary used notes from one presented decades later in San Jose, California. It has not been published. The baccalaureate addressed to 1965 Tabor College graduates in Hillsboro, Kansas, was published in the June 8, 1965, edition of *The Christian Leader*. I said that this text recommended imitating the faithfulness of past leaders in the context of changing times and of the consequences of their actions and interpretations. I now

intended to contribute, what I wrote, and that I needed to understand why many had misinterpreted that long analysis.

It will become apparent to readers of this book why a book about me in 2015 was titled *A Dangerous Mind*.[9] Its editors intended it to be taken ironically, but after several challengers began with, "That thing you wrote, 'New Wine for . . .'" and then couldn't complete a logical title, I began to suspect that the too-persistent length of my critique led many to forget it was the *old wine* I wanted to celebrate. The present book is addressed to a larger audience, and I hope that the pilgrimages we share with larger ethnic and Christian audiences can be fulfilled. Where I err, I ask for correction. If I am unclear, I ask for forgiveness. And I mostly tell stories.

The congregation to which I belong has recently been officially severed from the denominational heritage I continue to cherish and I hope that fellow pilgrims will help each other to respect our heritages and to wrestle with each other that we may learn to point more truthfully to what fulfills them. In this book I urge, that in some respects, a large number of my people have departed from the traditions of their elders and that I have been freed to speak for it more boldly, as I trust my home congregation will continue to do.

Indeed, many of us have been separated from our heritages. I hope to speak clearly enough to help us to reinterpret our pasts to our heirs and to encourage others to reclaim their own. And then all of *them* and *us* can help each other to rebuild our civilization's falling cities.

THE MATTHEW 14 SERMON

I had learned from classical writers that *boats* symbolized "ships of states" that, more or less safely, navigate the *seas* that image chaos. Jesus was not in the boat. He had told his disciples to take to the other side of the lake after his feeding of five thousand with five loaves and two fish. All ate and the leftovers filled twelve baskets. These images and even these numbers symbolized the social order and its sustenance. Five thousand symbolized a suitable number of male citizens for a Greek *polis*, a city-state, and twelve sons of Israel symbolized a complete number of tribes.

The first paragraph of Matt 14 described a birthday party for Herod Antipas, son of Herod the Great, who had been so pleased by the provocative

---

urge that in Rom 1 and 2 Paul was also urging that mere repetition of words and imitations of actions better fits what we must call "ethnic righteousness" than the genuine "heart-righteousness" of thoughtful Christ-followers who must correct unfaithfulness.

9. Johnston and Crosby, *Dangerous Mind*, 36–59.

dancing of his stepdaughter, Salome, that he stupidly, if not also drunkenly, offered her whatever she might ask. Prompted by her mother's suggestion, she asked for the head of John the Baptist on a platter.

Jesus, who had been teaching about the coming of the "kingdom of heaven"[10] in the region of Galilee ruled by Herod Antipas, withdrew "in a boat to a lonely place apart" upon hearing of the decapitation of John the Baptist.[11] Like seas, deserts were understood to be a natural home of demons who also disordered civilized places. For Matthew's readers, the five thousand males following Jesus symbolized those seeking the fulfilled *shalom* Jesus offered in a kingdom of God. The "other side of the lake" was the Valley of Gennesaret, sometimes referred to as a "valley of Princes" and was a symbol of heaven in first-century Galilee. Matthew framed the story of this ark of salvation for a land disordered by wrathful rulers.

It fits this staged story that when a figure came striding over stormy waves, the disciples assumed it was a demonic phantasm. Before Peter accepted Jesus' invitation to step out of the boat, he must have remembered that demons take the guise of whomever they choose. Perhaps he realized that if it wasn't Jesus, he was doomed, and he dared to walk on water.

Of course, only very gifted saints can do that for long, but Jesus took his hand, lifted him out of the water, and helped him back into the boat. Peter continued to learn that the One who created and the Son who healed had to be masters of chaos as well as of the earthly arks of salvation that were needed to reach the enduring order they could not themselves enter unless invited and guided.

He had also to learn that those called to captain boats had to learn the patterns of winds and waters to manage their sails and rudders and how to interact with an always dubious crew. The earthly captains of the churchly boat, *and all those in it who plan its missions and participate in its tasks*, have to step outside it and "walk on water." They, too, must faithfully serve within them and move beyond them to image God and to exercise dominium over the fertile earth.[12] Those who mentored HR and were elders of *Korn* had also learned to walk on water, to die—even daily—and to live truly.[13]

A student who had heard my sermon confronted me several days later with, "Wiens, I've figured out why we tolerate you always trying to shovel us back into the boat. It's because we know that you're telling our parents that it's time for them to get out of it." He knew, of course, that what he had

---

10. Matt 13.
11. Matt 14:13.
12. Gen 1:26–31.
13. 2 Tim 2:12; 1 Cor 15:31.

said also required an ironic interpretation to point truthfully. I interpreted it to define much of what I have wanted to contribute. After he graduated from Tabor College and spent several years in the US Army in Vietnam, that student had reentered the "boat" while continuing "to walk on water." Dale Suderman was one of the students who mentored me.

In seminary, and especially while attending Willow Avenue Mennonite Church, my "boat" that consistently understands the relevance of using lectionary texts guided me to Ps 96 in a later sermon on Matthew's text. Its invocation extols God's "salvation . . . glory . . . [and] marvelous works" (vv. 1–4). This Creator of the cosmos is the king who is worshiped (vv. 5–8). "Say among the nations, 'The Lord is king!'" For this, "let the heavens be glad, and let the earth rejoice; let the sea roar, and all that fills it; let the field exult, and everything in it. Then shall all the trees of the forest sing for joy before the Lord; for he is coming to . . . judge the world with righteousness, and the peoples with his truth."[14]

The lectionary included a passage about Cyrus, a Persian emperor.[15] This passage began with messianic language that, among "these things," Cyrus will "subdue nations" and do that "for the sake of my servant Jacob, and Israel, my chosen." Isaiah then quotes God's statement that "you do not know me." And it ends with "I am the Lord, and there is no other. I form light and create darkness. I make weal and create woe. I the Lord do all these things."[16]

The Gospel has the Pharisees and Herodians ask Jesus if it is lawful to pay taxes and Jesus asks whose picture is on the coins used for paying this tax. When told that it is the emperor, Jesus says, "Give therefore, to the emperor the things that are the emperor's, and to God the things that are God's."[17] But since they believed that God created and rules what is, they could not answer and departed. His hearers knew that they should always obey God; but when and how should one obey actual earthly rulers? Matthew knew that the answer to both questions requires careful discernment and guided faithfulness.

In the text from the Epistles, Paul commends the *chosen* and insists that their "faith and labor of love and steadfastness" has made them "imitators of us and of the Lord . . . inspired by the Holy Spirit" after abandoning

---

14. Ps 96:9–13.
15. Weisberg, "Cyrus II," 200.
16. Isa 45:1–7.
17. Matt 22:15–22.

idolatry.[18] One must carefully discern and interpret idolatry and competing spirits!

These texts and their images sum up much of the Old Testament's linkage of creation to God as the Lord of all and of God's *chosen* as those gifted to image God. Paul quotes 1 Thessalonians comparing bad news with radical good news and with Jesus "who rescues us from the wrath that is coming."[19]

Radix is the Latin word we translate with radical, to contrast human wrath with the patient love of God that creates harmony and justice. And my application of that meaning to reinterpreting Paul is my labor of love for all heritages. That reinterpretation begins in Romans[20] with an introductory argument that opens his comparison of his good news and bad news of the health and woe of civilizations—and of the histories of their cities.

In a baccalaureate address in 1965, I used Heb 10–13 to compare wrathful bad news with the good news debated in the Hebrew and Christian heritages instead of the lectionary texts used in the 2008 sermon on Matt 14. The writer to the Hebrews spoke to readers who had learned to identify with those like Abraham and Jacob-Israel, who learned the childlike openness to wildernesses where demons dwell, but are also the places from which that is learned that creatively restores life to what civilization enhances and disorders.

Noah had been told to build an ark of salvation and, for Galilean disciples, Jesus had modeled walking on water. For the heirs of Abraham, the writer of an epistle to Abraham's heirs appropriately used tents and encampments when traversing deserts to image what Galilean fishermen experienced in boats crossing dangerous seas. And how could they be built to be arks of salvation rather than fragile rafts, canoes, or boats for fishing? And what did Peter have to learn to captain the boat that took what kind of fish to the other side, symbolizing the kingdom of heaven?

NEW WINESKINS FOR OLD WINE

In 1965 our denomination's magazine, *The Christian Leader*, published a lengthy analysis of practices and attitudes that I thought had succumbed to popular evangelical models of "faithfulness." I wrote "New Wineskins for Old Wine,"[21] asking its MB readers to acknowledge that after one hundred

---

18. 1 Thess 1:1–10.
19. 1 Thess 1:10.
20. Rom 1:16—2:11.
21. Wiens, "New Wineskins," 1–28.

years of the formation in Ukraine of this Mennonite sect, our "skins" were smothering old wine that needed new skins that more adequately expressed the old wine for a new era. I continue to contrast contemporary attitudes and lives with those of our elders and to insist that in addition to coping with modern and postmodern worldviews, we needed to reincarnate an older spirit and wisdom I had recognized in still-living elders that I thought was being lost.

I was not refuted, though many disliked my analysis. I was often accosted by those who began by citing it as "New Wine for . . ." and then were unable to complete the title. For many, apparently, a sustained critique of *practices* implied heresy. Though I had not directly challenged taken-for-granted doctrinal formulations, an insightful essay by Paul Toews that traced our tradition's response to it has helped me to realize that I needed to become explicit about denominational controversies within its initial century that revealed the influence of alien modernism that distorts how we think about "what-is" (the created cosmos) and how to organize human interactions (businesses, schools, interest groups, schools, and churches).

In addition to suggesting some of my limitations, Paul Toews, a close colleague at Fresno Pacific College (now Fresno Pacific University), modeled a historian's recognition that interpretation of the pilgrimages that result from presumed new beginnings depend upon the historian's sensitivity to the possibilities and the limitations imposed upon even those who seek to reform it. He modeled the methods and attitudes needed by historians to illuminate the meaning and consequences of reformations by explaining the contexts and tracing the results of reforms achieved by founding fathers. I am shaping much of the rest of this chapter as a review of his essay, "New Wineskins for Old Wine: A Fifty-Year Retrospective."[22]

His opening paragraph acknowledged that "Wiens, ever since, has been an intellectual gadfly for the MB."[23] For me, his comment expresses my wrestling with the difficulty of understanding old-wine truths and with expressing them to those who have not grown up in cultures more attuned to the worldviews of the biblical and classical ages that often more patiently distinguished good and bad news. Prof. Toews then addressed the historical context that had motivated my attempts to help students in "a bewildering religious culture."[24]

He also speculated that 1965 appeared to climax an era of "MB intellectualism," citing the increasing accreditation of its schools, the creation of

---

22. Toews, "Retrospective," 36–62.
23. Toews, "Retrospective," 36.
24. Toews, "Retrospective," 36–37.

a historical society to study its past, the progression of its publications, and the apparent willingness of MBs to listen to sympathetic outside scholars. He thus justifies the courageous editor of *The Christian Leader* for publishing an "extended critique [of] almost everything in the MB churchly world" that had emerged since its founding. The editor's announcement of its imminent publication admitted that it would be controversial and insisted that the changes that had happened needed to be faced at this point in our history.[25]

Having approved of the editor's decision, Prof. Toews began his summation of my critique with a description of what schismatic MB founders intended and the antagonisms they encountered from the Mennonite culture that had emerged in the Ukraine that they had criticized. In his description, he cited the apostle Paul's metaphor of old treasure that becomes encased in earthly vessels,[26] adding that perhaps it is more difficult for immigrant groups to negotiate always difficult transitions.[27]

I call attention to the summary of "New Wineskins" offered by Prof. Toews rather than attempting my own because I suspect that his more clearly explains what happens to the *treasure*, the old wine when it is decanted into cultural skins that are meant to preserve it while encouraging its becoming mature wine. When Jesus explained the relationship of wine to the skins, that in his time were its cultural containers, he agreed that fully mature wine is the good wine.[28]

I urge that readers of this book who share our traditions read Prof. Toews's review of the response of MBs to understand what I had been trying to explain without directly discussing recent evangelical interpretations of the inspiration of the Bible that hinder understanding of traditional ways of opening ourselves to be grasped by the *treasures* revealed in ancient texts. What must be understood is what the apostle Paul meant when he wrote: "But we have this treasure in *clay jars* so that it may be made clear that power belongs to God and not to us."[29] I return to this when I try to clarify good news by comparing it with bad news.

Prof. Toews explained the intentions of the MB founders to create the new forms that would enable their successors to reexperience the dramatic conversions that led to transformed lives. He noted that immigrant groups "must negotiate different cultural realities," separating themselves from the

---

25. Toews, "Retrospective," 37–39.
26. 2 Cor 4:7 (KJV).
27. Toews, "Retrospective," 41.
28. Luke 5:39.
29. 2 Cor 4:7. Emphasis added.

supposedly unreformed patterns of the past, and that their children often suffer the tension that results from growing up differently but who are expected to repeat the dramatic changes their elders had made.[30]

Both new forms of nurture and of the achievement of communal consensus must be discovered. This was especially true when "lay leaders gave way to a new professionalized and trained ministry," often received from outsiders. The meaning of biblical authority also changed when relatively traditional godly communities sensed a need to *defend* the Scriptures in addition to *using* them to achieve guidance and consensus.[31] Even the systematization of right beliefs is similar to the earthly development of ideological systems used to insist on *certainties* rather than upon a confident *faith* that also requires continuing reinterpretations.

Prof. Toews admitted that my call in "New Wineskins" to return to the past might be taken as the incurable romanticism of those who try to turn the clock of history back, and this calls attention to the importance of thinking carefully about modern worldviews. He also notes that our heritage had waited "for the spirit of God to move . . . the church" to a "revitalization" that enabled it to "shape the future."[32]

After reviewing the large number of affirmations of my essay that were sent to the editor of *The Christian Leader*, he addressed the one sharply critical letter to the editor and three that expressed disquiet. In its April 13, 1966, edition, the *Mennonite Brethren Herald* printed three thoughtful responses to "New Wineskins" solicited from Canadian leaders that expressed approval for an authentic and imaginative faith, acknowledged the problem of behavioral legalism, and admitted that what had been analyzed needed to be evaluated.[33]

A very thoughtful assessment of "New Wineskins," published in *The Christian Leader* edition of April 26, 1966, was written by Jacob Loewen, a missionary translation consultant sent by the American Bible Society to help many Bible translators in South America and Africa. He insisted that only a very pointed analysis could stir up action, adding that "in such a wide-ranging study one could quibble about many assertions. Perhaps Wiens had overstated his case."[34] One of my few responses was to the Southern District pastor who wrote the one entirely critical letter to the editor that my inclusion of his congregation among rural churches not likely to double

30. Toews, "Retrospective," 41.
31. Toews, "Retrospective," 40–41.
32. Toews, "Retrospective," 43.
33. Toews, "Retrospective," 43–48.
34. Loewen, *Personal Reaction*, 4–6.

in a decade had been the result of my failure to research the possibility of differing circumstances among them. I did not take my failure to be a mere quibble.

I also appreciated the comment in one of the three extensive reviews in the *MB Herald*, referred to earlier, that the concepts of such evaluations "may easily run rampant and become the master rather than the tool."[35] This was from the Canadian pastor quoted two paragraphs prior to this one who urged a public evaluation. Although nearly 90 percent of later letters to the editor expressed gratitude for helping readers to understand what had also troubled them, a number of pastors and leaders were expressing fears that the ensuing debate might split our denomination.

Paul Toews speculated that my "traffic in sociological and historical analysis . . . may have been unfamiliar to most of . . . the hierarchy."[36] He was sure they would have responded had I boldly departed "from normative theological understandings." Or had some not understood the essay? Granted that such calls for renewal and revitalization "are almost sacred themes in MB history," Toews realized that a muted response had to be accounted for, and he commented on a handful of possibilities.

The editors of the *Herald* and of *The Christian Leader* and Jacob Loewen urged that what puzzled them was the absence of a response from MB leaders. Even calls from pastors for such a response were ignored. Paul Toews cited a small item in a later edition of the *Herald* noting that there was "an official decision not to respond." The editor of *The Christian Leader* wrote me that he had found no evidence "of such an official decision" though it was apparent that "our ministering brethren were determined not to respond."[37] What Janz, the editor of the Herald, later reported was that "a letter" written by a seminary professor reported that a committee had been formed "to respond to Delbert" and had decided that "the best way to let the whole furor raised by the essay die would be to say nothing. And so nothing was said."[38]

A second possibility had been suggested by a comment from the president of the MB Bible College in Winnipeg. A response from a conference official or even from an individual would make it easy "to label the school or the individual, and thus to dismiss the subject."[39] The time of the publication's appearance also accounts for the muted responses. In that era

---

35. Toews, "Retrospective," 47–48.
36. Toews, "Retrospective," 49.
37. Toews, "Retrospective," 48.
38. Toews, "Retrospective," 48.
39. Toews, "Retrospective," 49–50.

there had been significant controversies over the doctrine of scriptural inspiration and how science faculties in conference schools might interpret evolution to apply to the creation of "what-is." Scheduled conferences and discussions had been held and even those appointed to defend orthodoxy agreed that, for example, there were "divergent understandings in the evangelical world on the meaning of inspiration" and that differences had not been "superficial."[40]

Prof. Toews then suggested that not all individuals could understand that "practices that were supposedly rooted in scriptural understandings often turned out to be cultural markers."[41] If the structure of conversions can also be sociologically explained, this might "demystify the sublime and ineffable." I again suggest that MB-informed laity, pastors, and their leaders need to ponder Paul's essay to think how to respond to present challenges.

A final explanation was that conference leaders were so preoccupied with the Decade of Enlargement that there was little time to consider other issues. Prof. Toews wondered whether a response to "New Wineskins" might have "produced more authentic growth than the misconceived program."[42] This title had replaced the original "Double in a Decade," and those ten years ended with an increase of 8.6 percent, not 100 percent. The phrase "authentic growth" hinted that maturational growth might be more significant and might even have led to greater numerical growth.

Prof. Toews had begun his review of the response to "New Wineskins" with the suggestion that 1965 had appeared to mark the maturation of its schools and of intellectuals capable of leading vigorous discussions of critical questions. But the absence of response had revealed "the emasculation of the academic class in MB circles." And the Board of Reference and Counsel, within the year, identified among their major concerns "the widening chasm between church and school." This problem is reflected in the very long use of images of "town" that is suspicious of "gown" influences throughout Western history.

I, too, had inherited such suspicions. My decision to apply to Yale Divinity School ranged from the suspicion that an impoverished young man might want to attend prestigious richer schools since where there is money, some of it might rub off. Much more important for me was the more or less unsolicited advice of a very knowledgeable theologian and consultant with many years of experience in Asia that I should attend YDS. When that was also suggested by a missionary I met in India, whose character and insights

---

40. Toews, "Retrospective," 50–54.
41. Toews, "Retrospective," 54.
42. Toews, "Retrospective," 55.

I admired, I decided to visit its campus after landing in New York. Since unready to come home, I had known that it was time to leave Vietnam, and I had, for six months, wandered west. I quickly sensed that its setting and ambiance had the monastic serenity that could foster my recovery from culture shock.

Since the early seventeenth century, many brilliant discoveries in the physical, biological, and other sciences could not be denied. Some, and especially interpretations of the theory of evolution, were intensely debated. In March 1925, Tennessee legislators voted that it could not be taught in public schools. In July 1925, John T. Scopes was tried and convicted of breaking that law. Though that state's supreme court quickly released him, citing technical errors in the course of the trial, the debates of the prosecuting and defense lawyers stimulated so much controversy that the trial has symbolized the supposed *war* between science and religion.[43]

Despite the fear that science undermines faith, almost no one is willing to give up the technological advances made possible by scientific advances. Despite the recent controversy about dangers inherent in artificial intelligence, few will discard their computers. I will argue that technology has been more seductive and modernizing than is real science. I remember that my early fear of skepticism dissipated when I realized that its debilitating effects were more the result of the failure of would-be skeptics to fulfill their vocation by also becoming skeptical enough to question the limitations inherent in skepticism. The goal of an open mind is to close it upon defensible truths as others have pointed out. The true skeptic who recognizes his or her creaturely limitations welcomes reproof and correction.

I sum up the admittedly controversial effects of my wish to contribute to the heritage I inherited. I have consistently intended to defend what I have called the old wine of that heritage. I also admit that many who share that heritage, including some of its pastors and many lay conservatives misquoting my title, has convinced me that they believed that I was recommending a vintage of heretical new wine. It has taken a long time to suspect that their misreading of what I intended to be a plea for old wine might have resulted from my having been infected by a virus so subtle that it has been present in all eras, and not only the modern. That *virus*, I now suggest, had led me to use too relentlessly the rhetoric of modernistic "I-It" analysis more appropriate to manuals sent to those who repair technological equipment than to those who interpret canonic texts or meditate upon a heritage we prize.

The precision of "I-It" analysis and the critical exactitude of ideological certainties is needed even by theologians and historians, but that kind of

---

43. See ch. 10 of this volume.

scholarship is better understood by academics. Of course, academics might also remind each other that they may absurdly resemble foxes or hedgehogs and I acknowledge having inadequately disciplined my foxiness. Foxes so often dart off the track of their chosen prey that they end up "knowing nothing about everything." Hedgehogs so thoroughly dig up a narrowly defined turf that they end up "knowing everything about nothing." Since no one can learn everything about everything, it is necessary to learn as much as possible about what is truly important.

My next chapter clarifies the methods and metaphors I use to compare the good and the bad news of ancient cultures and of our own. And I again confess that I hope to clarify some of the past attempts to shape the progress of civilization. In the rest of this volume, I explore what I have learned from growing up in *Korn*, Oklahoma, its short-lived name that, for me, points *mythically* to its roots in a still premodern world. I compare that with what I think those now growing up experience.

Along the way I suggest that several simple directional metaphors help to illuminate some of the differences between "top-down" and "bottom-up" varieties of worldviews and attitudes. In addition, I sketch the differences between those that are *circular* or *linear*. Beyond that, I compare *simplistic* and *radical* forms of worldviews. Each of these lead to different natural or metaphysical (and theological) conceptions of what actually is in the cosmos and/or beyond it and whether "what is" evolves *incrementally*, *radically*, or both. Though these metaphors are too simple to be fully adequate, I hope they clarify many of the disagreements among us.

Paul's Epistle to the Romans clarifies my interpretation of the apostle's *radically* evolutionary worldview and with his comparisons of the causes and consequences of what is good news and bad news and of how the Divine *Presence* works in the natural world and in human history. We will also need to ask why postmodern humans are confused about their relationship to the natural and the supernatural *presences* in our actual world, and are confused even about their own identities.

In this book, I meditate on my early experience of growing up in a *Korn* community still in living contact with a premodern worldview. I do that to suggest that my heritage helped me to survive culture shock and to define my identity as created to image God,[44] when truthfully interpreted. I also argue that though our relationships to powerful institutional principalities and powers and to strange others have subtly shifted, we have to rethink what constitutes heresy and idolatry.

---

44. Gen 1:26–31.

We must again *wrestle bravely* with each other and with feared strangers, with our abuse of natural ecological forces that we have alienated, with God, and with our own taken-for-granted assumptions and attitudes. In doing that, I ask us to go *beyond* what *Korn* took-for-granted and to *return* to some of its attitudes and disciplines to regain its quest for health and holiness.

I add to my repentance for having too much succumbed to the *virus* of a rigorous analysis that repelled too many readers and try to return to images, metaphors, parables, and stories that characterize a rhetoric that fits the nature and importance of interpersonal relationships. I am, however, too much a student of philosophy and theology to deny the relevance of critical analysis to careful thinking.

CHAPTER 3

The Images, Metaphors, and Stories That Shape This Meditation

My attempt to interpret the signs of these times has led to a search for what would clarify and illustrate what I wanted to understand. Two groups of metaphoric images proved to be so compelling that they opened up new topics for exploration. Indeed, the readers who understand these will find most of the rest of the book easy to read and will be able to add chapters of their own. The master metaphors around which I construct this book are so bare that perhaps they should be called images. The first pair is *concrete* and *abstract*. The second group is *village, town,* and *city*.

CONCRETE

The way I use *concrete* takes us back to the word's original meaning in the Latin language. Its second syllable is from the verb *cresco*,[1] "to spring forth, to come into existence." When applied to what already exists, it meant "to grow, to increase in size." When joined with the prefix *con*, it named the process of growing together, as of organisms that mature and flourish. The noun form of the word was *concretio*.[2] It was used of living, growing plants or animals or persons. When secondarily used of what we think is mere matter, it spoke of "congealing, condensing, thickening," as happens to cement.

What does it mean, "to grow together"? Whatever grows must be alive. What grows together implies a living entity that is complex, one that consists of various parts so interrelated that they form a greater unity, a one that

---

1. Simpson, *Cassell's New Latin Dictionary*, 257.
2. Simpson, *Cassell's New Latin Dictionary*, 128.

is greater than the sum of its parts. I am a concrete human being. I consist of organs that are quite different from each other: heart, liver, stomach, lungs, and all the rest. All of these are perched upon or cradled within or hung from a skeleton. This body is surrounded by skin, activated by muscles, and animated by a nervous system. Blood and other fluids coursing through the parts make it possible for the body and its unified *self* to flourish.

In the introductory chapter, I used *mythos*, the ancient Greek word translated *story*. Every concrete individual creates a story, a history, and even if all its bodily parts decompose into its objective molecular or atomic parts after death, its living *self* was a subject that transcended mere objectivity. A *Thou*, as in Martin Buber's comparison with *Its*, exerts a *Presence* that interacts with other *presences* to form a "world" that even if small and passing can really be experienced as "heaven on earth—or as hell."[3]

So long as I am alive, I am a single human being, someone with a singular name. The moment I die, the parts are still all there, hardly at all changed. Yet I have ceased to be a unity. Because the parts no longer work together, the forces of decay that have always been present in the body, are no longer countered. Though all of the parts briefly remain what they are and might even be able to start up again, the larger living unity that is myself is gone. I have then ceased to be a concrete human creature.

I ask you to imagine that the *Korn* I knew as a child was a concrete community. We were all engaged in the process of growing together to create a living "self" that was greater than all of us seen only as a collection of individuals. I end this discussion of concretions by using the old Anglo-Saxon word *Halig* to characterize the *Presence* and *presences* that are holy, sacred—or who can aspire to that status.

Korn had its skeletal structure and its arteries. Many creeks fed the Washita River west of the village. Cobb Creek defined part of our eastern border. Corn Creek flowed around two sides of the village and behind our back yard, though it took a citified California cousin to show me how to catch the tiny sunfish in it. These arteries and capillaries and an occasional pond supplied the water table and shaped the drainage patterns that made life and agriculture possible. Roads were the arteries for the passing of the people and the skeleton that divided the land into sections one-mile square.

---

3. Niebuhr, *Responsible Self*, 72–73; Buber, *I and Thou*, 1–34. I recommend both books as "moral masterworks" and I closely link Niebuhr to Buber's classic contribution to the field of social psychology. Niebuhr cites this Jewish scholar's distinction between "I–It" objective relationships and "I–Thou" subjective relationships. The entire second chapter of this volume, and all of Niebuhr's book, illustrates the importance of these distinctions and the books should be read in connection to each other. Like Niebuhr, Buber was also a significant theologian, philosopher, and biblical scholar.

Fences squared the quarter sections that had been the original holdings, and more fences confined cattle and horses to the pastures and bordered the "eighties" and "forties" (acres) on which their crops grew.

Just beyond the skin of *Korn* were the cities of Weatherford, Clinton, and Cordell that linked us to the always enticing, and often alien, outside world. We usually drove three miles east, ten miles north, and then another mile east to get to Weatherford. From there, Clinton was fifteen miles west along Highway 66 (now I-40). Cordell was fifteen miles south of Clinton. Our southern boundary extended about sixteen miles east of Cordell. None of the local roads inside this rough square were paved while I was growing up. Nor was there a paved road near our wobbly eastern boundary.

Of course, our "skin" was not that geometric. Substantial portions of the inside edges of these boundaries did not belong to Dutch-German Mennonites. Nor was it possible to draw a line, however curvy, which did not include outsiders or exclude insiders. I remember pressing my face to the car window after turning west six miles south of the village of Corn to look at the handful of homes of insiders who lived on the wrong side of the highway. Etched in my memory is an image of Mrs. Deutschendorf standing alone in her bare yard.

I wondered what it was like to live so near and yet be on the outside. After her husband died, she moved to Corn. Later, when her grandson John Denver sang about his grandma's feather bed, I liked to imagine that she was the one who owned it and was glad that she could live her last years in the center of the community. A bed with a featherbed and some of her descendants upon it appeared on a float in the village's centennial parade. In 2005, *Korn* was proudly claiming the song. As stated earlier, I use "Corn" to name the village and *Korn* to name the *Geist* of the larger community.

Actually, I knew quite well what it was like to be on the outside, for that road led about a dozen more miles west to Cordell. For five years, including my first four years of grade school, we had lived in this county seat with the "English" and perhaps a half-dozen families from our country church. This church had been built east and north of Cordell for members of the *Korn* community who lived on the west side of the Washita River. Bessie, where I was birthed in the home of father's parents, was a hamlet a few miles north and west of the church and lay a bit west of the highway that linked Clinton and Cordell.

The concreteness that was *Korn* included much of this. Its interrelated parts were the fields and the streams, the cows and the horses. These, too, were *presences* that mingled with the spirits of the people and the families and the clans. And there was the united spirit that was the *Geist* of *Korn*. That is a German word for *soul*, or *spirit*. *Korn* had a personality, a spiritual essence that we created and which, in turn, shaped us. A related ethnic who had never been there but who had known others of us might remark, "I might have guessed," when discovering we were also from there.

Therefore, *Korn* also had its nervous system, a web of communication that held us together and expressed the mind and will of the *Geist* that we had created and that continued to shape us. Gossip could be cruel, but it was a defense against what was supposed to be alien to the *Geist* of *Korn*. The words of preachers and teachers kept our ideal ways and thoughts before us in the form of language that worked to shape us into the character we held dear. Perhaps most important of all were the stories that were told and retold, from the Scriptures and from our history.

The party lines that were installed a decade or so before I was born illustrate the web of words and feelings that bound us to each other. Telephone poles were planted along the road and down the lanes to each home. Each line connected a dozen or more houses, and every phone on that line would ring when any one received a call. Each telephone had its own code of long and short rings, so everyone on that line knew who was supposed to answer. All of the others could lift the receiver and listen in. If too many listened to an incoming long-distance call, the power could be so drained that the one receiving the call would beg the others to hang up so that the message could be heard. My mother and her sister could secure privacy. As I've mentioned, they were both *Hutters* from South Dakota who had married in. Though also Mennonites, they were from a different ethnic branch and spoke a dialect incomprehensible to the Low German speakers of *Korn*. After counting a suitable number of clicks, they could choose whether or not to continue in *Hutterisch* or switch to English.

A series of short rings alerted all along a line that a public announcement was about to be made. Since each line led to a switchboard in the village where an operator could connect it to any other line, the central operator could make public announcements on all the lines. Since she could listen in on all the calls, she was almost omniscient. It was not unusual to get her response when trying to reach a friend on another line, "Oh, they're not home; they went to Cordell for the afternoon." Or, "He took his tractor in to DeFehrs to be fixed. I'll connect you there." Through the web of talk and the help of "central," all could share in the significant knowledge that defined the community.

Imagine a concrete community in the form of a giant web with tonus. Each line in that tight web is connected, eventually, with every other line. When any line is plucked it quivers, and it passes that vibration to every other line until the whole web resonates. When anyone weeps, all grieve together. If anyone laughs, all rejoice. Through the tautness and interconnections of the web, all can share in the significant emotions and feelings of the community's members.

Imagine a concrete community as a giant folk dance with everyone holding hands or touching shoulders. Someone moves, tugging upon a hand or pushing against a shoulder. How shall the second one respond? Should she pull back the other's hand? Should he yield to the push? Should each pass on the motion to yet another? All the actions of the community can be thought of as a dance of initiations and responses. To grow mature in such a community is to learn the dance, to know when and how to initiate new actions in response to prior actions and to do so in the light of future responses and the initiations they call forth.[4] Through the tautness and interconnections of the dynamic web, all can share in the construction of the village's institutions and the ethos, the manners and morals and morale, that incarnate its *Geist*.

Sociologists, whose job includes discovering the obvious that is not noticed until pointed at, tell us that bounded concrete communities are also primary. That is, they grow from the inside. One has to be born in them to belong fully. Hardly any families from the outside wander in and settle down. A small group of Catholics had settled on our turf; but they did not stay long, and after they left even their tiny cemetery was effaced. Distant members from the larger tribe are accepted because they can trace membership in one or more of the local clans. The "English" could marry in; but it might take a lifetime to be fully accepted.

Such bounded primary communities are basic. By this I mean only that all that is essential for an ongoing communal life is present. The village may be small and its life may be constricted, but it contains most of the essentials that are needed to build an economy, a society, and a *Geist*. Each of its members grows up with intimate knowledge of what is essential to make

---

4. Niebuhr, *Responsible Self*, 61–68. Niebuhr summarizes four aspects of all of our actions. They are actually responses to previous actions upon us. All our reactions all are guided by our interpretations of the actions to which we respond. Our actions become responsible only if we anticipate how they will be interpreted and responded to by a relevant community of agents and our anticipation of their appropriate responses. Finally, social solidarity points to the continuing community of agents that is the context enabling coherent patterns of responsibility. Chapters 2 and 3 place responsibility within society and in time and history. The fourth chapter describes the "absolute dependence" of the responsible self. Perhaps it is appropriate for me to express this as recognition of myself as an earthly creature, as in Gen 3:19. His fifth chapter is titled "Responsibility in Sin and Salvation" and, in it, he treats his understanding to be one of the ways to interpret the Christian life and the biblical ethos by asking, "To whom or what am I responsible and in what community of interaction am I myself?" Perhaps it is appropriate for me to express this as recognition of myself as also "created in the image of God," as in Gen 1:26–28.

a life. We grew up, moving in enlarging circles until we knew the shape of the whole. We could recognize its members and assess the importance of the clans to which they belonged.

Our eighth-grade teacher, an *Englisha* whom the board had hired during the Second World War, explained the national census one day. "Let's do one," enthused a student. She had not planned a field trip, but the class would not be denied. She was greatly relieved when the census was made without anyone leaving the room. Several went to the blackboard, drew all the village streets, and chalked in the houses. Then, among us, we counted all who lived in those homes. My memory claims to remember that there were 319. There were many more living on the outlying farms, and we would have had trouble trying to count them. Because there were still several one- or two-room schools in the countryside, no one from those townships was in the class.

We were also learning the basic facts of life and how the community worked. While still children, we knew the sounds of birth and the smells of death. We watched the adults at work and imitated them in our play. Even the few of us whose fathers were not farmers were hired out to hoe cotton and to pick it. By the middle grades, many of us were driving tractors, plowing and harrowing for long hours at a time. Most of my friends grew up able to do almost everything that adults in the community could do; and, since a farmer must be at least an amateur of many trades, by adolescence many of my peers had the rudimentary skills to move into the service trades and other occupations.

We acquired a "common sense." We were learning how things worked and how to fix them. We were also imbibing a sense of the common, how the parts of the whole fitted together to create the larger ethos. With that sense of the whole, we could also hope to grow into the mature judgment of those who moved beyond simplified recipes to cobble solutions to problems that defied the normal procedures. With the holy shrewdness that can come from concrete experience, we, too, could aspire to become elders who had the gift of resolving moral contradictions, of bringing healing to broken individuals, and of reconciling shattered relationships. Such a community was necessarily small. But it could produce individuals who achieved depth and height. In mastering the comprehensible whole, we could transcend it.

Such a concrete community could also transcend itself. As in many communities containing tribal members, the web extended beyond our boundaries. There were friendships and occasional intermarriages with the "English." The most common relationships, however, leaped across hundreds and thousands of miles to those Low German Mennonites scattered across the Midwestern states and Canada and California. There were related tribes, like the Hutterites from whom my mother and Aunt Emma had come. Three of the smaller country churches around *Korn* were part of the community and most of their members shared a Dutch-German-Russian history, though some of them might have a slightly different dialect and belong to a different Mennonite denomination. Even on our own turf there were differences to be surmounted.

Even when the differences were significant, they had to be reconciled; for a common *Geist* implies a common goal. The purpose for all that work was to perfect a *Halig Geist*. I claim that the Germanic word for *Korn* because the root was *hal* and was a name for the concrete wholeness of things. The present German word is *heil*. When a life and a community were almost entirely concrete, that word named its total well-being, its *commonweal*, another old word that implied both spiritual health and material wealth.

Though *whole* retains much of this earlier sense, the word lost its fullest meaning when the consciousness of concreteness began to dissolve. Then the root *hal* gave birth to two words to characterize the ideal qualities of the now separated aspects of a fading concreteness. For its now distinguishable materiality, we gained the new word *healthy*. To praise a saintly soul, the word became *holy*. To remember the ancient link between these words, we need only to associate them with a fish that was frequently eaten on Friday when, for religious reasons, fish was the only meat that could be eaten. When the Middle Low German name for such flatfish, *butte*, came to be added to *Halig*, one of the species of those fish came to be called the *hali-but*, the holy flounder. We, of course, were not so Catholic.

I have read that some of the early settlers in *Korn* deliberately chose smaller plots of land than they could have freely claimed on the grounds that what they chose was sufficient for a healthy family in a holy community. Though it did not take long for such sentiments to seem extremely shortsighted, I will claim them as evidence that those who formed this community had more than wealth in mind. They wanted a concrete community with a nervous system and arteries and organs enclosed in a skin, the whole of which would be *Halig*.

Because most of us were farmers, the common *Geist* was closely related to the spirits of the earth and the flora and the fauna. Our mini-ecology was to be part of God's holy court, though I doubt that they would have expressed it in that imagery. At least they would have assented to the image of the creative, sustaining, redeeming *Presence* of God that hovered over them as a sacred canopy yet another kind of "skin" that defined their *Halig* concreteness.

I occasionally contrast the word *hairesis* from *Halig*. That word is related to the ancient Greek verb that meant "to take, to choose." Any person or group that adopts a particular point of view as the key to interpreting aspects of a concrete whole is a *hairesis*. New Testament texts speak of "the *hairesis* of the Pharisees." Anyone who tries to write an account of *Korn*, as I am now doing, must choose which aspects of the whole to use as themes for such a history. Then particular truths can emerge by which to understand its character. From this process, insight can emerge. Important heresies are always based on important truths. That is what gives them the power they have to make a simplified sense of things.

They become dangerous when a single aspect of the whole or a limited set of truths about the whole is treated as the whole truth. Worse yet, any group that makes up its mind to live out such a partial set of insights will gradually produce a way of life that is a cartoon version of the *Geist* they had intended to preserve. If *Halig* can be interpreted as "having it all together," then un*hal* means living "at loose ends" among the fragments that come from heresy.

ABSTRACT

I use the word *abstract* to image the breaking apart of the original concreteness. This word is based on the Latin verb *traho* or *tractare*, "to draw, drag, pull about, as a tractor pulls the plow." The prefix ab(s)- denoted motion away from a fixed point. *Abstract*, then, names the act of pulling something out of or away from its place. As contrasting with the concrete, I use it to speak of something separated from its living whole. When one of my teeth ceases to be an interacting part of the concrete whole that is myself, I go to the dentist, who will probably abstract it. I trace the process that is the loss of concreteness by describing three different sorts of abstraction. These may be summed up in a sentence: *Persons were abstracted to specialize in functional abstractions that became abstractly rationalized*. Its three phrases will be the subheadings for my descriptions of increasingly abstracted cultures.

Persons Were Abstracted

Perhaps because part of my young life was lived "on the edge," I was very aware of the promise and the danger of straying beyond its boundary. How was I to live beyond the web that sustained me? How was I to live well beyond the ethos that defined me? What would I be when what I had was the knowledge of where I had come from? The heresies that could emerge upon the turf of *Korn* seemed less drastic than the chaos that lurked beyond the fence.

On the other hand, the grass out there often looked a great deal greener. Some of my father's generation differently experienced the *Korn* I knew as a child and were anxious to flee as soon as they could. Some were born with a differentness that was not tolerated by adults or by their peers and were treated like the aliens they became. Even these often had gained enough strength of character to achieve success in some other part of the world. To their later shock, they might discover that those still in *Korn*, whom they had fled, were speaking of them with pride as living proof of the worthiness of *Korn*. Many of the best of my father's generation abstracted themselves from the community, often because they felt a call to take the *Halig* they had found in *Korn* to those that did not have it. When my wife's grandparents felt called to China, they attended a German Baptist Seminary in Rochester, New York. Both grandparents studied in its extensive program for missionary medicine and were able to build a small hospital, a mile from Shang Hang, Fujian Province, China. Walter Rauschenbusch was its leading theologian. He has been celebrated as the father of the American "social gospel."

To emphasize that this was not heretical liberalism, I add that Walter Rauschenbusch and Ira Sankey coedited a popular evangelical hymnal, *Gospel Songs*. When I was young, I took for granted that all MB congregations used the German version of this hymnal titled *Evangeliums Lieder*, for their German services. Ira Sankey collaborated with Dwight L. Moody in a series of revival meetings that stressed God's merciful love.[5] When the young couple who became Marj's grandparents went from a rural MB church in Nebraska to Rochester to learn how to be pioneer MB missionaries in rural China, they knew that they would be taught the wholistic "good news" that they had long shared with faithful Christians.

Many members of our congregation illustrate this *Halig* orthodoxy. Prof. Delores Friesen is a marriage and family therapist who taught in the Mennonite Brethren Biblical Seminary at Fresno Pacific University and headed its accredited family therapy program. She and her husband were missionaries in Africa and he subsequently received his doctorate with a dissertation that traced the contribution of missionaries who helped shape the methods and discoveries of the early development of anthropological science. He had grown up on a Mennonite mission field with a wholistic program that included homes for orphans and widows, promoted agricultural

---

5. Rauschenbusch and Sankey, *Gospel Songs/Evangeliums Lieder*. The song book was cherished by MB congregations in the USA and Canada. I suspect some Canadian MB congregations still use it. Like Rauschenbusch, the "Father of the Social Gospel" and a Dwight L. Moody colleague, *Korn* traditionalists and many traditional evangelicals shared the biblical conviction that holiness and concrete wholeness had always characterized the traditional Christian "good news."

developments, and built schools and hospitals. His dissertation[6] reports on a consultation in 1910. Friesen examined other writings of missionaries who collected early folklore or who closely observed concrete village life in his book.

I add that the sense of concrete *Halig* I absorbed is reflected in a brief essay.[7] In it I argue for the authority of sages and parents reflecting the loving image of the Messiah Jesus who exhibited the image of God. My essay was a meditation on the simple chorus "Jesus loves me, this I know, 'cause my mommy told me so."

Prof. Alvin Dueck, author of the introduction to this memoir and also cited in the preface, is professor emeritus of cultural psychologies at Fuller Theological Seminary's School of Psychology. For two decades he led student and faculty groups to China to meet Chinese seminary faculty and pastors who were concerned to take more seriously the Chinese cultural context of their ministry. Not surprisingly, given a more collective cultural context, the Chinese churches had a profound love for the church as a community. Prof. Dueck met also with Chinese psychologists who had been trained in the Western models but were now wondering what a psychology "with a Chinese face" would look like.[8]

Many other *Korn* young adults wanted to be educated so that they could return to enrich the mind and *Geist* of the community. The young man who married one of my father's sisters was one of the first to go away to college, and he told me of the pressure he felt to stay at home.

He then helped my father to follow him. Both of them returned to teach in the community and to become superintendents of *Korn*'s church-sponsored academy. Both of them became ministers and leaders within the churches of the larger tribe. An astonishingly large number, for such a small place, became missionaries, pastors, teachers, professors, doctors, and other members of the service professions. A few became entrepreneurs and scientists and corporate leaders. That generation sent a wave of talent and reforming zeal out from the boundaries of *Korn*.

Many of my generation left for the same reasons, but, by now, more insidious forces were pulling us out. The land had been filled up. There was no room for most of the large number of children who had earlier been needed to do all the handwork that was required for a family to cultivate a quarter section. Larger tractors had arrived. Now one person could do the work of several. Most of my friends were pushed out, whether they wanted

6. Friesen, *Missionary Responses*, 135–49.

7. Wiens, *Making of Sages*, 99–102.

8. Dueck and Reimer, *Peaceable Psychology*, 179–200.

to go or not. Those just older than I got caught up in the turmoil of World War II. Many of the young males had to leave because of the draft, at least for a few years. Most of them never came back. The war that forced farmers to labor-saving mechanization also brought agricultural prosperity.

Korn paid the price of economic success. By the time I returned for one year to teach, there was seldom a large family on a quarter section of land. There were more often a middle-aged or elderly couple with one or two sons or grandsons who farmed many sections. Those who retired moved into the village. Even remaining active farmers moved there and now drive to their scattered holdings. The village of Corn now has more inhabitants than it had when I lived there, but their farmyards, what we called *Hofs*, have disappeared into the fields that once surrounded them. Most everyone still goes to church. But there are perhaps a third as many worshipers as when I was young.

To Specialize in Functional Abstractions

What shall those of us do who either fled or were pushed out of *Korn*? Only a tiny handful found a home in another concrete community, perhaps by becoming a pastor of a country church or a village school teacher or by marrying the daughter of a farmer successful in everything but having, or retaining, sons. The rest of us moved where there were jobs to be had, in often-distant towns and cities.

A job and a profession are what results when one aspect of the full round of activities that constitutes a basic society is abstracted out of that comprehensiveness and becomes one's occupation. Most of us made good employees and professionals. We were accustomed to hard work. We knew how specific tasks could be connected to fulfill a larger purpose and had developed appropriate varieties of common sense. Our experience with farm machinery had taught us at least rudimentary mechanical skills. And our relationships with animals and elders and peers had prepared us to cooperate with others.

The opportunity to specialize in specific tasks or professions brought the thrill of mastery. Abstracted people concentrating on specialized aspects of already abstracted functions become incredibly skillful at what they do. A farmer who can mend his horse's harness or even patch his own boots must appear clumsy to a skilled shoemaker. A "shade tree mechanic" repairing his harrow is an amateur compared to skilled machinists and mechanics. A farm wife spooning her string beans into jars cannot match the production of a cannery worker surrounded by mechanized equipment. The teacher of a one-room school will seldom match the detailed expertise mastered by a specialized instructor in a large urban school.

There is also the joy of working with those who share similar interests and serve a common goal. Instead of having to learn to like and to live with the relatives and neighbors who are one's lot in a small concrete community, we mostly learn about coworkers and what makes them birds of a feather who, in choosing that abstraction, have also chosen the flock with whom at least their working hours are spent.

With this narrowing of focus and increasing skill comes a new kind of creativity and a corresponding spirituality. Because they are focused around specific tasks, a network of communication emerges, and a *Geist* develops to serve the goal that is materially defined by the bottom line even if it includes more. The ecstasy that sweeps aside all doubts is the practice and the "theology" of progress. The old has given way to the new and the new yields to the newer. Every day abstracted individuals are swept into the future that is the goal and meaning of our routines.

Professionals joined with other professionals to offer the services that divided into increasingly complex subspecialties. Specialized people and specialized machinery made it possible for production lines to move faster and faster to turn out more and more items. Other departments had to be created to keep records, to design new products, and to sell what was being made. The original secondary association that was a group of the like-minded in a simple workshop gradually spawned a complex of secondary associations linked into what would eventually become a large corporation.

The new gods of the gospel of progress deliver much. But with every good there is a corresponding possibility of disorder. Pride in growing skill is swiftly replaced by boredom if one's job is narrowly defined, as on a swiftly moving assembly line. The satisfaction of speed and efficiency entails pressure. Like-mindedness breeds jealous competition. Even the highly skilled worker in a very complex operation may discover that the joy of a narrow mastery entails the loss of a concrete sense of how that effort contributes to the larger process. At a very high level, all these abstracted functions interweave with the others to create an economy and its ecology. But does anyone who experiences a vast cohesion fully understand it? Though progress must be welcomed, it remains true that, like traditional prophets, many philosophers, historians, and theologians discern the disordering consequences of *haireses* and heresies and what inspires idolatry.

The town and city that dissipates concreteness offers other secondary associations to compensate for the narrowness of one's occupational abstraction. Yet other groups of the like-minded gather around the interests for which one's occupation does not offer scope. One can join a softball league or a health club. Artists and musicians form their own secondary societies, as do those interested in camping or hiking, or in saving souls or whales. In the city all of the functions that were once part of the round of a single concreteness are multiplied and subdivided into secondary associations that enable us to flourish. Progress comes in many sizes and shapes and flavors.

The gods of more abstracted communities promise much but they also exact their price. They offer wealth and personal fulfillment as compensation for the loss of the satisfaction of shepherding the entire process of the tilling of the soil, the birth and maturation of one's livestock, and the building of a concrete community. Even the memory of a sacred canopy that nurtures a *Halig Geist* can disappear. But a powerful civilization can be built.

That Became Abstractly Rationalized

A progressive civilization must be built upon previous knowledge and continues to give birth to new information. For this, a third kind of abstraction becomes increasingly important. The farmers of *Korn* had already recognized this and had more or less joyfully accepted the challenge. The machinery they purchased came with actual or implicit diagrams or even blueprints that gave an abstracted two-dimensional explanation of how it was to be assembled or repaired.

The engineers at the factories that had manufactured these machines had given more elaborate versions of these diagrams to the machinists. Behind the engineers were the yet more abstracted laws of mechanical motion and of thermodynamics and of chemical interactions and of electricity. And behind these were the even more abstract ideas developed by great mathematicians. "I wish that I had learned more math in high school and had then gone to college," mourned my uncle Ed, who had become an expert mechanic. "Any idiot can repair what another person makes. I wish that I had become an engineer who could design them."

He was showing me around the large repair shop he supervised and partly owned. It seemed to me that he was wrong about one thing. I had been awed at the complexity of the huge wheat combine he had been working on. Not any idiot could do what he was doing. He clearly had the intelligence to apprehend the levels of scientific and mathematical abstractness implied in what he confidently handled.

The key to success in the new world was education in the layers of abstractions that were being built upon the brilliant abstractions of the great scientists and philosophers. Every department of the corporation, from designers to accountants to personnel directors to the sales force, governed its actions by the carefully rationalized corollaries that had been deduced from more basic principles. Behind each of the professions were equally impressive systems of rational abstractions.

Progress requires the discovery of more complex and mysterious levels of abstractions. When I was young it was almost true that any "idiot" could repair most farm implements. One could see the way power was transmitted from the belts to the gears to the action that was wanted. One could even repair a machine that one was seeing for the first time. But then came electronics and computers and mysterious little black boxes so complex that the eyes could no longer follow the flow of the action. With each new level of abstractive rationality comes a new symbol system for describing what is going on. With each new symbol system another large group of us become the "idiots" who are unable to comprehend the civilization in which we live.

Village, *town*, and *city* are images that expand into metaphors that evoke stories.[9] I have used both *Korn* and village as metaphors for the kind of concrete community I have described. I suppose there have been hundreds of thousands of small agriculturally based "*Korns.*" From the beginning of the agricultural revolution until the last century or two, most of the peoples of this world have lived and died in this kind of place. In some parts of the world, they still do.

But there have been, and are, forms of concrete community that do not look like *Korn* and which are not accurately called a village. Before villages there were hunting and gathering groups that gleaned their livelihood while wandering over large areas of grasslands and forests. These would have had a very different sense of boundedness and a very different relation to the land and to plants and animals. Some still exist.

Immigrants in their chosen countries often dominate distinct parts of large cities and build relatively concrete communities despite not having land to farm. Instead of walking out to fields, they took public transportation out to their jobs; or they built small stores to sell to each other; or they created cottage industries for their exports. For several generations they could hold to important elements of their languages, their religion, and their old-world ethos. I suppose some "ghettos" still exist.

Factories and other commercial organizations sometimes organize schools, clubs, shops, and entertainments in an effort to become more like a concrete community. Certain sorts of religious groups also try to become the center of many of the aspects of the lives of their members. If they succeed, the rest of us might think of them as cults.

9. Wiens, "From the Village," 98–149.

I consider groups of people who work at growing the parts of their lives into a living whole to be concrete communities, and I use village as a metaphor that also names them. I try to remember that what I say about *Korn* may apply to them, and I invite readers to rewrite what I say to fit their own histories. I have already hinted that other *Korn* exiles will have to do that when their memories of *Korn* do not fit mine.

Korn is more than a metaphor for me. It is also an important part of the larger *mythos* I construct to take account of my life. I know very well that the actual village was often a very uncomfortable place for me. My parents moved there so that my father could become the head of its academy. I lived in its center from grades five through nine. I had been an outsider. To repeat from the introductory chapter, I was a nerd and a preacher's kid.

We are free, however, to work at shaping our futures both through our hopeful anticipations and by the use of memory to make past goods the material for creatively dealing with the present. I have included in *Korn* the smaller community that was the Bessie country church that my father helped to pastor for all of my first fifteen years. It was an extension of the *Korn* congregation for its members on the far side of the river.

As embodying my earliest memories, *Korn* also provides me materials to construct my own understanding of innocence. As an ideal, it images for me the garden of Eden. I am very grateful for that, though going back to Eden is not the future that I would ever choose for myself, nor would I want to regress to my childhood or any other period of my life.

What I mean by *city* has been made fairly clear, I hope. City is what happens when abstraction and progress has most fully done its work. Life in a city does not have a single boundary around the places of one's activities. One can live anywhere in the city and travel to any other part of it to take care of the abstracted functions of work, shopping, recreation, and worship. Nor is a city a primary community. We exist in it as individuals who have chosen to go there to join the secondary associations it offers and to attend the schools that educate us in the abstractions by which it lives.

Despite its cultural richness, the city does not strive to be "basic." It can only exist by importing the food by which its people live. One can grow up in it without any real sense of the source of some of the basic elements that go into the construction and maintenance of a life. Finally, the *Geist* of a city is both larger (it is the summation of many lesser *Geists*) and thinner (it does not sum up a genuine concreteness).

A city separates most of the functions that were all grown together in the life of the village and puts each into the zones that have been designated for that function. Citizens leave their homes to drive to their jobs in the commercial sectors. They go to malls to shop. None of these zones are skins that contain a life. They are areas that define the performance of specialized functions. Not even the neighborhood one lives in is a primary community. They too, like the businesses and factories and schools and hospitals are, at best, quasi-abstracted. Individuals choose where they live and work and play and worship. One even chooses one's friends, and it now becomes true that birds of a feather flock together. Houses are purchased on the basis of what one can afford, putting one with others who are mostly of the same economic and age level.

I have been astonished at the instinctual skill by which children work to create some sense of concreteness in city and suburban neighborhoods that seem to the adults who also live there to be little more than an amorphous collection of individual families. But it remains true that the children grow up without a sense of how the basic aspects of a life and a society cohere. Common sense diminishes, but a new kind of sophistication becomes possible.

A vestige of the village remains. For most citizens, each family's home becomes a shrunken village. It is the bounded center that is the exit and place of return for all the forays of its members into the secondary spaces. It is the space of the primary unit of society, and it is where the most basic processes are supposed to happen for nurturing the deepest meaning of an adult's relationship to another adult and for the creation of new citizens with the moral and social skills needed for the well-being of the larger society. It is also supposed to create the kind of *Geist* that leads to the *Halig* that can still be imagined as good.

No doubt this sounds very negative. Most of the time I will be critical. Therefore, I must insist that the future I foresee for all of us is existence in a city. Almost all of my adult life has been spent in cities. The ones I have known best are Saigon (Ho Chi Minh City), Chicago, and Fresno, California. The seer of Patmos, who wrote the book of Revelation, described two kinds of cities. The metaphor for Rome his heritage taught him was "Babylon." It was the abstracting epitome of war and commerce and "progress." His name for a city worth living in forever was the "New Jerusalem," a bounded city where perfected individuals lived in the eternal concreteness of a transcendent *Halig*.

It is harder to describe what is a *town*. From the point of view of my metaphors, *village* and *city* are at the extremes of the single continuum that defines *concreteness* and *abstractness*. Some vestige of the village must endure in any possible city. At the same time the germ of every city is cradled in the village.

For the purposes of this book, the *town* is not a place that introduces any fundamentally new virtue or vice of its own. It is that place which can still live out of the living memory of what it meant to be a *village*. It deliberately develops the abstracting rationality and institutions that come to perfection in the city and its natural destiny is to grow into a city. I suspect that its *Geist* remains vibrant so long as it can believe that it will progress toward that goal. It may be possible for the town to shrink back into a healthy existence as a village but I cannot predict that it can remain a perpetual town without becoming rancid.

The towns I lived in were Reedley, California (during my high school and college years), and Hillsboro, Kansas. I went to Tabor College for two years, taught for three years, and to which I returned often to visit my mother and, now, a younger sister).

To sum up, the master metaphors that shape this book are the words *concrete* and *abstract*. A concrete community is one whose land and creeks and fields and living things are all grown together to create a single organism that has a boundary, a web that links its separable parts, and that embodies a unique personality, its own comprehensive *Geist*. The humans who live themselves into this web adapt to the ethos they build, learning the appropriate initiatives and responses that embody their manner of life. Such communities tend to be self-contained, providing most of the basic elements that are necessary for their survival. Because it tends to grow from within (is primary) and is limited by its boundary, it remains small enough that its members can comprehend the functions of its parts and develop a common sense of how they fit together. The goal of such a community is to become *Halig*, both healthy and holy under the protection of a sacred canopy.

Although all the levels of abstractness are always present within it, at least in germ, the time came when the village that I use to illustrate these processes filled up, and many of us were drawn out of *Korn*. Then persons were abstracted to go to towns and cities to join the secondary associations that collect individuals with suitable talents to specialize in functional abstractions. Their shops and industries and institutions produce the specific goods and services that had been knit together in the ordinary rounds of village life. The focused effort that ensues brings new levels of mastery and creativity. Secondary associations give birth to new specialties and sub-specialties. All of these depend upon knowledge that has been, and is being, organized into the rational patterns of shop manuals and textbooks that teach the abstractly rationalized principles which have been discovered to underlie the processes of natural and human interactions.

The goal of the new societies that are being built is progress. Some of the virtues and ideals of the concrete village are lost, despite intense efforts to build some of its more important functions into the life of the nuclear family. In any case, the three levels of abstractness make it possible to build great civilizations. They die when too much abstraction crowns their progress.

I continue to use *Korn* and *village* as metaphors for all sorts of concrete communities, even those that look very different. Despite its many faults, *Korn* is also the myth I create to illustrate the sensibilities and relationships that Jews and Christians have read into the biblical picture of the garden of Eden. I assume that every culture develops a myth of innocence from such materials.

I use *city* as a metaphor for the process by which the common sense and concrete character of its citizens continue to be nurtured in families and in clan and ethnic loyalties. At the same time, their interests and talents can be nurtured and expressed in the secondary associations that concentrate on the specific interests and needs of all viable cultures. These include the institutions of the economy and of the groups of social services that educate the minds, heal the bodies, express interests and talents, and elevate the souls of its citizens.

Whether or not they are fully aware of it, I assume that all humans are in search of either "Babylon" or the "New Jerusalem." I use *town* as my metaphor for the transition from *village* to *city*. Towns nurture the early mind and hopes of the city while retaining much of the memory and soul of the village. When I use village and city as ideal types at the two extremes of a communal continuum, all of us can claim to live in town. However, it remains appropriate to think of many small communities as villages and very large ones as cities.

The rest of this book is a deeply ironic attempt to give those who inhabit and construct nations to encourage creation of neighborhoods and ghettos, both within and outside urban boundaries, that evoke more of the concrete character of villages and towns.

In this meditation, I abstract several of the interrelationships that grow together in the village and that become progressively abstracted in the town and city to help us to understand what is lost and gained in the progress of civilizations. It is my hope that readers will be helped to think how to recreate within a larger ecology enough of what village and town has meant that the arrow of progress bends upward and not just outward to express our aspiration for prosperity and fullness of being—for *shalom* and *Halig*.

In the preface, I mentioned the biological maxim "ontogeny recapitulates phylogeny." But I intend my description of a relatively insignificant ethnic rural group in western Oklahoma during the era of the Great Depression and the years of World War II to show that the ethos of a community still in touch with a premodern and even biblical-era ethos may need to be somehow recapitulated in the lives of our heirs.

I do not assume that readers should want to build the *Korn* I describe. I do hope that readers will be guided to take their own heritages more seriously. If that past is largely forgotten, there are cultural historians and elders that teach about them. And I hope that stories of my odd life and its heritage can evoke insights that enable readers to construct the kinds of communities, towns, and cities that liberate, nurture, fulfill, and sanctify the lives of succeeding generations.

Excursus B
On Learning from Korn: *Misplaced Idealism?*

To invite the kind of readers I hope will interact with each other in this quest, the following paragraphs summarize an essay in the June 25, 2023, issue of the *Fresno Bee* titled "The Past Seems So Much Better Than Today."[1] It is written by Andrew Fiala, a philosopher and ethicist who consistently contributes enlightening op-ed essays. He begins this one with a scholarly study titled "The Illusion of Moral Decline" authored by Adam Mastroianni and Dan Gilbert.[2] He reports in the *Fresno Bee* that on average, modern humans express greater kindness and honesty than did previous generations. Prof. Fiala added that recent social and political life is better, women have been liberated, and there have been improvements in science, medicine, and technology.

He then cites a recent poll revealing that 58 percent of Americans think that our lives are worse than those who lived fifty years ago. Why do so many believe that? Prof. Fiala notes that historians have discovered echoes of this nostalgia throughout the historical past. He also suggests that the recent pandemic, political polarization, the war in Europe, climate change, and "rapid shifts in cultural identity" make our wish for a supposedly simpler and a more stable past understandable. But there has been no golden age to which we can return. I agree with his concluding advice to "get to work to build a future that is a bit less crooked, and a bit closer to the ideal."[3]

I repeat that there has been progress and that, on the whole, I do not judge that we are morally worse. And yet, I think that more must be said to account for the 58 percent of us who are more pessimistic and, also, to

---

1. Fiala, "Past Seems."
2. Mastroianni and Gilbert, "Illusion," 1–8.
3. Fiala, "Past Seems."

justify this book's meditation that I do not take to be merely a nostalgic exercise.

Premodern villages were less ideological than those of us progressing beyond the limitations of provincialism imagine. It is true that challenged provincials often circled their wagons and insisted on old status quos when forced to defend what they knew had been important. When I was a child, few young adults had patience to rethink the difference between living seeds and husks protecting seeds when too many "conservatives" resisted every change and—as I have mentioned before—too many "liberals" were sure that elders had become old fogies clinging to outdated husks.

Webster's New Collegiate Dictionary defines ideological as "a systematic body of concepts especially about human life or culture."[4] Or, when applying the word to political parties, it defines "the integrated assertions, theories, and aims that constitute a sociopolitical program."[5]

I sometimes encouraged students in history courses to think that American democracy had survived as well as it had because many citizens developed a *ratio sapientiae*, a reasoned wisdom that concrete proverbial communities modeled. Learning communal patterns of initiatives and responses to supernatural, human, and natural *presences* had defined the communal "soul" or "aura" that was more than the sum of its parts, a communal identity that reflected ideals and guided actions. A sophisticated common sense could cautiously embrace changes.

Drawing overlapping ellipses on the blackboard, I suggested that major political parties had platforms that exhibited significant disagreements and attitudes on the left and right side of my sketch. Nonetheless, a shared core of attitudes and convictions encouraged adjustments, permitting progress and patience until disagreements could be dissolved or resolved. Older Americans remembered growing into our common sense. It is also true that strong ideological commitments led to a devastating civil war.

Present politics reveal that we are increasingly fearful because consensus is unraveling and there are good reasons to fear that a disastrous way of thinking appears to be winning—one based on simplistic moral relativism and agnosticism about the affirmation of any justified convictions regarding any "way, truth, and life" or about faithfulness, hope, and love. Where anything goes, angry fear increases. For example, the March 3, 2023, issue of *The Week* magazine's cover headlined "An Epidemic of Anguish: Why Depression and Despair Are Soaring . . ."[6]

4. Webster, *New Collegiate Dictionary*, 430.
5. Webster, *New Collegiate Dictionary*, 430.
6. This article is based on this research report: Allen, "Long-Term Mental Health,"

As a cultural historian I knew of other eras when assumptions long taken for granted had to be rethought. Complex societies produce rival ways of thinking that replace common sense with the *ratio scientia* that deduce certainties from apparently irrefutable assumptions. Unfortunately, when one set of certainties confronts sets that stand over against it, simple agreement becomes difficult. For example, the axioms I learned in a plane geometry text "contradict" those found in texts giving the mathematics of spaces not flatly three-dimensional. Fortunately, most of us have learned that these contradictions are resolved by differentiating which types of mathematics applies to which types of space.

It becomes more difficult to reconcile opposed sets of certainties in the moral *scientiae* (ethics). Deontologists developed moral rules (the "thou-shalt" type) by deducing them from a compatible set of assumptions that defined fundamental rights and duties taken to be either natural or God-given, like the Ten Commandments. Utilitarian ethicists worked out moral recipes that aimed at "the good" ("by the fruits of actions you shall learn what works out for the best"). About a hundred years ago, ethicists began to give up reconciling these very different ideologies and began to search for other ways to explain their inability to harmonize sets of moral "certainties" employing very different moral logics.

As in the politics of abortion, when the moral compasses of legislators are committed to the supposedly most rational certainties of different versions of what is right or of what is good, they often can't agree with each other even within the same political party. If belonging to a different party, and especially if their moral compasses point to different poles, they may end up screaming at each other. Now it is difficult to wait patiently for compromises that often appear to be irrational or flatly wrong.

In the more or less hard sciences, fundamental assumptions were called hypotheses to emphasize that they must constantly be tested. Scientists confronting unexpected data and conflicting hypotheses can learn to enjoy mysteries while patiently testing even "mythical" hunches that might harmonize anomalies and become overarching theories that better explain facts that don't fit with theories.

Cultures expressing proverbial wisdom had a similar advantage. They knew that proverbs regularly complemented or flatly disagreed with each other. The difference between a sage and a fool was the ability, or the instinct, of intuiting the appropriate proverb. *Homo sapiens* could retain faith and hope in the face of life's inevitable uncertainties and erring judgments. Those now relying on "certainties" deduced from sets of ideas and ideals begin to lose the common sense that allows adjustments. Then minorities with opposed certainties sulk, convert, leave, and may face genocide.

The Greek word for parties confronting each other with different assumptions was *haireses*. The New Testament mentions the *haireses* of the Pharisees and Sadducees. First-century Jews agreed that *Yahweh* was the *Presence* guiding them to the *shalom* promised to Abraham. Pharisees recognized that old statutes and laws had to be streamlined and made more relevant to changes in the real conditions of their social and economic lives so that all or almost all Jews could understand and keep them. Sadducees assumed that God could act if elite representatives punctiliously made up for the failure of the poor and desperate people of the land to live up to covenant demands that seemed impossible or irrelevant. The sectarians of the Dead Sea Scrolls developed a more extreme version of a righteous elite that would free God to act. And from *hairesis*, English speakers derived *heresy*.

Jesus announced that he had been sent by Yahweh and that what he did and taught constituted "the way, truth, and life." After Jesus, desperate Jews chose yet another "solution." They mounted a rebellion against an imperial Rome, the enslaving *other* against whom virtually all its *haireses* could unite. That radical, but hopeless, "faithfulness" would supposedly free (or force) God to rescue them from Rome.

Whether or not ancient Hebrew *haireses* qualify as ideologies since they were derived from differently combined sacred texts instead of based on supposed abstract axioms, it is obvious that present Christians also differently point to faithfulness and fulfillment by basing their convictions upon carefully selected Scripture texts, like the *haireses* of the Baptists or Presbyterians whose churches do or don't resemble the church of a Mennonite *hairesis* which I attend.

Secular "sects" similarly differ from each other. When Democrats and Republicans meet to debate their platforms and to choose candidates for a national ballot, conventions can dissolve into angry debates among ideologues screaming their "certainties" against relatively different ideologues whose sets of political assumptions differ. At least temporary unity can be restored by resorting to demonizing the more or less opposed assumptions of the truly heretical *them* of the other parties which have their own conventions and platforms.

In our postmodern world, unfortunately, we lose the patience proverbial cultures had since they had understood that fools were not those who knew fewer or different sets of proverbs. Proverbs had countering proverbs. For example, "out of sight; out of mind" countered "absence makes the heart grow fonder." The significant difference between the wise and the fools was the experience and insight to intuit the appropriate proverb for the occasion. And since time might be needed to recognize what becomes the actual truth, individuals and cultures could more often be patient.

To sum up, all of us must constantly rebuild decaying cities as I must learn to rebuild what I learned as a child in *Korn*. All of us in North America are experiencing the consequences of "progress" from concrete, traditional communities that fostered a common sense. The quest for *shalom* and *Halig* were expressed in our racial and religious traditions, whether Judaic, Christian, Muslim, Hindu, Taoist, Confucian, or some other religious tradition based either on written sacred texts or on what I think of as unwritten or at least noncanonical Ur Testaments. Now all of us, including those who have been labeled the *secularized*, have to learn to live with our differences.

This book is a meditation on my distinct and relatively unimportant Mennonite sect even within the larger Anabaptist-Mennonite traditions. Though I cannot return to my mythic *Korn*, and none of my children and grandchildren will want to move to Corn, I hope that not only the 58 percent of us who fear what the abstracted modern era has done to us might learn something from this book that would help them interact with each other to learn how, in our own lives and ecologies, we can rebuild the kind of communities that help us and our heirs to both recapitulate what has nurtured our elders and to build a culture that better exhibits *shalom* and *Halig*.

I also write from the training of a cultural historian, and, so, I also hope that those who do not claim an ethnic or religious identity will want to dialogue with those of us who do and will also want to explore this or other resources that help to understand our different stories and to welcome each other to help rebuild our cities.

CHAPTER 4

The Places and Times of *Korn*

THE FOUR-BLOCK MAIN STREET of the village of Corn matched my memories despite many absent buildings and some new ones. Though not so tall and dramatic as the old church that had dominated the countryside for miles around, the modern MB building was spread over more of the double block that centered the village. There had always been gaps across the street from it, especially after DeFehr's still-small John Deere dealership moved to Weatherford. The flour mill and wheat elevator reminded those who entered from the east that the main business section of my mythic *Korn* was a diminished derelict. The block west of the church, *Korn*'s "shopping mall," still evoked its past. A small, well-designed Memorial Park now stood where Tina had built her first café and become a hub of the community.

PLACES AND SPACES OF *KORN*

I could recognize the older homes on the side streets, but the feel was different. Most of the homes were new, but it was the yards that seemed most changed. There were no expanses of bare dirt. There was no buffalo grass, or whatever it was, that we had mowed and pretended were lawns. Now the grass was smooth and green all the way to the creek that defined the north and western boundaries of the village. The strip of weeds and canes that suggested wilderness between the creek and the homes had been tamed.

I had driven from Weatherford in Uncle Ed's van to visit some friends and kin in the nursing home, and to see if I could attend the Alumni Banquet of the Corn Bible Academy. I had no reservation, but I was passing through Oklahoma at the right time and had learned that one of the features of the program was a tribute to the fiftieth anniversary of the class of 1949.

I would have graduated with them had we not moved to California at the end of my freshman year. They were happy to sell me a ticket at the door, and I enjoyed meeting old friends and others I had known when I taught there in 1961–1962. In the days that followed, however, my thoughts circled around the alien emptiness that had haunted me while driving through the countryside.

The larger *Korn* had become beautiful. It was only a few weeks before the wheat harvest, and the long green stems holding yellowing heads of grain pulsed gloriously to the rhythms of a moderate wind. The harvest would be bountiful, if it didn't hail, but it puzzled me that many fields were being cut. Instead of waiting for the grain to mature, farmers were binding the stems and milky heads into large rolls. The market price for mature wheat was so low that many of them thought it more profitable to store the unripe wheat as winter food for the beef cattle grazing the stubble of already cut fields. My older memory of the natural and sacred rightness of traditional harvesting was offended, but that was not the only cause of my unease.

Ironically, the glorious beauty of the countryside hinted at the source of my discomfort. I reveled in the sweeping vistas of rippling fields and green trees. There were fewer of the straight lines of trees that had been placed around especially exposed fields as a government program to stem the terrible dust storms of the thirties and to provide income for the farmers who planted them during the accompanying depression. Now many more trees and bushes curved naturally through valleys between the hills, covering the steeper slopes. The effect, at least during this brief season of the year, was both stunning and disquieting. It was as if a landscape architect had created a mannered park from what had been a small farmer's West with untamed edges. An occasional dead armadillo along the road showed that new species of wildlife had moved into the new areas of brush, but the new wildness no longer had the feel of unfinished business in the settling of this place. It now seemed to have been planned. As in Switzerland, what was left was a civilized natural beauty.

Had I come later when the fields were disked, or during some earlier drought, I might have responded differently. When I turned from wondering at the scene to noticing my wondering, I knew two things. I had changed. I could take that for granted. What I had not expected was that my stance for seeing had changed.

I was no longer a chubby, late-getting-his-growth-spurt boy stretching to peer over the lower sill of a car window. I was an average-size adult sitting tall in the driver's seat of Uncle Ed's large van. I was not driving over often-rutted dirt lanes between steeply pitched ditches full of tall weeds, looking through and over them at the equally tall weeds that had lined the fences and obscured the fields beyond. Now most of the roads I took were graded up and paved. The ditches had been gently contoured into shallow depressions to permit easy mowing of grasses that could also be baled for cattle feed. No weeds obscured my view of the nearby fields and distant hills. I had been raised far enough above the land to see a more distant horizon. From the taller swells of land, I could imagine what it would be like to comprehend the entire space of *Korn*.

The village was still the center of the community and it did not feel empty. In fact, it had grown larger. Most of the old homes had been replaced with larger, modern houses set on larger yards. Though there were fewer children, its population had grown. I knew that most of the children that had lived on the family farms when I was growing up had moved away. But it was obvious that most of those who had remained now lived in the village, near their surviving aged parents. Apparently, the successful farmers who had added field to field had fled to the center of the community to escape the emptiness of farms without traditional farmyards.

That was it! The *Hofs* were gone, and with them their families. Years after leaving *Korn*, I had come to think that most of them had been ugly, but now that they were gone I missed them, along with their two-story wooden houses, big red barns, smaller granaries, chicken houses, hog pens, and patches of rusting machinery. Horses, milk cows, chickens, and pigs were also gone. Even the fences, many of them, were gone. A handful of twisted windmills had not yet been removed.

The *Hofs* were gone, along with what it had meant to be a family farm. The *Geists* of the *Hofs* were also gone. Each had had its distinct *presence* that revealed and then molded the character of those who created and maintained it. No wonder the land seemed so empty despite its beauty. They were gone, whether or not a house and a shed or two remained where a farmer still preferred to live outside the village.

The English word *farmyard* signals poorly the concrete reality named by the German word we used, though it is true enough that a large, bare yard was always its center. This yard was so pecked over and walked over and driven over that its many paths merged into a single bare dirt flatness connecting the buildings and pens. From its circumference, defined arteries led out to all parts of the farm, ranging in width from the driveway and the broad fenced lane that guided cows and horses between the barn and the pasture to the parallel tracks made by wagons and tractors moving to and from the fields. The narrowest trail led to the one- or two-holed privy behind the house.

The yard was the center for the farm's most basic functions. From the barns and granaries, pigs were slopped and chickens fed. Cows came willingly from the pasture to receive a portion of grain and hay as a reward for their milk. In the winter more of their time would be spent in or near the warmth of the barn across the way from the warmth of the house. The *Hof* was the entire circle of those buildings and their inhabitants. *Hof* named the pulsing heart of the living organism that was a farm. The word allows even those of us who lived in the village to remember the *Geists* that filled them.

Each *Hof* lived between two aspirations. Each sought the self-sufficiency of material concreteness. Its existence would never be threatened if all the basic needs of its members could be produced inside and if it could be defended from outsiders who coveted its goods. This was impossible. Tools, fuel, and much else had to be imported. Even food staples, like sugar and salt, could not usually be produced. Each also sought the spiritual wealth of a larger spirit. Complete concreteness would have ruled out the rich gifts of others. Isolation would have thwarted its family's urge to fulfill itself in the meanings of larger wholes. Its *Geist* was enlarged and fulfilled in merging with those of its neighbors into the larger *Geist* of the richer concreteness of the entire community.

The *Hofs* of the countryside had been scattered originally on each quarter section. In the Dutch-German settlements of the Ukraine, from which most of these people came, the *Hofs* jostled each other along both sides of the roads so that people could live nearer each other. The fields stretched long and narrow behind them so that oxen, which were much harder to turn, could efficiently plow long furrows. In this corner of the new world, it had been decreed that at a certain moment on a particular day, the original settlers could race to the one hundred sixty acres they wanted and lay claim to that quarter of a section if they tilled it and lived on it for at least brief periods of each year.

Though *Hofs* in this new land were now more separated than in the old country, I don't think that I have ever seen one in the middle of its holding. Around *Korn*, as elsewhere, a lane of a hundred feet or so led to the section road that connected it to neighbors. Here a mailbox nailed to a post linked them to the rest of the world. The road also led to the elevated central yard toward which almost everyone funneled on Sunday morning to honor the God above the larger *Geist* of which all their smaller *Geists* were parts. This church was at the intersection of the wider roads that led to other villages and to the towns and cities that formed the ever-larger spaces and more abstracted *Geists* that were the county, state, nation, and world, of which they were also parts.

I want to believe that *Korn* retains a concrete *Geist*, though I suppose that it more often excites nostalgic gratitude for the past than grand hopes for the future. I also imagine that its *Geist* is less complex, for it has lost the many smaller *Geists* of the many family farms of which it had also been composed. The village of Corn may always have been the heart of the larger *Korn*, but now the village web is almost the whole of the local human concreteness that remains. To live outside the village would seem to suit either those who have become more isolated or those whose inner sense of themselves is linked to larger, more abstracted, communities.

For all I knew, the space that could be claimed by present citizens of *Korn* had expanded to match the ambitions of its remaining farmers. Even if I had been sure of the present boundaries, I would still have experienced that space as a homogenous quantity. What I missed were the varied qualities of the places that had once graced it. The *spaces* of the *Hofs* had never been absent from surveyors' maps; what could not be mapped were the *presences* that had defined them as significant *places*.

Even wildernesses contain a variety of spaces, like a grove within a forest that imposes a sudden hush upon an intruding wanderer, as of a revelation of a sentient spirit who makes its dwelling there. Perhaps farmers who give careful attention to each field continue to sense the special qualities of each, but what was left for me was the impression of a quantity of space that had been emptied of its most significant *Geists*.

Just as the fields and creeks of the larger *Korn* were a part of the incarnation of its larger *Geist*, so the entire spread of the farm had participated in the *Geist* of the *Hof*, which was the central place for the ordinary business of living and working. It both secluded its members from neighbors and strangers and furnished them with the means and the desire to interact with that larger world. Yet each of its parts possessed qualities of its own. I was sometimes tempted to linger in the private darkness of an outhouse to daydream and to observe the dust motes dancing in the thin slits of sunlight that filtered through the cracks of its walls. Like pigpens, however, the pungent smell of the place did not encourage loitering. By themselves, the smaller sheds and pens had little quality. Only the barn and the house combined qualities significant enough to project personal *presences* of their own.

Intimacy and transcendence were built into both the barn and the house as soon as it was possible to build something better than half-sunken sod houses for the family and lean-tos for the animals. Except for sleeping, the kitchen and its adjoining living room was the homey space for family life, for eating, for schoolwork and for playing games. Here the family focused around itself. Here neighbors were invited to share the family warmth.

The formal parlor, for those who could afford to add one, invoked a more elegant *presence*. In my memory, the parlors were sometimes dark and musty, with dust covers spread over the finest furniture of the house until the time for the serious hosting of important guests. Because music was highly valued, a piano or a pump organ was often present. Some featured a large wooden gramophone and a small rack of precious records. Guests were invited to enter for serious conversation. Church ministers and deacons were ushered in for ritualized spiritual checkups. The family Bible and at least a few books would be there. This was the special place for "higher culture."

I have thought that even the barns possessed a sanctum for more private reveries and elevating meditations. The arched spaciousness of large haylofts above milking parlors and horse stalls resembled the interior space of churches, inviting individuals to stretch beyond the smells and textures of the ordinary places of the *Hof*. A cupola at the top invoked the aura of a steeple and funneled stale warm vapors upwards, allowing fresh air to enter under the eaves. Our large wooden churches heightened the formality of the parlors and the expansive spaces of the barn lofts, while adding floors and benches made of varnished hardwoods, throne-like high-backed chairs for the ministers, and tall arched, frosted windows through which the sun bathed the startling whiteness of walls and ceilings in natural light.

The *Hofs* that had once given a human aura to the spaces of the countryside had shriveled into the yards and homes of nuclear families and had mostly retreated to the central village, which had lost the imposing *presence* of the old wooden church. Its new campus covers a larger area, adding spaces useful for the many functions that now are abstracted parts of the program of a modern congregation while preserving a sanctuary large enough to seat many more worshipers than normally attend. Since it has no windows, my first impressions of its interior matched my memories of the dark intimacy of older parlors. In the past there had been ornate plaques with Bible verses and, perhaps a painting of the head of Christ. Now there was a baptistery beyond the pulpit. Behind that was a lighted cross.

A later visit, when the lights were on, revealed a latticework of brown-stained beams that arched to support walls that sloped upward in the shape of an enormous tepee that culminated in a large circle of colored frosted glass through which at least some natural light could penetrate. Just as my first impressions of the larger space of *Korn* had suggested that the living *Geist* of the community had shrunk to the place that was its village, so now it seemed to me that God's invisible canopy over the entire space of the community had descended and congealed into a visible shelter for its remaining elect.

My stance for seeing had changed. More importantly, *Korn* itself had changed. Perhaps most importantly, all of us at the alumni banquet had also changed. I had lived in Asia, had traveled around the globe, and had attended two of the world's finest universities. My knowledge *of* this place was no longer the direct knowledge of continual lived experience. For me the world had both expanded enormously and had shrunk dramatically. I had been abstracted from this place and thrown outward into a multitude of spaces. I could only partially master them as places by enclosing them within myself through the abstractions of thought *about* them. I had become esthetically aware of many *presences* and had been enriched by my appreciation of their qualities; but I had not lived deeply enough into any of them to make my own the concrete heritages that they possessed.

I, too, had become modern. Though occasionally weary of abstractions and unsatisfied with mere esthetics, I am profoundly grateful for the life that I have lived. I was born at the right time to enjoy the gifts offered by modern technology, the cultural sophistication made possible by interactions with many peoples, and the intellectual stimulation of some of the world's greatest thinkers through their books and as interpreted by some of the best teachers of the preceding generation. At the same time, I was born in the right place to have been essentially formed by a community still sufficiently concrete to instill the blessings of pre-modern *Halig* while modern enough to prepare me for my future. I have been privileged to add the intellectual and material coin of modernity to the inherited spiritual capital of an older way of life.

Though nostalgic, I had not wanted *Korn* to be entirely unchanged. I knew very well that I had never wholly felt at home while I was living there. Part of me, however, still longed for the comfort of a primarily human *place* to shelter me from the alien differences of other places and from even the most beautiful spaces marked mostly by degrees of latitude and longitude. I also wanted that human place to be larger than the home that I enjoyed in a far-off city. Yet I was now judging my natal place with the tools and habits shaped by abstractions. I was ironically enjoying the esthetics of concreteness remembered.

I am, therefore, amused when I think back upon these feelings. I remember the instantly revived camaraderie of former classmates. All of them, even those who had remained, had also moved beyond the older boundaries. All of us, I think, were grateful that *Korn* had given us the desire and the abilities to move beyond it. We were its alumni, telling the old stories that expressed the ethos we had lived and the *Geist* that continued to nourish us. *Korn* was a success, and so were we. Most of us had become adapted to the abstractness of a modern world that destroys the unique qualities of individuated places and that expresses its own fundamental emptiness in the functional spaces of bare rectangular skyscrapers sheathed in monotonous green glass. I share with you again what the beautiful and sophisticated young lady had said to me a long space ago in Saigon could have been said to all of us. "We envy you . . . we really do. You seem to know where you come from."

It is true that recent architects have recognized our recoil from the modern ideal of abstract geometric spaces, adorning newer structures with nonfunctional shapes and decorations borrowed from many places and long-passed eras. We have fled the wearying spaces of our daily rounds and retreated to the family rooms and dens that we have built into our homes. Like the *Korn* sanctuary, we have then filled them with relics that incarnate aspects of our past concreteness. Then we add souvenirs that remind us that we have gone beyond *Korn*, that we have also been there and done that in the larger world.

In the end, all of us in the city crave something like the varied concreteness of a *Hof*, if only to have a bounded space that both defines a personal and familial *Geist* and also mediates our own to the *Geists* of our neighbors. As huge government projects to warehouse the poor have proved, the lack of appropriately varied spaces with inherent qualities invites alienation. As even luxurious apartment buildings show, closeness does not evoke neighborliness.

Of course, not all of our old comrades returned to this reunion. Some had escaped with memories dominated by dark places and angry *presences*. All of us who were present were marked by a few such shadows, but we were the fortunate ones. I strongly want to believe that we were true representatives of the very large majority whom *Korn* birthed and nurtured. The rest of this book is devoted to illustrating my conviction that everyone needs to have had a place which does for them what *Korn* had done for those of us who were happy to return—and again to leave for the real and imagined richness of the larger spaces and the private places—from which we came.

After taking back his van, I mentioned to Uncle Ed how landscaped the borders of Corn Creek had become on its way around the north and west of the village. Its edge of wildness had been tamed. "What kind of vegetation do you remember along the creeks?" He paused, and said, "I loved walking along the creeks and noticing the variety of trees and plants." Then the litany spilled out, like an incantation:

> China Berry, Sand Plum, Hack Berry, Elm (two kinds), Oak, Jack Oak, Black Walnut, Red Bud, Dogwood, Sassafras, Sumac, Blue Grass, Catalpa, Osage Orange (it's also called Hedge Apple and Bodark), Willow, Cottonwood, Maple.

I knew that Uncle Ed had given up on farming and had followed his father to the dealership in Weatherford. I wanted to know about his feeling for the earth. "What did you like best about farming?" I asked him. He thought a bit and answered, "Standing out on a field, feeling the wind in my face, and feeling free." I visualized him standing in his fields, perhaps in the prairie to the northeast that had never been plowed, with a circular depression where the buffaloes had often come before their near extinction. This buffalo wallow had entered into my imagination during the late thirties when he was still farming the home place on the eastern edge of the boundary of *Korn*. From the pasture, one could look far to the east, toward the less productive, sandy fields beyond *Korn*'s richer soil and, turning toward the south, almost to Colony, where Cheyenne and Arapahoe had been settled only a handful of years before the Mennonites appeared. Sometimes Uncle Ed turned up arrowheads while plowing.

I remembered staying several days at their farm, probably a weekend when Dad was away preaching somewhere. The house was a lonely one, down the wrong side of a hill to the west that seemed to me to be a barrier to the *Korn* beyond its crest. There were few, if any, trees to soften the barren yard that was defined by a barn, a shed or two, and a creaky windmill. At night Aunt Emma, my mother's sister, took me to the almost unused and unfurnished second story of the house. In one small room was an iron bedstead with a mattress and some bedding. I felt very small and dreadfully alone when she returned to their downstairs bedroom. The eerie cries of not-so-distant coyotes knifed through the wind that was howling around the corners of the house and whistling through the iron of the windmill. Too ashamed to ask to sleep on the floor downstairs, I fought my fear and loneliness until, eventually, sleep came.

I had also been feeling free, dreadfully so. Only Uncle Ed and Aunt Emma, sleeping below, connected me to a familiar web. I was a child. Perhaps I would have been brave enough to walk alone beyond the pasture during the day, but I doubt it. For me, that buffalo wallow was the beginning of the wilderness.

"Feeling free," for Uncle Ed upon his field, was not at all the same as feeling disconnected. He knew that his field was linked to the fields of his neighbors and to the entire community. It was also his turf, accentuating his individuality. At the same time, it connected him to possible friends and neighbors on the far side of his pasture. To the east, beyond Cobb Creek, there were other sorts of communities. He had later rejoiced with them when desperately poor hardscrabble farmers on too-sandy soil had discovered that it was perfect for peanuts and when World War II prices made them unexpectedly prosperous. He could also applaud their need for expensive new John Deere equipment.

I realized that he had always lived on borders. He almost always referred to *Korn*, with an ironic edge to the words, as "Cobb City." He had been glad to step beyond *Korn*'s northern boundary. He was also content that he was close enough to remain connected. After I commented on how clean and pleasant the nursing home in *Korn* was, he even allowed that it was a possible resting place to prepare for his last transcending freedom.

While still thinking about the places and the spaces of *Korn* to write this chapter, I learned that Uncle Ed had moved to a small apartment in that home. Then, while working on these pages, I heard that he was no longer able to handle the round of daily activities and had been transferred to a room in the assisted-living wing. Like most of those in his generation, Uncle Ed had enjoyed becoming modern, but he had always remained near enough to keep a critical eye open to the traditional qualities of *Korn*. And now, sensing his frailty, he has moved back to close the circle of his life surrounded by others who have been formed by the *Geist* of this place.

THE TIMES OF *KORN*

Those who have been shaped by *Korn* know well that there is a time for everything, "a time to plant and a time to pluck up . . . a time to mourn and a time to dance . . . a time to love and a time to hate . . . a time to seek and a time to lose . . . a time to live and a time to die."[7] Like places, times also have qualities that cannot be measured by modern devices.

Time, for my elders, had not been an endless sequence of abstracted moments. It was rather a moving nexus of cycles composed of distinctive and repetitive periods. Each day was a cycle of known qualities, from the set routines of the morning and evening chores that bracketed the varying morning and afternoon tasks on the fields and the *Hof* to the evening family time that ended, for many, with Scripture-reading and prayers. A minister friend of mine from a "*Korn*" far to the north twice told me about his father who, for many years, had been convinced that God had rejected him. Every night he continued to read from the Bible and to ask one of the other members of the family to pray. Despite his despair, the daily rhythm of work and prayers could not be abandoned. My friend's eyes misted and his voice quivered as he testified how much this faithfulness had affected him. Before he died, my friend concluded, his father had joyfully experienced God's loving *Presence*.

The week also had its particular rhythm. Chores had to be done every day, but Saturday afternoons were given to Sunday preparations and to an expedition to the nearest town or village to buy and sell and to visit with friends from other *Hofs*. The summing up of each week took place in and

---

7. Eccl 3:1–8.

around the sacred place of the central sanctuary. Each day and each week climaxed in the family and communal celebrations that lifted up before God the ultimate meaning of its spirals of time.

These shorter circuits fitted into the experience of the seasons of each year, which climaxed in the sweaty labor and the joy of harvest and which received its glorious exclamation point, again at the church, in the annual Harvest Festival.

The year was also a parable of the great rhythm of each lifetime. The seasons expressed the fresh beginnings of childhood and youth, the steady years of productive work, the fulfillments of providing land and livelihoods for one's children, and the shortening days leading to the honor and the promise of old age as well as to the coming cold.

I had not deeply known the reality of *city* until I was hastily transferred to Saigon to face hundreds of thousands of refugees whom I was supposed to help to feed and clothe and resettle. Since no one had told me about culture shock, I had to try to figure out by myself the confusion that I experienced. The simplest explanation, of course, was that I was too young and too inexperienced for the work that I was doing; but I also sensed that there was something more.

Finally, I stumbled onto the recognition that an important reason for my distress lay in the disruption of my sense of the movements of time. All my life had been governed by the cycle of the seasons and the two rhythms that had been governed by this cycle: the patterns of seedtime and harvest and the complementary alternation of school studies with physical summer labor. I had been so profoundly shaped by these that my inner clocks could not readily adjust to haphazard transitions between frustrating inaction and bursts of frenzied effort. Only gradually did my body and my spirit accommodate to the shift from the only slightly cooler time of rains to the hotter, but slightly less humid, dry season. I later realized that there is more to culture shock than a changed experience of time, but I continue to be convinced that spiritual and psychic health depends upon fitting into the seasons of the natural world, discovering a productive rhythm of work and rest, and maturing with the larger cycle of birth to death.

The *Korn* that I knew had probed the secrets of older sorts of times before reapers and tractors introduced them to the productive power housed in the clanking, roaring heavy metal beat of endlessly repetitious moving rods and spinning wheels and turning belts. But our elders could enclose these early signs of modernity in the forever rhythms of recurring times with timeless qualities. Those early machines also rested most of the year. Our elders knew the weariness of long and heavy labor, but they did not yet guess the triumph of one-damn-thing-after-another in the rat races of late modernity's radically compressed, yet endless time.

It is true that time as a sequence of featureless moments so impressed our elders that they reverently hung wood-framed clocks on the walls of churches that had no crosses. Yet the Roman numerals on their large faces, their ominously spear-like hands, and the solemn ticking of their pendulums somehow emphasized the relation of our fleeting times to the eternal. The early discovery of abstracted time added another mystery to the magic that was time. As if in preparation for the triumph of abstraction that would displace the older magic, we youth had also discovered the fascination of clocks, taking them apart to discover the secrets of their motions.

We could hardly imagine a timelessly abstracted soul or even a purely nonspatial heaven. Nor, whether or not we consciously thought of it this way, did we live as if our embodied selves occupied only the space enclosed by our skin. Each of us organizes the space around us so intimately that the horizon reshapes itself to all our movements. Only during times of intimacy, when we allow the spaces of others to merge temporarily with ours, can we endure the too-close presence of another without discomfort. Therefore, as times for intimacy illustrate, both space and time are aspects of concreteness.

The conception of either as a measured quantity wholly distinct from the other is entirely the product of abstraction. Whatever Einstein meant when he spoke of "space-time," we may claim the term for our older recognition that the qualities of both came together in a concrete world. Our own time-space was a nexus of all the other times and spaces with which we interacted.

TIME AND SPACE IN *KORN*

The union of our earthly places and times was dramatized at funerals. I know that by the 1930s funeral directors brought the bodies to the little country church of the Bessie Mennonite Brethren, but burials were still a powerful communal tribute to the place where we had lived and to the completed circle of a life. Men of the church had hand-dug the grave. After a service inside the church, the congregation walked with the casket to the cemetery and prayed and sang and heard another, shorter homily before the body was lowered. Then the men, in some kind of order determined by churchly rank and closeness to the deceased, passed around a shovel to throw earth into the hole. I can still hear the first clods hitting the drum-like caskets. As the earth piled up, the horror of the first hollow thuds faded. More men took shovels, and the filling grave returned us to the almost comfort of the sounds of ordinary digging. Most of us stayed until the earth was lovingly patted into the finality of an enduring mound.

After the burial, we shared a meal in the church basement and the mood changed. Stories were told of the deceased that might bring chuckles to the most bereaved. When paper plates began to be used, we boys might gather up a handful and return to the cemetery, where we sailed them into the wind.

We are nourished by the earth from which we come, and to the earth we will return. The earth, however, did not have the final word. It was the ground of our concrete existence, but not the entire substance and time of it. The community lived on to mark a larger rhythm, as did our memories of the deceased. Because the whole was held in the eternal faithfulness of God, the late loved one could be trusted to the care of God, who would someday reunite us as concretely reembodied selves, however unlike present earthly stuff might be our resurrected bodies.

It felt appropriate, therefore, to know that our bodies would soon complete the cycle of dust to dust, nourishing the earth and the worms and the ants and the smaller living organisms that nourished the plants that made possible all higher species. In some dim sense we may always have understood that we had the right to live off this chain of life only if we offered our entire bodies back to the large rhythm within which the life of each is made possible only by the gift to it of the lives of all the others.

That was not the only possible reason why my elders were horrified by cremation, which scattered most of the body's elements through the vagaries of the wind to no particular place. They recited "ashes to ashes" with "dust to dust" only because it was part of the entire biblical phrase. But surely that part of the image was to be taken literally only by pagans who starkly abstracted their souls from their bodies, believing either that the soul died with the body or that it was an eternal "real self" that either went directly to its dis-placed afterlife or first transmigrated through an almost endless succession of animal and human bodies.

Marj and I were startled, therefore, when her mother announced that she wanted to be cremated. She had gone to her potter's wheel to shape an urn that would fit inside the cemetery's box for burial above her husband's vault. Had this nearly ninety-year-old daughter and wife of Mennonite missionaries and ministers become so modern that she wished to celebrate the abstracted integrity of disembodied souls? Had she abandoned the idea of an earthly resting place? Though modernity had been at work, those conclusions were unlikely.

I have since wondered whether Mom understood that modernity has so changed the manner and meaning of burial that what looks like the conservative continuation of village practices is now almost its opposite. The process now begins with an attempt to make the face of the deceased so lifelike that fundamental change can almost be denied. Embalming fluids preserve the rest of the corpse long enough that family members and friends from spaces around the globe can gather for a final viewing and the ensuing rites. The body is no longer interred in a simple pine box that will decompose with it into the nourishing earth.

Because the fluids used to embalm are so poisonous that they sterilize the soil, the embalmed body is usually housed in a metal casket or in one made of exotic hardwoods that almost never decompose. To guarantee the continuing integrity of that box, it is enclosed in a cement vault. Because burial now serves to deny the body's concrete connection to natural cycles, the corpse remains in a state of slimy putrefaction as long as its enclosures seal it from the healing earth. Mom's decision has led me to suspect that cremation is now the most conservative way to honor the older orthodoxy, short of an almost immediate burial outside a public cemetery. I am glad that what are now called "green" burials are being offered.

What is not returned via smoke to the natural cycle will be placed in the clay urn that she has shaped. Before the urn was fired, she asked her two daughters to paint symbols on it of the two most significant place-times of her pilgrimage. Marj painted a bamboo to represent the place in southern China where she was born to missionary parents and where she grew until the age of twelve. Carol painted a tepee to represent the twelve years her mother and father pastored Comanches around Post Oak, Oklahoma.

The urn with her ashes was to be interred above Dad's coffin in the cemetery outside Reedley, where her father, stepmother, a brother, and many of her husband's siblings and their wives were also buried, along with a wide circle of friends and relatives. Her ashes remain in a communal place accessible to people. She happily invited her children to take advantage of the cemetery's policy to accept five urns above the plot necessary for a single coffin. She had discovered the best way to honor our past love of time and place and community. I have also become convinced that being buried together with more of her family had been her conscious reason for cremation.

I had written these wonderings about her wish to be cremated long before she died three days after we celebrated her one hundred and one years of life. Mom had actually shaped a smaller urn, also decorated with bamboo and a tepee, and, by then, Marjorie had decided that Mom had "told" us that she also wished to be buried in Indiahoma, Oklahoma. During their ministry among the Comanches, they had grown so intimately into the *Geist* of Post Oak that the Quahadi clan, to which the last Comanche war chief, Quanah Parker, belonged had honored them in a ceremonial "adoption." We later took that urn to Indiahoma where those buried at Post Oak had been reburied after an army base expanded its artillery range. About a half-dozen of her immediate family were surrounded by two dozen of her enlarged family who planned and led the burial of the smaller urn with some of her ashes.

During an earlier visit to Indiahoma, a very well-educated young lady asked me how to think about a photograph taken when a carload was given permission to accompany someone with official permission to revisit Post Oak. On a photograph of the site of the old burial ground, a circle of dancers in full regalia hovered above the bare ground. She acknowledged that older Indians were not as puzzled as was she and those like her. When they wrote to ask the large automated facility how such a double-exposure could happen, they were curtly told that it was impossible.

I responded with a story told me by a *Hutterish* aunt whose aged father had agreed to pastor a small congregation in South Dakota and whose mother had announced to him that she sometimes heard a crying baby. Since the nearest neighbor lived perhaps a mile away, he assured her that was impossible. She persisted, and soon he, too, began to hear it. After tracing it to the wall of an upstairs bedroom, they contacted the farmer who had rented them the house. When he heard it, he cut a hole and lifted a tiny human skeleton from between the studs. He admitted having rented the house to a young couple who had mysteriously disappeared several years earlier. With a brief funeral service, they buried the skeleton and the crying did not return.

I hope to remain sufficiently childlike to enjoy mysteries. I also confess that I doubt the appropriateness of granting legal status to the presence of individual concrete citizens to corporations even though I know why our legal system does that. And even abstract legal fictions reveal actual quasi-presences.

All of Marj's parents and grandparents came from places like *Korn*. All of them had been abstracted from their natal villages. Dad's parents and his five oldest siblings emigrated from the then-Russian province of Ukraine and settled in Saskatchewan until drought and depression drove them to Reedley. Mom's parents left Nebraska with a strong sense of calling to China, where her mother died and was buried. Between Dad and Mom's marriage and retirement, their twelve years at Post Oak and in nearby Indiahoma was the longest period that they had lived in a single community. Clearly, the first level of abstraction had become part of our lot.

I was born and raised in the space-time of *Korn*, but I did not live long with the illusion that I would remain there. Uncle Jake, who had married one of my father's older sisters, had earlier left to attend college and had then helped my father to follow him after he had almost given up on finishing high school. The 1930s forced the departure of many more. World War II guaranteed that most young men would leave—and that few would return. Not many of my classmates remained in *Korn*. "Modern times" had fully arrived and had abstracted us from our homes. Such departures are always painful, whether individuals depart out of ambition or in anger. Perhaps it is even more painful for those who, like me, were just beginning to have hope that they belonged.

The larger horizon that I had seen and imagined while driving around *Korn* in Ed's van was the boundary connecting all its enclosed parts into a home for a people. A boundary, of course, is also an edge; and edges in a larger landscape are links to the otherness of alien concretions or even more alien abstractions. An edge is a comfort when it defines one's place. It is a promise when one's place becomes a prison. It is a threat when it becomes clear that one will be forcibly abstracted.

I had not wanted to leave *Korn* when my father agreed to become the superintendent of a larger Mennonite high school in Reedley. I had known what it was like to live "on the border," among the "English" in Cordell and, later, among the half-strangers of *Korn*. When I was old enough for high school, my bookishness was less of a social handicap. Students from Bessie and up to a hundred miles away came to their academy, and some of them were also bookish. Some of my *Korn* grade school classmates now turned out to be more like me than I had thought. I was beginning to belong and dreaded to again be the outsider in communities owned by others. I was just beginning to stretch above the windowsill of our car to see more than the steep ditches and tall weeds along the road. I was just beginning to comprehend the character of a community that could furnish materials for a myth of Eden.

Had I remained longer, I would have become too aware of the serpents that lurk in every Eden. The original serpent also spoke significant truth, as the text of Gen 3 acknowledged before abstracting Adam and Eve. My elders also understood that *Korn* existed in part to help us move beyond it. There is loss, but also great gain, in exile from the Garden. There are also profound, and profoundly ironic, gifts that come with the knowledge of Good and Evil.

I count myself among the greatly blessed. I was fifteen when we moved and not merely five or ten. I had lived in *Korn* long enough to be able to learn many of the steps of the giant folk dance I had joined and to remember stories from the levels of interrelationships by which I and my friends were being formed. I had a taste for the concrete and a desire to explore abstractions. Nor was I a sophomoric eighteen, anxious to judge all flawed concretions against impossibly pure abstract ideals. I do not think that I can imagine a more fortunate introduction to the world.

CHAPTER 5

The Work of *Halig*

IN CHAPTER 3 I compared a concrete community to a giant web with tonus. Each connection in that web has sufficient tautness to pass on its vibrations to the entire web. I also likened both the sharing of emotions and the work of building its *Halig* to a giant folk dance with each hand holding a hand or resting on another's shoulder. Someone moves, tugging upon a hand or pushing against a shoulder. How shall the second one respond? Should she pull back the other's hand? Should he yield to the push? Should each pass on the message to yet another?

To grow mature in such a community is to learn the dance, to know when and how to initiate new actions in response to prior actions, and to do so in the light of future responses and the initiations they call forth. Through the tautness and interconnections of the web, all share in the construction of the village's institutions and the ethos that incarnates its *Geist*. To talk about the qualities of our spaces and our times, as in the previous chapter, was also to talk about the qualities and the contexts of its dance floor.

To imagine dancers with multiple arms, some extended in time and space invites us to comprehend a complex, constantly changing set of movements responding to deep rhythms over time and space. Life itself becomes an extended dance that is not an endless grind if rest and play are built into its rhythms and if the whole of the dance achieves its transcendent purpose. The metaphor would be more appropriate, of course, had *Korn* not so sternly frowned on dancing.

The three aspects of the work of *Halig* can be illustrated by three positions of the dancers. They stood upright or knelt in contact with the earth they tilled and upon which they moved and built. This chapter reflects on labor and on work upon their soil. In the next chapter we reflect on the second position of the dance in which their hands stretch out to touch each other and to share the privilege of constructing their characters, their ethos, and their institutions. It was also true that at any moment their arms were poised to sweep upwards in awe of God and in gratitude for the sacred canopy that hovered over them and that is the theme of a third *Halig* chapter. The earth, the others, and God were three great themes of the entire pageant. These three themes converge in the individual, each of whom is a nexus of all these relationships.

WITH FEET UPON THE GROUND AND HANDS IN THE SOIL

The rhythm of each day began with chores for all except the infants. Small children gathered eggs from the hen house. Older children fed and watered the animals and were soon able to milk a cow or more. A friend commented that two more milk cows appeared whenever another sibling became strong enough to handle the job. After an hour or so of chores, the members of the family gathered for breakfast and then moved out to the one- or two-room country school or to the seasonal tasks that defined the rhythm of the year. In the early evening the chores were repeated before supper could be enjoyed, homework done, and games played. Family prayers often completed the day.

Just as the fields and the house flowed into each other on the *Hof*, so the boundaries between the work of men and the work of women and the work of children were seldom fixed. Here too, the dance with the earth and nature called forth surprising patterns. Men could neither give birth nor suckle the young. Women, therefore, were primarily responsible for the home and the youngest children. But the prosperity of the farm demanded another focus for her around the *Hof*. Virtually all of the farm wives milked cows, slopped the hogs, and fed the chickens.

In addition to their use for food, income from the sale of chickens, eggs, and cream was an important contribution to the success of the whole operation. During the busiest periods of the year, many of them also worked in the fields. A farm was a family business, and many women had a strong voice in its management. Neighbors might even speculate which of the women had the smarts and the drive to "rule the roost." I suspect that much of the early-modern "domestication" of women was a result of the demise of the *Hof*.

The women were also farmers in living contact with the soil. Perhaps their fingers more often entered the soil than did those of the men. For them and for their men, a hoe or shovel was a direct extension of their arms, permitting them to touch the earth while standing up. Indeed, the most intense farming of the entire operation was theirs to supervise. After horse- or tractor-drawn implements had dug and smoothed a plot, they planted and tended a large garden. Many dozens of quarts and half-gallons of meat, fruit, vegetables, pickles, and pickled watermelon joined crocks of sauerkraut and smaller jars of preserves in the cellar.

For both spouses there were special times to play and to pray, times when the play that was implicit even in work was lifted into the shared communal work of a hog slaughtering or "bees" when they gathered to can food or to quilt. For all, there were regular times when the prayer that was felt on the *Hof* and on the fields was solemnly raised to God in the church even if, as in our country congregation, the leaders standing behind the pulpit saw most of the women sitting in the rows of benches to their right while most of the men sat to their left. Whether or not on the *Hof* or in the church, there were times when the essence of work and prayer and play and friendship was distilled and savored, when all times were revealed to be God's gift to all God's children.

My parents had no farm; but, like all children in the community, my sister and I grew up with our hands in the soil. At first it was in play that loose dirt was our sandpile. Then gardens kept us in touch with the feel of earth and seasons. Soon we, also, were working in the fields, whether the cotton fields in Oklahoma or the vineyards of California. That meant my mother had to work with us; her supervision of us in the field was part of the tacit bargain that induced farmers to hire us.

Finally, I realized that poverty was only half the reason she needed to goad my sister and me into hard labor. We were the excuse she needed to do something other than house chores. She had been the fifth child in a family that pioneered in central South Dakota. Her two older brothers were not as many hands as were needed by their ambitious father. Her two older sisters were mostly kept busy helping to sew and cook and clean. Mother, unfortunately for Grandpa, was the beginning of a string of five girls. She and the sister who followed her were treated as boys and sent out to the fields she learned to love. Then Grandpa had his reward. Three more sons followed all those girls to help in his last years of farming.

My father later enjoyed revealing that it was he who had taught her how to bake bread. He had been kept at home during what would have been his eighth-grade year to help his ailing mother. He had learned to cook and to mix and knead the bread on a table dragged beside her bed. Tradition held that one of his two older sisters should stay home, but his progressive parents decided to allow the older sisters to finish high school.

NON-HUMAN PRESENCES

I had been prepared for thoughts about our relation to the earth and the animals when Uncle Ed had taken me on a tour of the DeFehr dealership the day before I drove his van to Corn. The DeFehr who was then the general manager of the entire operation had declared an open house to show off the new space for garden tractors and other smaller machines, but what had stirred my imagination were the monstrous diesels parked outside. The floors of the glass-sealed cabs were high above my head and the inside, said my uncle with a grimace, was "more like the cockpit of a 747 than of a tractor."

When I was young, we had *driven* tractors, but I could see that these required *piloting*. I remembered his almost scorn during an earlier visit to the service department he supervised before his retirement. "Look at me, I used to be a tractor mechanic. Now I'm a hi-fi technician." Little noise and no dust from the field being tilled would disturb the pilot's enjoyment of high-fidelity cassette players and CDs or his cellular phone connections to his wife or to his brokers at the Chicago commodities market. He might even be buying cattle loaded on trucks that were already moving along a far-off highway in anticipation of such a call.

I chose to walk back to his home. While pushing my way through the grass beside the road against a strong wind, I tried to imagine what a farmer would see and feel from so lofty a perch. What had become of his relation to the land? Had anything changed in his feel of the earth? When I arrived at Ed and Emma's, I had shaped my question.

"Ed, what was a farmer's relation to the soil when he tilled it with oxen and horses? How did that change when tractors first came in? And what is it now when piloting a huge machine from an insulated cabin, listening to talk radio and music?" Unfortunately for me, Uncle Ed had been one of *Korn*'s early moderns. "I didn't like horses. I didn't even like to ride them. And I hated sitting on a cultivator a couple of feet behind two big, fat horses' rear ends all day long."

I could appreciate the sentiment. For the two summers after my sixth and eighth grades, I had worked for Adolf Klause in place of the son he never had. One of those summers he decided to harness the team he kept for what I took to be mostly sentimental reasons. They had been used so seldom that they were a little wild, but he put me on a two-row cotton cultivator and put the reins in my hands with injunctions not to dig out the plants at the end of the rows when I turned the team. For two days I was alternately terrified and bored. At one end of the field the rows came so close to a barbed wire fence that only a split second separated us from tearing up plants or running into the fence. I will never know how I got the horses out of the fence when, just as I was calculating the turn, a large horse fly stung one of them and she lunged forward. I have a hazy memory of returning to the field with Uncle Klause, a shovel, and a lantern late one evening to reset plants at the ends of numerous rows. I am quite sure that this memory is not a frozen remnant from a later nightmare.

    I have been glad for those two days. Terror and boredom had not been my only emotions. I was appropriately proud when I managed a well-timed U-turn and awed that two such large animals usually obeyed me. I enjoyed the squeaks and clatter of the cultivator and the gentle slaps and rubs of the harness. Though the blades did not go deeply into the earth, they turned up rich looking loam and destroyed most of the weeds. At least I had escaped the roar and smell of the Farmall tractor that I usually drove when fieldwork was to be done. Best of all, I was gifted with a memory that has inspired me to wonder what it might have been to be shaped into this disappearing way of life.

    I could barely imagine what it had been like to break the sod with a handheld plow, but I had known some who did and I wanted to understand them better. Emma's father, my Grandpa Kleinsasser, had done so both in South Dakota and in California's San Joaquin Valley. Uncle Jake, who helped my father go to college, remembered the sod house in which he had been born and in which he lived during his earliest years.

    Since Uncle Ed did not like horses, I later asked a former classmate about working with them, and he told me that he had recently been regaled by his ninety-plus-years uncle with stories and exact histories of the dozens of horses his family had owned. In the old days, when life had been concrete, a horse was more than a fun ride; and a good team was more than an extension of one's muscles. A good horse, for a farmer, was also the relational "other" with whom he united to focus the energy of the soil.

    Many yeomen loved their horses. Some farmers do yet. At the turn of this century, a cousin's son who was a fully scientific South Dakota farmer and rancher was dreaming of the day when he could handle all his cattle operations with horse-power alone. His perfectly matched horses were twins and had won that state's horse-pulling championship. The Amish naturalist, David Kline, celebrates the sensual and spiritual joys of this way to farm in two books of graceful essays.

> And then there are the pleasures of plowing—plowing encompasses more than just turning the soil. Although I can't fully describe the experience, it is like being a part of a whole. In early spring, my son and I, each with a team as eager to be out as we

are, turn the mellow soil, feeling its coolness and tilth. We take pleasure in the transient water pipits and pectoral sandpipers feeding on the freshly turned earth abounding with life. As we rest the teams, I listen to the joys and uncertainties of teenage years.[1]

Unlike cows, horses were not milked or eaten. Dogs and cats also escaped these fates and could join the family play in addition to the special uses that earned them their keep, but horses were essential partners for tilling the soil and harvesting the crops. Their intelligence, strength, and latent skittishness earned them cautious respect and they took on human traits. The distasteful task of turning their bodies to other uses after their death seemed mostly to have been consigned to outsiders.

Since horses needed times to rest and to catch their breaths, even labor on the field was a rhythm of work and rest. If two farmers were resting their horses on the line between their fields, they might well take the time to discuss church and community business. For them it would have been arbitrary to assume that they had divided their afternoon among work, rest, and committee meetings. These activities were experienced as interpenetrating facets of a single time. No one needed to take a vacation to recreate from the burdens of labor. "Recreation" had been built into the entire rhythm of the year. The purpose of travel was to build the *Halig* of one's larger clan by visiting relatives, to serve the mission of the church by being a delegate to conferences of like-minded disciples, and to go to cities to search for things and experiences that could enrich their lives and the life of the community. Perhaps all of these would be combined on the same journey.

Rhythms of work and rest shaped even the intense labor of harvest. Three hours would hardly pass between breaks for lunches and drinks that were taken to the fields. Those were in addition to elaborate breakfasts and suppers for which the workers came to the *Hof*. When Marj was fourteen, she was sent to the Oklahoma Panhandle to help cook for a harvest crew. What she remembers is that it was the women who had little time for rest.

A farmer did work alone in his fields for days at a time; but harvest season was not the only time that his labor was lightened by sharing it with others. The earth itself, with its own energies and rhythms, was the active partner that elicited relationships with neighbors and with God.

---

1. Kline, *Great Possessions*, xxii.

HUMAN PRESENCES

"In the old days, I would work for my neighbor for several days when he needed help, and then he would work for me. We never thought of paying each other. We never even kept track." Uncle Ed hesitated, and then stammered, "I guess it all came out even." He was silent a moment, recognizing how odd it sounded. Then he finished in a final burst that managed, somehow, to combine the comfort of certified fact with unease about its virtue. "But nowadays you can't work for each other without being paid immediately, cash on the line."[2]

Work had not been important enough to keep track of! It was no wonder that my increasingly modern uncle had faltered after framing the thought. Work was necessary, of course; but neither skill nor sweat could guarantee a harvest. The same amount of work and careful management that preceded a bumper crop one year might lead to crop failure the next. Failure could be guaranteed by refusing to work or by doing it badly or by doing it outside the fitting times, but success was never a certainty. Therefore, work could not be the only measure of the value of a person and time could be given away.

The rain came or it did not come. Hail and killing frosts came or they did not come. Insects and disease moved through the fields or they did not. And there was little they could do about it. "Success" was not alone their doing, and so they depended upon others and on God, and not only on themselves. Through the anxious days of waiting and the agony of watching hopes being blasted, they either learned to be bitter or to trust; and in this trust they learned to see their work as not their own. Their energy flowed out into the greater energies of God, the energy that was—had always been—the source of their own strength.

Work was not so all-important. And then again it was, for it united them with God. There were times when work was worship, and this was its ultimate meaning. There were mornings when the gates of the soul swung wide to mystic interpenetration while the body moved along the furrow made by horse and plow. There was a fluid sweep in the rhythm of a scythe, and a sweaty ballet in the movements of the harvest crew. There were also afternoons, for one must learn endurance. And there were times at close of year when, moving through the smokehouse and the granaries, they felt the rhythm of the year summed up as a psalm of celebration.

Then, there had been a time for everything: a time to work and a time to rest, a time to play and a time to ponder the mysteries of God and of

---

2. Uncle Ed, personal communication.

God's world. Indeed, when the music of the dance was strong in them these times flowed into each other and were one time.

When they theologized their relationship to the land and the community, their activities were summarized as *stewardship*. The parables of Jesus about stewards made good sense to them. A steward was entrusted with the important task of taking care of his lord's property. To improve the community and to find new land for sons and daughters were as much the extension of the kingdom of God on earth as was the careful personal use of any of the gifts of God.

Being generous for the sake of the *Halig* of their *Hof* and community was as much a mission as sending missionaries to heathen lands. Since many of the necessities of life could be produced at home or secured in barter, money was only one aspect of the bounties of God. Therefore "stewardship" applied to all the goods of life. To limit stewardship to the tithing of their money would have required the assumption that only a part of God's bounty belonged to God.

There was a word for the virtue of effortless action and of caring serenity. It was *Gelassenheit*. My father defined it for me as a state of relaxation that was neither fatalism nor mere resignation. It implied an action that was and was not ours, an action born in trust, of letting God work through one. It named a release from anxious responsibility for the goods for which they worked and a joyful participation in the labors that helped to make them possible. Those who had it could share their action as freely as God shared nature's bounty. They could kneel while standing straight even as they stood up straight while kneeling, for they knew themselves to be children of God who shared in God's creating power. When Sunday came they shared their worship and their celebration with those who understood with them the Sabbath rest of God.

I am grateful that I lived long enough ago to have known old men whose lives were at one with earth, animals, and neighbors. I, too, have sensed the strong tenor of their relation to the soil. I, too, have walked through fields with my elders.

Except for morning and evening chores, most of the work that I had done for Uncle Klause was done with a tractor. After a summer of picking fruit in the orchards and vineyards of the San Joaquin Valley of California, I knew that I preferred to work on tractors and traveled back to work for Arnold and Edna Wedel during the summer after my third year of high school. Though still simple and close to the ground, their machines testified to the fact that modern technology was forever changing traditional yeomanry. Yet the setting for my work was still pre-modern.

For the three summers that I worked for the Klauses and the Wedels, I was integrated into the concreteness of a *Hof* and was at least an honorary member of its family. *Tante* Klause was a doting "grandmother" and their daughter Sophie combined the best traits of a younger "aunt" and older "sister." She was a coworker on the *Hof* despite the continuing effects of a childhood bout with polio that lamed her. Edna Wedel was a member of our extended Wiens clan.

My first day at the Wedels was painfully symbolic of the lingering *presence* of the past. I had arrived in time to help thresh a field of oats the old-fashioned way. Arnold's semi-retired father and I pitched bundles of oats from the shocks in the field onto a wagon to be transported to an ancient stationary thresher. Unfortunately, the effects of nine months of school and a tonsillectomy received within the week made me a victim of Uncle Wedel's taunts that I could not keep up with an old man, until I sagged against a haystack and was sick.

During the length of my first summer with the Klauses, I had no idea what I would be given at the end of seven weeks. The thirty-five dollars that I received had more the feel of an honorarium than of a salary, though I could do the math and suspected that Saturday chores had been discounted. In any case, who could calculate the value of the work that I had done and deduct the cost of board and room? A church friend who lived in exile among the *Englisha* of Cordell was given a calf at the end of that summer's labors on another church member's *Hof*. Uncle Klause must have pondered long what he should give. It is hard to know what is right when traditions shift. I, too, struggled with the past. I knew well the old rule of straight lines when I was thirteen and learning how to plow that late in a *Korn* boy's life.

My elders, like other European immigrants to the vast American Midwest, imposed the methods of the old world onto the new. In Prussia and then in Ukraine, they had gradually adapted older European methods of farming to the Vistula Delta and then to the Ukrainian steppes. What they learned was passed on from fathers to sons and grandsons as elements of a long tradition. Not even the systematic efforts of a few progressive reformers in Russia toward the middle of the nineteenth century had fundamentally erased time-honored wisdom.

Fields in their parts of Europe had been long and narrow because the oxen it took to pull a plow were difficult to turn. Over many generations, they had taken pride in keeping their long furrows as straight as possible. In Oklahoma, land came squared in smaller plots, but our pioneer elders had adapted to shorter rows since horses could manage turns much better. When tractors were accepted, they could box the fields, proudly ending perfectly straight rows with gently furrowed corners that converged with geometric exactness to the middle of the field.

Beside the fact that I was young and small for my age, and a bit too fat, the two front wheels of the Farmall I first drove were so close together that the tractor resembled a tricycle. This was fine for row crops but made it easy to waver out of line while plowing. Worse yet, when I looked back to see whether my wobbles were obvious, my arm on the steering wheel would move and, when I looked again, I would see a bigger wobble. I remember vividly a furrow with two large curves that I then tried to straighten out so gradually in the subsequent rounds that my shameful double lapse might not be noticed.

The folly of plowing straight lines was already becoming obvious. Pounding rains on fresh-turned earth were not absorbed. On every hill, gullies had appeared, over which the plow had sometimes to be lifted. Some hills were so steep that they should have been left in pasture. For part of one anxious day of seeding wheat for one of Klause's neighbors, I wavered between fear of crooked lines and dread of tipping over.

Three years later, while pulling a combine in one of Arnold Wedel's fields, I had to slow the tractor, turn directly down into a deep wash, and then curve up its other bank. Twice I came so near botching the two gear changes I had to make that the momentum of the combine almost overwhelmed the tractor at the bottom. Each time, Arnold screamed and, after I had stopped at the top, came running to me, visibly trembling. I learned well to respect erosion.

I was glad, however, that I was working for traditionalists. Other farmers had begun to challenge the righteousness of straight lines. They responded to the natural action of the soil and listened to the government's agricultural agents who taught them to sculpt low swells of soil around the hills to hold the water from rushing down. I appreciated the need for contouring the land. I could even admire the graceful curves of the contours. But I was not sure that I could till such land without damaging the mounds. Keeping a tractor straight was hard enough.

Worse yet, I worried about the souls of the progressive farmers who were willing to change the traditional moves of our dance upon and with the soil. They were vaguely dangerous. They were listening to the doubtful science of skeptical university professors rather than to the settled wisdom of the past. They were probably the ones who had begun to wear khaki work pants instead of divinely designed bib overalls.

Unfortunately, contours do not solve all the problems of erosion, as I discovered when I went back to *Korn* in 1961 to teach at the academy. I arrived in the middle of the week before the start of school and remembered that this was the season for preparing ground for the fall seeding of wheat. Suspecting that farm hands might be in short supply, I went to Main Street and let it be known that I could do a day or two of work before school started the following Monday. One of the farmers looked me up, took me out to his field, and did a round with me to show how he wanted it harrowed.

His tractor was similar enough to those of the thirties and early forties that I did not have much to learn. Though windy, the air was still clear when he left. Before long I found myself in the middle of a heavy dust storm. An earlier rain had left a hard glaze on the field, which soon began to be scoured by dust blowing from neighboring fields to the west. Ever the conscientious one, I knew that the only hope of saving some of his topsoil was to continue to break it up. Soon I could barely see beyond the front of the tractor. By the time I got to the end of the field and had doubled back, the furrows I made had already filled with the dirt of his and neighboring fields. To make it worse, I could no longer see the wet hollows and twice had to disconnect the harrow to get it out of mud. Somewhere I found a chain or rope to pull it far enough that it could again be hitched to the tractor. At noon I went back to my lodging and got a large sock to tie around my nose and a bottle of water to keep it wet.

It was an afternoon from hell. The next day I learned that the old-timers were comparing the previous day with the dust storms of the "dirty thirties," and I was told that they knew of only one other person who had stuck it out all day. I knew that soil is precious. We are all both linked to it and nourished from it. I had a duty, even at the risk of "dust pneumonia."

Despite my youth, and despite the smell and roar of the tractor that came between me and the smell and feel of earth, there were times when plowing became a sacred act. Some mornings, when the mix of mulch and soil and moisture was ideal, the earth curved smoothly and willingly inside the shiny arc of the steel shares, and I could feel that I was part of a larger communion with the process of creation. Despite the tractor, I was part of a *Geist* that linked the earth to heaven.

There were also times when I heard music out of the roar of the tractor. I knew very little about classical music, but I seemed to hear symphonic movements. I hardly trust my memories when I think back upon it now, but I do remember wondering about my mental health. The music was so beautiful, however, that I could let myself enjoy it. It has more recently occurred to me to pretend that I was hearing the music that underlies the greater dance, but I don't quite believe it. Surely, my head was trying to subvert the tractor's steady roar. I wonder, though, whether what I was hearing was closer to that music than the canned stereophonic fidelities resounding in the plugged-in heads of drivers in lofty cabs. In any case, I suspect that if I had to do it over, I would prefer the modern pilot's throne. I would know, however, that there was something important that I had lost.

THE REVOLUTIONARY PRESENCE OF MODERN TECHNOLOGY

Few of my *Korn* elders questioned technology. Apparently, the elders had hoped that its advantages could enhance their cherished ethos and that we children would receive a double blessing, weaving the throbbing of the future into the rhythms of the past. By 1961 Uncle Cornelius knew better. We had been talking about the old days while sitting on a cement stoop close to his home in Corn. Suddenly, with quiet intensity, he exclaimed, "I can't tell my sons anything anymore." I protested, "That's not true. You have good sons. They love and honor you."

He waved aside my misunderstanding and, after a short silence, explained what he meant. "In the old days, I bought a cheap, weak tractor. Everything was about staying out of debt." Then, holding his hands less than a foot apart, "We plowed so deep. In a good year we got eighteen bushels an acre. Now my son goes deep into debt to buy a big tractor." Moving his hands much farther apart, he concluded, "Now he plows so deep, and he gets forty bushels an acre."[3]

He gave me time to digest the message. The problem lay between him and modernity. He was an old man whose thoughts and ways had been shaped by an older wisdom that was no longer relevant and he had nothing to say. Melancholy hung in the air. A short time ago old age would have given him the right to transmit practices honored for generations along with the opportunity to give good advice distilled from life-long relationships with the soil, with animals, and with others. Old age was then the crown of life. That traditional world would have acknowledged him as a sage. His descendants and the larger community would have valued every word.

That world was disappearing. The old rhythms had not found a way to grant the modern beat an appropriately limited place within its patterns. The yardstick and the metronome had won. The progress made possible by abstraction had the last word. Now farm animals existed only to be milked or shorn or eaten. Distant cities had extracted almost all the children. The earth was losing its qualities and being reduced to quantities of chemical ingredients as measured in test tubes. It had become dirt that could be enriched with artificial additives.

---

3. Uncle Cornelius, personal communication, spring 1962.

Uncle Cornelius may have been saddened, but he was not bitter that his status had been usurped by university-trained agricultural agents preaching to farmers eager to learn the latest scientific good news. Had I thought of it then, I might have protested that his story dealt only with plowing and that his hard-won wisdom might still be true of more significant aspects of their lives. I think he would have waved that aside as another proof of my failure to understand. To appeal to "other aspects" would have acknowledged that scattered abstractions remained. An older, concrete common sense is essentially irrelevant in a modern world, even for those of us who continue to remember the past with gratitude. Even the most trivial product of the modern factory is a strident evangelist for the new worldview.

The new science was heresy, of course, in the strictest definition of the word. It was based on the decision of early Enlightenment philosophers to abandon the worldview of a concrete traditionalism that was becoming idolatrous. They adapted the older rationality that sought to comprehend many complex interrelationships dimly revealed by an unshielded light scattering its rays from the top of a hill to the analysis of what could be revealed by a narrow beam of sternly focused light to analyze a physical world that could be rationally deduced from the kind of data available to a single, colorblind eye.[4] As in Martin Buber's elegant prose, they were reducing the *presences* of the inter-relational "I-Thou" cosmos to objective "I-It" relationships among *things*.

Descartes made a crucial division between the realm of mind/soul and the realm of matter. Mind was substance that possessed the attribute of thought without extension. This was the reality of God and, within this world, of human minds. Matter was substance that possessed the attribute of extension without thought. Therefore, the entire created universe, everything that defined a space, including the bodies of animals and humans, could be thought to be reducible to assemblages of matter operating according to mathematical and mechanical laws. Machines had become so important that they now became the model for understanding all things physical, and, for some, subhuman animals.

Subsequent philosophers and physicists mostly agreed that matter could ultimately be understood to be atoms that were, more or less, solid, extended, shaped particles in motion. In themselves atoms do not have color, sound, taste, or odor, though they can cause human minds to have these impressions because external atoms can move the atoms of our bodies that can, mysteriously, affect our minds. In themselves no atoms, not

---

4. See ch. 10 for a different view of science (Prigogine) that is not rooted in Enlightenment rationality.

even our own, can possess the heat or cold or pain or pleasure that can be experienced only by our souls. Since no other animals have souls, they were mere machines that had no consciousness. Some thought the cry of a beaten animal to be as meaningless as the screech of tires driven too fast on a curvy road. For many, animals were merely livestock to be exploited for profit. How much less could trees and plants and the earth itself have *presence*?

The generation or two between the elders and myself harbored few doubts. The new technologies made possible by the focused vision of the new worldview promised to make the earth more fruitful and their labors easier. The scientists could even teach us how to heal the damage created by the inappropriate application of old-world wisdom, like the law of straight-line plowing, to the different conditions of this new land. They were messiahs proclaiming a new gospel for a kingdom of this world.

Modern zealots were sure that the traditional view had no real defense against the new. It, too, had valued efficiency. Better methods for growing and preserving food had been celebrated as gifts of God. Nor had the earliest mechanical cultivators and reapers distanced them much from the soil and natural rhythms. When an explosion of new techniques opened the late nineteenth century, few of our elders had understood the underlying factors that led to a "bottom-up" materialistic worldview that produced astounding technologies. There were good traditional reasons to welcome the new ways that would destroy the old traditions. Like Uncle Cornelius, many of my elders must have become uneasy, but they could not foresee the consequences that inevitably followed.

Few of them were the kind of sages who could trace the long-range effects of this all-conquering revolution. Their convictions and sensibilities had been shaped by concrete older patterns, and these remained mostly intact throughout their lives. They could respond with spiritual fervor to the gifts offered by a worldview that implicitly denied the real existence of *Geists*. The new gospel was good news. Their labors had been eased. The earth was becoming more fruitful. Erosion was being tamed.

The Amish, among the Mennonites, were sufficiently suspicious of the new to wait until it became clearer what effect the new inventions would have upon their way of life. Eventually they agreed that tractors with the wheels removed could furnish power for processes like milling and lifting grain and sawing wood without destroying their relationships with the land and with their animal coworkers. Many accepted telephones so long as they did not disrupt their families within their homes. A few Mennonites compromised by imposing upon themselves the penance of suffering the rough ride of tractors with iron cleats on iron wheels instead of accepting the comfort of pneumatic tires.

The villagers of *Korn* scorned halfway measures. They were happy to accept the mindset of the town. Especially the young of the preceding generations would have it all—the living memory of tradition with the heady excitement of modern progress. Males eagerly studied the action of levers and belts and flywheels and gears and power takeoffs. Few of them faltered before the mysteries of incandescent light and of simple electrical controls. They became at least "shade tree mechanics." Boys dissected clocks and whatever else they were permitted to overhaul. Hundreds of thousands, if not millions, of new moderns across the American heartlands traced the flow of energy through the fantastical contraptions drawn by Rube Goldberg for almost every newspaper's Sunday comic section.

One-Eyed Pete, of course, was an embarrassment. He took the obsession much too far. He was our next-door neighbor the first year that we lived in Corn, and I was afraid of him. He stared fiercely out at the world through his one good eye while the other socket revealed only a deep and shadowy hole. Fortunately, I do not remember that he ever directly looked at me. Like Superman's use of X-ray vision, he seemed to focus his attention narrowly on what lay far ahead as he lurched swiftly but awkwardly forward with his spastic stride. One-Eyed Pete was an inventor, potentially *Korn*'s McCormick or Edison. We lads were sure that he was mad.

One day, when I was older, I snickered to Uncle Ed that One-Eyed Pete had been said to be working on an invention that would produce perpetual motion. It is my only memory of a swift rebuke from Ed. "Never laugh at One-Eyed Pete," he chided. "Many years ago, he announced that he was inventing a machine to harvest cotton." We also laughed. Years later, after someone else invented and marketed cotton-pickers, I went out to look at the big pile of rusting metal that he had abandoned out in the corner of a field. He had done it. All the essentials were there, even the spindles. The problem was that his motor was too weak to power it.[5]

Since then, I have wondered what would have become of us if some had believed in One-Eyed Pete enough to subsidize his efforts. I have also come to imagine him as *Korn*'s far-seeing prophet of modernity. I do not know whether he was colorblind, but surely his single eye furnished him the monocular vision of early modern physics. Unhampered by the complexities of binocular perspective, had he transformed our fascination with early machines into an obsession?

Had he really tried to invent perpetual motion? Or had someone else thought it was appropriate to project that quest upon him? Had he, with powerfully focused vision, grappled in earnest with the problem of entropy?

5. Uncle Ed, personal communication, summer 1999.

What would happen to all our machines when the fossil fuels that powered them were used up? Did he foresee our end in fire (a solar explosion) or in ice (the slow extinction of its fires)? What did his one eye see?

What should the rest of us see? On the one hand, the science was undeniably successful. I recently met a farmer who had also grown up in the Bessie church who built a large shop on the road to *Korn* to manufacture extra-wide cultivators. The one he made for himself folded itself down so that he could work hundreds of acres in a single day. He and two sons farmed between five and six entire sections of land without significant hired labor. No doubt he had worked out the problem of doing this without ruining the contours that preserved his soil.

Technology now allows one person to do the work of hundreds, and to do it sitting in the comfort of an air-conditioned cab. Even better, the methods by which the scientists do their work allow for self-correction. Specific processes or chemicals that turn out in the long run to do actual harm can sometimes be altered to solve the specific problems they create. In the long run, however, the results of mechanization may destroy the civilization that pursues this kind of "progress."

The natural resources of our earth are finite. The abstraction and concentration of toxic chemicals and radioactive elements necessary to keep the wheels of industry and modern agriculture turning poison the land and affect the bodies of living things. Hundreds of acres a day become infertile. That science will always be able to solve all the problems that an imperialist technology creates is not itself based on science. It is a faith that flies in the face of evidence and logic and entropy.

The number of days that I had worked with horses, or shucked corn, or pitched bundles for a stationary threshing machine can be counted on the fingers of my hands, but they were enough to make me happy to get jobs driving tractors. The problem with mechanization, for me, lay in the fact that I was among the hundreds who were displaced by the new efficiencies. In California I was not given tractors to drive. The "cushy" jobs were normally reserved for the farmer's sons. For many summers during high school and college I toiled for months, picking fruit and cutting grapes in the orchards and vineyards around Reedley, California. These chores had not been mechanized.

On the other hand, those primitive physical labors had become integrated into modern methods of agricultural production. In the cotton fields and vineyards and orchards, we were just hands, performing specific functions abstracted from the yearlong cycle of tasks the crop required. We were not integrated into a *Hof* to do this work; we went directly to the fields from our own homes carrying our sack lunches and contracted to be paid by the hour or by the number of pounds picked or trays cut. Labor is not inherently demeaning, but in comparison with the concretely organic labor I had earlier sensed, I disliked field labor in California's Golden Valley almost as much as I hated forcing farmers to accept or reject the abstracted hands to which I was debasing myself when offering them up for sale.

The large peach cannery in nearby Kingsburg introduced me to the next stage in fruit production and to the noise and sweat of still-primitive assembly lines. My mother's youngest brother, only three years older than I, drove with me to the hiring shed. We had high hopes of a quick hire and one of the better jobs since one of the cannery bosses was a not-too-distant *Hutter* relative. Several demeaning days of sitting on the grass outside the shed with dozens of others waiting a call had the paradoxical effect of stirring anger at our unhelpful relative while assuaging the guilt we felt at stooping to nepotism.

Only the fact that we were better paid than field hands kept Willis and me from quitting the job that finally became available because others before us had seldom lasted more than a few days at what was generally conceded to be the worst job in the entire cannery. Three of us were stationed around the end of the line that fed large cans of peaches through the labeling machine. On each side of the line, forklift drivers placed pallets of stacked, wooden, three-sided trays holding a dozen cans each. Two of us, facing each other, alternately stretched or stooped to take a tray and jerk it violently enough that the cans would remain upright while sliding off onto the rolling pipes in front of us. The unnatural rhythm we endured was an endless repetition of motions dictated by the unvarying speed of the machine, except when the line jammed and had to be unclogged. Every twenty minutes we rotated, so that two stints of jerking earned one period at the head of the line, catching and stacking the empty trays handed over by the other two.

Now we were completely abstracted hands and arms. Our minds counted for absolutely nothing. That was the one blessing of the job. We could sulk or think or fantasize as we pleased. Willis enjoyed regaling family gatherings with an account of a long silence that I triumphantly interrupted with, "I just knocked out Rocky Marciano in the eighth."

For a while we had hopes that faithful effort would be rewarded with promotions. Finally, we realized that our bosses were pleased that they had found two slaves too stubborn to quit and too proud to complain. We held that job for two full canning seasons.

"Progress" has come far since then. "Well, you know, Delbert," said a professor of engineering who designed computerized lines to sort the fruit by size and color and to box it, "our job is to design machines that minimize the number of workers that are needed and to so 'dumb down' what jobs are left that almost any idiot can be hired at minimum wage to do them." Marj had earned her way through college, earning more than the pickers in the field because this task was paid according to the number of boxes packed and her hands were very fast. Now this job also had been automated, greatly reducing the number of hands remaining on those lines.

Add to these trends the removal of entire factories to countries where hands were cheaper and it becomes obvious why even an "idiot's" job is harder to find. When found, it often proves to be just complex enough to require one's attention despite being too unchallenging to earn one's interest. Then even one's mind is not one's own and even fantasies are chained.

Pious or not, I do not remember being comfortable in bib overalls, and I could enjoy being out in the fields only during the early hours of the day. In agreement with even the most traditional farmers in *Korn*, I approved of the labor-saving machines that technology provided for the fortunate few who owned successful farms. However, since I was becoming increasingly skeptical of the advantages of "progress," I began to wonder about the hard labor of the "good old days." One Sunday morning, a year or two after my teaching stint in *Korn*'s academy, I was standing in a circle of mostly older farmers in the country church I had joined after moving to central Kansas. When the conversation began to drift among the tasks of the week, I decided to draw them out and asserted brashly, "You guys work much too hard. You work much harder than your elders did in the 'good, old days.'"

They turned on me to do righteous battle against such heresy. "Oh, no, we don't. They worked much harder than we do." I denied it, and they eagerly competed with each other to describe the intense physical labor of shucking corn and pitching bundles and scooping wheat.

I remembered my youthful body's agony during my own brief stabs at all those tasks and partly backed down, "All right, I'll agree that they worked harder during the harvest, but what did they do with all their time during the rest of the year? What did they do in winter after chores were done, implements had been repaired, and the harness mended?" The tone of the conversation changed as they began to put the rhythm of the year into perspective. I continued, "They could rest. But modern equipment allows you to add more types of production to your schedule. You now keep working all year round. You never rest."

They began to agree with me. "You know," one of them mused wonderingly, "You can't put lights on horses." Later, one of them sidled up to me and muttered softly, "Even in harvest we young men would often have time for a baseball game in the evening."

Newer machines had greatly shortened their times of intense physical effort, but these machines had chained them to an almost endless grind.

I had not yet fully realized that this also changed the quality of the experience of work. The early pioneering years had been harsh and grueling, but the quotations from the Amish farmer suggest that the work of fully traditional agriculture may not have been the purgatory we have claimed to remember. How could young men have had enough strength left for a game of baseball? Why had the threshing machine been turned off while there was still that much light? Modern combines don't stop until midnight condensation makes the grain too moist. Moreover, many of their hardest tasks offered the joy of communal effort. Even normally solitary chores were sometimes shared. And one might not truly be alone even when others were not present.

Farmers must still respond to the pushes and the pulls that come from the climate and the soil, but I fear that the insecticides and herbicides and fertilizers that have brought a short-term miracle of abundance also allowed farmers to listen less and to lead the dance more willfully. The old tractors were so noisy that they drowned out human sounds, but we were almost near enough to the soil to reach down and touch it. I wonder what can be seen and felt and heard from the lofty cockpit of a modern diesel.

Before huge tractors and the use of large amounts of chemicals, it was becoming clear that the nature of a farmer's relation to the earth had changed. The farmer was less a partner in nature's self-healing creativity and more a would-be creator of its potential. Because the earth had become a malleable resource to be endlessly reconstituted, it had ceased to be a partner in the dance. As never before, labor on it had become abstracted and quantified work.

Except for the limits of seedtime and harvest, the old rhythms tend to disappear. Lofty tractor cabs and even burial denies the closeness of our relationship with earth. Comradeship with at least a few favored work-animals disappears. Neighbors become competitors for scarce acres. No wonder those once anchored to the family farm tend to become abstracted individuals flirting with the diseases of modernity. No wonder their sometimes less desensitized children romanticize the natural world they are being denied and become vigilant environmentalists. No wonder they sometimes react against the objectification of living animals in huge, disease-ridden "factories" by becoming vegetarians or vegans. Do they sense, if dimly, that those of us who no longer offer our lives and bodies to the rhythms of the natural world are losing the right to demand that they be sacrificed for us?

REVULSION AGAINST SOME OF THE BAD NEWS OF MODERN PROGRESS

My one brother was born almost a generation later than I, during the summer that I had traveled back to Oklahoma to work for the Wedels. He grew up with only the reflected echo of a concrete village that was part of the ethos of the Mennonites in and around the town of Reedley until our parents moved to Hillsboro, Kansas, an almost-village small town that had a small college. Having learned to love the mountains from our Uncle Walter, who often pitched tents and created an all-summer camp in the mountains near Yosemite. Doug returned to Yosemite for summer work to pay his way through college. There he learned to ski and rock climb, returning later to teach cross-country skiing and the techniques of winter survival in the high mountains. From that, he was invited during the summers to be a member of high Arctic expeditions. He also kayaked the canyons of the Colorado River from somewhere in Utah through Arizona to Nevada and paddled the Inland Passage and open ocean from Seattle to Alaska. In between, he climbed sheer cliffs, including the three-thousand-foot face of El Capitan.

Practical town Mennonites were both fascinated and appalled. "Doug, you know what you have to do to become legitimate back home. You must either figure out how to make a lot of money at what you do or you have to make it into *National Geographic*." Doug grinned, "Guess which one I'm aiming for." Soon after a dramatic circumnavigation of Denali appeared in its July 1979 special edition celebrating the centennial of American national parks, he received a Junior Alumnus award from Tabor College and was featured in *The Christian Leader*.

Concrete village life necessarily included moving beyond the border to ponder the strange ways of neighboring villages and towns and cities and confronting the vagaries of nature that were forever outside our control, including, as well, the edges of wildness that lay inside our borders. When all these interpenetrating facets exploded into separated functions, it became necessary, somehow, to experience again the range of these new possibilities, if only vicariously. Human nature, too, abhors a vacuum. It then becomes the role of explorers to keep alive the aspects of our former completeness that are denied to those of us who concentrate on more conventional roles. Had I pointed this out to Doug, he would have smiled, "It's a tough job, but someone has to do it."

It was also dangerous. All four of the members of that expedition died too soon. Ned Gillette was knifed while sleeping in his tent in the high mountains somewhere west of Everest while tracing the ancient Silk Route. I have forgotten how Alan Bard died, but Galen Rowell perished in a small plane that crashed in 2003 in the eastern Sierra Nevada. Doug was blown apart twenty or so years earlier when the cannon exploded that he and his partners were using to bring down snow that otherwise might have avalanched upon workers on a large hydroelectric project.

Days after his death, our Mom admitted that she was comforted by the fact that he had died while gainfully employed. His expeditionary friends, who came to participate in his burial by interring with him his cross-country skis, a kayak paddle, and other items, expressed to me their regret that his death had been "wasted" in an ordinary job instead of on a trek over lonely mountains. I think they knew that such deaths were necessary to remind the rest of us that nature transcends our wish to bend it to our desires and our human-centered notions of justice and meaning.

Meanwhile, Mom had apparently forgotten her early tomboyish life as Grandpa's field hand. "I don't understand your life style. I don't understand at all," she complained while sitting around our dining room table with Doug, Jake (her second husband), Marj, and me. The rest of us tried hard to help her, but she ended the discussion by glaring at me, "For that matter, I don't understand either of my sons."

Jake, a retired prairie *Hutter* farmer, understood why Doug was attracted to his calling. While teenagers, he and some of his brothers had hitchhiked out to see the Barnum and Bailey circus and had been so fascinated by the trapeze artists that they rigged double trapezes high in the hayloft of their barn. Soon at least one of his brothers had learned to catch his free-flight somersaults between the trapezes and above the hay.

Jake also knew well that nature could be pitiless. He had kept his young family alive during hard winters of the Great Depression years by selling skunk pelts for fifty cents each. He snatched them out of their lairs and stunned them so swiftly that they did not (at least, not often) have time to release their scent. After age seventy, he strapped a sleeping bag to his bicycle and, in three stages, pedaled from Hillsboro, Kansas, to the North Dakota border, sleeping in haystacks and in barns along the way. His loyalty to friends within the Pine Ridge Reservation had brought him into physical danger during the "Indian Wars" of the 1960s. It is true that some were more daring than others, but *Korn* also bred those who challenged ever-present frontiers.

Most of the circle of retired Hillsboro farmers, who met almost daily to eat doughnuts and drink coffee, were not anxious to hear Jake expound on present racial and social issues, as he soon came to understand. His coffee-mates were good citizens who had worked hard to survive and to build a defense around their sense of social rightness and a cushion against the lurking threats of untamed nature. They were mostly content to complain about the present difficulties of modern farming and the restrictions imposed upon them by governments and mysterious economic forces, but many were unwilling to probe deeply into the distant and homegrown causes of their discontent. They would not happily rethink the farming methods that served them well or their distrust of strange others.

Plains Indians had learned to manage these spaces, supplementing their buffalo diet by tending plots of special plants and grains and nuts and fruit with minimal overturning of the ancient sod. There are students of their methods who believe that some of the prairie would produce more usable protein in the long run if we could return to their way of responding to the climate, to the prairie grasses and bushes and trees, and to the buffalo. Perhaps we will, when and where we will have used up the water that collected underground over thousands of years.

Some scientists believe that selective breeding and genetic manipulation of the native prairie grasses can lead to multiple harvesting of differently maturing perennial grains without any tilling of the sod. If so, abstracting science might ultimately teach us how to respond more wisely to the initiatives of natural life and soil and weather.

"I can't figure it out," said an accountant who did tax work for farmers in Ohio. "An Amish family can take over a small farm on which two or three conventional farmers have gone swiftly bankrupt, and within two or three years they are paying a significant amount of income tax." He shook his head and ended in a doubtful tone, "Of course, they don't need as much cash to pay for modern conveniences and food." But surely his puzzlement requires more than his surmise about simpler life styles.

Wendell Berry and others have argued that small plots of frequently rotated crops allow the soil to rejuvenate and suppress the pests that thrive on large fields dedicated to a single crop.[6] David Kline, the Amish naturalist, denied that they are opposed in principle to chemical fertilizer and pesticide. He hadn't needed any the previous year, but his neighbor spent eleven dollars on herbicide.[7] What's more, horses do not much compact the soil that their manure enriches. Meanwhile, birds and other wildlife thrive in the woods and borders they preserve between their fields. It is possible that in some areas traditional yeomanry may be the progress of the future—if, that is, government subsidies cease to give unfair advantage to huge factory farms.

While still in *Korn*, I knew that I would never be a farmer, though I did sometimes fantasize becoming a gentleman farmer after gaining wealth

---

6. Berry, "Renewing Husbandry."
7. Kline, *Great Possessions*, xvii.

some other way. What Reedley and the Kingsburg cannery reinforced was the misery of modern unskilled labor. I endured the fields and the labeling line, saving my earnings to invest in further education—the third level of modern abstraction that promised to grant me access to something vaguely like an integrative *Hof*, a profession that would unite my interests and talents, though it could never offer the satisfaction of building the *Halig* of a truly concrete whole and though it would forever abstract me from the earth on which all humankind must finally depend, whether or not we have learned to dance.

I admit that few of my friends from *Korn* or Reedley grew old while shackled to the drudgery of hard labor. We had learned the habits and the skills that allowed us to pick one abstracted function from the concrete life we shared and to become very good at it. With others who surfed the growing edge of modernity, we could experience the exhilaration of progress and the pleasure of self-expression in the businesses and arts and sciences that appealed to us. We were a fortunate generation, able to add the promise of the new to the living memory of the traditional past that continues to inform our lives.

I know I have been especially fortunate. I became a professor of ancient history and philosophy and enjoyed the challenge of helping captive college students understand the emergence of the basic institutions of early and later civilizations and the views achieved by thinkers who tried to comprehend the structures of the whole of things.

In turn, I was stimulated by the students, even in the required course in ancient civilizations, who became fascinated by old texts and who dared to counter my interpretations with convictions of their own. I was especially blessed by those students who chose the upper-level courses and seminars I led and who took turns sharing their discoveries in the research topics they pursued. I hoped that they would realize that at their most abstract, ideas jostle against each other to point toward comprehensions of concreteness beyond the literal power of words.

Every progressive Western culture began with more or less concrete villages and then, in different ways, succeeded in creating the progress that led to the abstraction of individuals and functions, as well as to the formal abstractions of advanced technologies and philosophies. The basic processes that I have ascribed to *Korn* have been present throughout much of human history. What is new is that science and technology have gone so far. What is also new is that now all "*Korns*" are dissected into modernizing abstractions. Until recently only a small percentage of citizens experienced the joys and losses of "progress." Until a few centuries ago, most all peoples tilled the earth in mostly traditional and conventional ways.

Then great civilizations could rise upon the backs of all those peasants to create the professional castes of armies and priests and merchants who became sufficiently abstract to enjoy the benefits of specialization. After earlier civilizations collapsed under the inevitable bureaucratized dead weight of their efforts to maintain control or at the hands of other civilizations with superior fighting skills, the great mass of its people would endure the chaos of subsequent robber bands and reestablish the local order that could in the distant future become the basis of yet another civilization. Until recently, these Dark Ages allowed village peasants to continue their lives almost unchanged except for the blessed absence of billeted armies and intrusive tax agents.

I do not share the desire of perhaps increasing numbers of "nativists" who are so alienated by our present civilization that they yearn again for such a crisis. In 2003 Marj and I visited the memorial to the victims of the bombing of a huge federal office building in Oklahoma City, and I marveled, yet again, at the depth of the hatred against our economy and governance that is possessed by many of our citizens who are disaffected by the rise of abstracting modernity. Thousands, perhaps hundreds of thousands of our citizens, are silently rejecting that citizenship and are organizing to overthrow the present order and return to their ideal of frontier individualism or autonomous small communities.

I wonder whether legislators and governing executive branches are half-secretly relieved to focus our attention on foreign terrorists to channel the hatred of homegrown terrorists to scapegoats far away. Unfortunately, the goal these citizens seek would be more disastrous than the collapse of previous civilizations, for almost all our food production is now concentrated in the hands of so few and is so dependent upon our top-heavy order that very little of it would survive a large collapse. It is now possible that not enough would endure to provide the basis for the ready emergence of another "higher culture."

Despite the occasional fears stimulated by my interest in the rise and fall of worldviews, Marj and I eagerly confronted the front and back yards of the first home that we had purchased. It had standard Bermuda lawns, but neither of us wanted the clipped grass and straight edges of our neighborhood. In our backyard we scraped out a dry creek bed, planted its curving edges with small redwoods, sculpted a couple of mounds to suggest hills, and determined to devote what was left of it to imitation of a small California mountain meadow. After several types of ground cover did poorly, something that vaguely resembled buffalo grass seeded itself, and we had the effect we wanted. Marj had also grown up in rural Oklahoma.

The parsonage she lived in was on the edge of pastures near the mountains once freely roamed by Comanche Indians, to whom her father was a pastor.

I am not a dedicated gardener, and I was shocked to discover that uprooting the Bermuda by hand became almost a summer's compulsion. After drenching a square yard or so of turf, I would push my fingers into mud up to my wrist and gently pull out all the intertwined roots. I was surprised how much I needed the feel of the soil again. Nearly thirty years later we sold that gracious old home with its maturing backyard forest and moved into a condominium with two small fenced-in patios. I complained much at the discovery that one of them was infested with nut grass. I had not known about this weed, which sends down a long thread of fragile root and then forms a peppercorn-like seed that cannot be pulled out unless one has completely loosened and raised the surrounding soil. Again, I was secretly content to spend hours sifting the earth with my fingers. Marj has been happy to use the fresh herbs that she planted in a raised bed nestled among flowers and climbing vines.

My hands in the soil and her herbs in the pot cannot be compared to the satisfaction of a farmer contemplating his ripening fields and the farmwoman's pride in a well-stocked cellar, but I remember my father's story of the ritual of his father's journey to the miller with a wagonload of wheat, some of which was immediately ground into flour and sacked for him. After returning, grandfather carried the heavy sacks to the attic. My father, then a boy, had gone to the attic with him. He still so vividly remembered his father's emotions that his own voice became hushed and reverent. Grandfather Wiens had stood there, looking at the sacks of flour. No matter how poor they were, there would be bread for his family to eat. God and he had provided for the winter ahead.

Excursus C
Treasures from the Past

THE SUMMERS AFTER MY sixth and eighth years of grade school were important introductions to my understanding of *Hofs* and of farm life. Jack R. Goertz, who grew up in the state of Washington, met and married Sophie's niece, Judy Schmidt. She was the daughter of Ruth, the third and youngest of the Adolf Klause family. Jack thus became Sophie's nephew-in-law who skillfully evoked Sophie's legacy to the large number of those who admired her by writing a seventy-page self-published book[1] with pictures of the family, the *Hof*, and even of the Farmall tractor I also drove.

Mennonite scholars will be glad if they find *Sophie's Story* in Mennonite archives. On pages 17–20, the fourth chapter of *Sophie's Story* traces the farm's history since it had been homesteaded by Jacob Klaassen in 1894 who paid only a ten-dollar filing fee for a 160-acre plot of land a handful of miles east of the village of Bessie. Historians will wish that the writer had expanded on the transition from groundbreaking to farming and from learning how to construct a sod hut until a framed wood house could be built. Though he created a viable farm, by 1908 his wife had died after bearing six boys. In 1918, fearing their conscription for military service in World War I, he sold the farm to the family of Adolph's wife, Anna Block, of Hillsboro, Kansas. They bought it since Adolph's options for evading conscription were farming or building ships for the navy. Though a still young emigrant from Poland, he had there attained great skills as a builder.

In addition to fascinating historical tidbits, Mennonite historians will be intrigued that on page 19 is a picture of Jacob Klaassen and his boys, one of whom is the Walter Klaassen who wrote *Anabaptist: Neither Catholic nor*

---

1. Goertz, *Sophie's Story*.

Protestant,[2] persuasively explaining that Mennonites were a third wing of the Reformation. A member of the Thursday-morning coffee group I attend, who has retired from teaching at the University of California, Santa Barbara, told me that Walter's father had been the son of Martin Klaassen.

Prof. Abraham Friesen is an important Reformation scholar[3] who refers to Martin Klaassen's excellent study. He had been a teacher in the village of Koppenthal, near Saratov. This was the first history written by a Mennonite in Russia. His book is a history of Christian pacifism from the apostolic era to the time it was written.

The *Mennonite Encyclopedia* has entries on both Martin and his son, Michael, who moved to the USA in 1880.[4] In 1894, he filed a claim for a quarter section plot of land about five miles east of Bessie, Oklahoma, for which he paid ten dollars. While attending the Herold Mennonite Church (organized in 1899) that could be seen from the site later chosen to build the Bessie MB church, he became an active itinerant minister in Oklahoma. For seventeen years he also taught German and English in an elementary school. To protect his sons from being drafted during World War I, in 1918, he moved to Morden, Manitoba, along with a number of the Herold congregation's families and there organized another Herold Mennonite Church.

I have written so long an excursus to provide further evidence that, like immigrants, the *Korn* Mennonites among whom I had lived had inherited a tradition that sought enlightenment from the treasures of the Western classical and Christian past. As I have noted, the Adolf Klause who had been an eighteen-year-old immigrant Lutheran lad from Poland who had appeared to Hillsboro, Kansas, with significant architectural and building skills and who became a Mennonite illustrates this pattern. For him to evade the option of either becoming a farmer or applying his skills to building ships for the USA navy, the parents of his bride loaned him the funds needed to buy the Klaassen farm. He became a deacon of the Bessie MB congregation, and I remember Sunday lunches when my parents were invited after some Sunday services. He and HR long debated theological issues like the dispensationalism presented in the Scofield Reference Bible and expounded on essays written in a journal titled *Our Hope* edited by Frank Gaebelein. His able, restless mind led him to withdraw from the Bessie Church for a number of years, but that, too, reinforces my sense of the inquisitive intelligence of the larger *Korn*.

2. Klassen, *Anabaptist*, 13–14.
3. Friesen, *Defense of Privilege*, 66–67.
4. Quiring and Thiessen, "Martin Klaassen." Krahn and Thiessen, "Michael Klaassen."

CHAPTER 6

Reflections on Mutual Aid

AT THE BEGINNING OF the previous chapter, I stated that the three positions of the dancers who wove the patterns of the ethos and the *Geist* of *Korn* illustrated the three aspects of the work of *Halig*. They stood upright or knelt in contact with the earth they tilled and upon which they moved and built. In the second position of the dance, their hands stretched out to touch each other and to share the privilege of constructing their characters and institutions. It was also true that at any moment their arms were poised to sweep upwards in awe of God and in gratitude for the sacred canopy that hovered over them.

In chapter 5, I concentrated on their relation to the land. I now speak of their hands stretched out to each other to share the privilege of building the *Halig* of the whole on this space and in this time. I begin with *Korn*'s concreteness to sketch what happens to human life with continuing abstractness.

Of course, my attempt to describe each stance in a section of its own has failed. I could not talk of our elders' position in time and space and their relation to the soil without also talking about their arms extended to hold the reins that guided the horses who shared their labor. In truth, animals bridged their physical and social worlds, and the animals who partnered in their work and play entered into humanness. I had also to speak of the neighbors and friends who assisted in many seasonal chores and whose cooperation was necessary to bring in the harvest.

Nor could I avoid the worship that was evoked by the recognition of their share in the continuing creativity that linked God's arms to theirs. As in that chapter and as in the all-grown-together concrete village, this chapter must also allow these themes to knit together as they will.

The earth, the others, and God were three great themes of the entire pageant. A fourth theme, to be built up through all the chapters of this book, was their convergence in the individual, each of whom belongs to all these realms by virtue of being a nexus of all these relationships. Just as each of us becomes a physically embodied person as a nexus of relations to the physical world, so also, each of us becomes human to the extent that we enter into larger nexuses of relationships.

WITH ARMS STRETCHED OUT TO EACH OTHER

"In the old days, I would work for my neighbor for several days when he needed help, and then he would work for me. We never thought of paying each other. We never even kept track. I guess it all came out even. But nowadays you can't work for each other without being paid immediately, cash on the line." In the last chapter I used Uncle Ed's remarks to emphasize the relation of their own labor on the land to that of their neighbors and to God. Then, work was only relatively important. Since it could not guarantee their success, it could not be the sole measure of their value. Work, at its most profound, was an instrument of all these levels of relations. Therefore, work could be given away.

Uncle Ed had been thinking back another twenty years or more to the hard, dry years just before World War II. Crops had been poor and the prices received for the crops had been so low that there had often been little to show for a year of work. Neither he nor his neighbor would have had cash to lay on the line for the other's help, even if it had been expected. Aunt Emma once described getting together with those neighbors for an evening meal, each bringing whatever remained in their pantries. It had been enough for just that meal. Surely, they scarcely noticed who had brought the most. She long relished the memory of that evening. Later prosperity never took from her the joy of giving and receiving. I use *mutual aid* to name this aspect of their co-inherence.

In addition to "I guess it all came out even," two other clauses had rung falsely. Those were the claims that "I worked for him" and "he worked for me." Though true, they obscured the truth that all in the community were also working for themselves when working with and for the others, because all were a part of something greater than themselves. To help the neighbor was to improve the whole that, in turn, defined and exalted its members. A prosperous and a healthy and a holy *Korn* implied the virtue of all who shared its *Halig Geist*.

To be an individual did not mean that one was enclosed within one's own skin needing to grow always from the inside out. We have seen that even our physical self requires us to extend beyond that skin in metabolic interchanges with the rest of the physical world. Each of us was also a "place" where the selves of all the others in the community entered into our own concreteness.

Each of us was a one who was also a many. Each personal *Geist* was itself because it uniquely incarnated the larger all-grown-together *Geist* of *Korn* as well as all the other *Geists* with whom it interacted. Each person was inspired by and contributed to a quest for excellence. I use *mutual nurture* to name this aspect of our co-inherence and will speak of it in the next chapter. The rest of this one is about mutual aid.

Perhaps because their German dialects did not have common words derived from the Latin root for *mutual*, Mennonites were slow to claim that English word to name their ideals and practices. *Mutuus*, from which the word came, proves, of course, that concrete communities have normally practiced this virtue. From its beginning, the word referred to that which is done or felt by each of two or more for the others. In biology it names those forms of symbiosis that result in advantage for all of the organisms involved. In sociology it means a life lived in interdependence, as opposed to individualism.

Mutuus had been derived from another ancient Latin word, *mutare*, that which endures change. It is precisely because humans are able to change that they can engage in mutuality. To enter deeply into a common life, our own character is changed and molded. We are created and created anew when our selves move beyond our skins, entering into and being penetrated by the selves of others and by the Spirit of God.

That vulnerability also makes it possible to stretch beyond our communities and to come into fruitful interchange with the larger world beyond our boundaries. But change has always a double face, and *mutare* was also a name for the inconstant, the unsettled, the unstable, the fickle, the vacillating and the mutant. *Mutuality* ironically implies the chaos to which it constitutes a partial answer.

MENNONITES AND MUTUAL AID

I knew that the community could not make failure impossible for all. But how, I wondered a few years later, had mutual aid been handled? I asked my then ninety-year-old grandpa Kleinsasser what it had been like to be a deacon when he was young. "Well, I'd take the wagon and load it full of stuff, and go over to the people who needed it, and give it to them."

"You can't do that," I protested, reacting to the utter matter-of-factness in his voice. He had made it sound too easy, almost careless. Where was spiritual sensitivity to the problem of the poor neighbor's embarrassment at having to receive help? I tried briefly to explain that, but his look silenced me. I had again confirmed his conviction of my generation's lack of common sense. I should have remembered that he was a *Prairie Hutter*, one who had grown up poised between the ideals of the full economic mutuality of the "Christian communism" of colony *Hutters* and the ideals of personal Christian stewardship on one's own landholding. When orphaned as an infant, he had lived briefly in a colony; and he continued to relate to them. He told one of my cousins that after marriage he and his bride had considered joining a colony.

I doubt that it is ever easy to give and to receive help. But for Grandpa and his neighbors it was still possible for charity to be direct and personal. In fact, *charity* is the wrong word. As brothers in a fraternity of common dependence they could share if God had, unaccountably, given some a larger handout than others. Almost all gifts could be shared, since each person was fundamentally a gift to all the others. The sharing of selves with selves contributed to the health of each and the *Halig* of the whole.

Each could mediate to the others the *Presence* of God, especially during those heightened moments when illness and death and tragedy called for others to hold one in faith and in hope before God. Mutual aid, in other words, was truly *mutual* aid. One was always giving, even when receiving. One was always receiving, even in the act of giving. Therefore, the sharing of material goods was a sign of more significant sharing even as it was a sacrament of the community-creating gifts of God.

Ever since the many decades of persecution following the rise of their Anabaptist forebears during the Reformation, Mennonites have had a profound sense of their need for help from each other across ethnic and national borders. Within concrete communities, this could be as informal as delivering a sack of potatoes to a neighbor. In *Korn* we took for granted that others would show up to help with daily chores or to work on the fields of a farmer who was ill or had to be away for a while. An Amish barn raising is a popular image of what is mostly ad hoc mutuality. There was usually little need to make that big a fuss. It just happened and sometimes it evoked a party.

And, of course, a group of the wise and caring had to make sure that aid was appropriate and that some were not neglected. That was only part of the reason why the churches took great care in the selection of deacons.

The greater reason was that spiritual and material needs had not yet been separated in communities that remained concretely integrated. So long as we could believe that whatever we received was a gift from God, we also were clear that the qualifications needed by those who helped to guide the sharing of those gifts were as much spiritual as practical. Those who were charged with "soul care" were responsible for the spiritual, moral, and material well-being of their brothers and sisters in the congregation. Then moral admonishments and managerial counsel might, or might not, accompany a needed sack of potatoes.

MUTUAL AID AND THE CHARITY OF THE AMERICAN TOWN

Concrete communities that encourage mutuality will also experience *mutare*. They will change. For one thing, they are likely to prosper, and prosperity inevitably ushers them into the three abstractive processes described in the introductory chapters. Mennonite communities became too crowded, and many of their youth were abstracted to a town or city. Now, needy brothers and sisters might not be near enough for ad hoc aid, or even near enough the slightly longer reach of deacons. Nor could a neighbor or clansman who had mostly time and muscled out-stretched arms to "give away" supply new cash-based needs.

In the latter part of the nineteenth century, North American Mennonites from east of the Mississippi, many of whom had arrived well before the American Revolution, recognized that informal aid could not cope with the changes that were happening to their communities, and they began, almost feverishly, to organize responses to fires, storms, and even the costs associated with deaths. Mutual aid societies sprang up by the dozens. By the middle of the twentieth century, Mennonite credit unions were formed to assist entrepreneurs and organizations that specialized in one or several of the functions that had earlier been grown-together.

It was also just before the middle of this century that a Mennonite sociologist adapted the phrase *mutual aid* to link their traditional communal mutuality with modern vehicles of charity in order to convince the older traditionalists who were profoundly suspicious that the adoption of these forms of "town" constituted a way for modernism to creep into the spaces that had nestled under a sacred canopy. Both parties to the controversy were right.

The phrase *mutual aid* did aptly name the meaning of the older pattern, and by now most of us would be surprised to learn how recently it was adopted. Those young progressives were right to recognize that the inevitable growth of all three levels of abstraction in their communities called for modern ways to preserve the Mennonites as a people. The conservatives were right to recognize that their adoption of these ways might hurry the end of the rural context that had fostered their older practices of mutuality. All concluded that the spirit and ideals of the old should shape the construction of new forms of mutual aid.[1]

All of these merged hardheaded business sense with their commitment to the mutuality that works with others for the *Halig* of the whole. Yet others applied the same mix to nonprofit insurance institutions. Mennonite Mutual Aid is now a nonprofit medical and general insurance company that enlists a small army of church respondents who advise the central offices of the "hard cases" that require help, which often goes far beyond the company's contractual obligations. Increasingly, these organizations adapted the modes of other organized charities. The debate continues about how to hold mutuality and modernity together while more fully becoming "town" in their reach for the good and "goodies" of the city while also trying to retain the memories and the virtues of the village.

Despite their different origins and a long history of separate development, the spirit of mutuality among the Mennonites who had arrived earlier led them to assist the Mennonites in Russia. The Mennonite Central Committee (MCC) was created to help these distant kin. Many of their Russian/Ukrainian neighbors also were given food.

Later, that organization moved beyond its focus on fellow-Mennonites to bring relief to sufferers around the world. In the same spirit, Mennonite Disaster Service (MDS) created enduring frameworks for harnessing the responses of hundreds and thousands who were trained to be effective during catastrophes to nearer neighbors. They help to rebuild the lives of victims of floods, tornadoes, and fires who may never have known a Mennonite. These organizations also strive to build the motives and spirit of mutuality into the charities they have become.

What I have claimed of *Korn* and other Mennonites applies, at least in part, to other concrete communities and half-abstracted towns, whether or not they embrace the language of mutuality. Mennonites were, in fact, enthusiastic latecomers to building the organized charities that characterize the American town. During the early stages of modernization in North America, there were few state institutions to pick up the burdens and opportunities of assistance that had always been borne, more or less informally, by concrete communities across the land and, earlier, by the homeland clans

---

1. Swartley and Kraybill, *Building Communities*, 192–243.

and villages of immigrants. And so, replacing mutual aid, *charity* had been reinvented.

Many of the new citizens in towns and cities, had earlier been formed within concrete societies, and they accepted the responsibility to extend aid to their neighbors. They had the capacity to envision a communal, even a national, common good; and they organized with each other to feed and to clothe and to nurture those who were no longer able to take care of themselves. They remained motivated to build the *Halig* of ever larger, now more abstracted, communities. Aid, however, could no longer be ad hoc, and it could seldom be as direct as delivering a sack of potatoes. Abstracted individuals separated from traditional communities could only be reached by equally abstracted secondary associations with a rationally institutionalized *modus operandum*.

"Charity," therefore, is the creation of the "town." It depends on a lingering recognition that each of us is a nexus of relationships and on a memory shaped by the experience of concreteness. Charities continue to need donors and volunteers who desire *Halig*, but those who hire the administrators of these programs look for a mix of youthful energy and mature managerial competence rather than for the seasoned wisdom of the godly.

Meanwhile, the advance of abstractness threatens to erode the qualities cherished in the village. In the city the memory of concreteness and its *Halig* necessarily wanes. Individuals continue to extend kindnesses and aid to individuals they meet, but serious charitableness mostly takes the form of donations to specialized agencies. Concern for communal *Halig* increasingly gets channeled through organizations that lobby state and federal governments to change specific policies. If this is right, "charity" is a concept and a practice that is likely to wane during the long periods of transition between concrete and abstracted societies.

"You know," said Dale Suderman, the farmer's son from a "*Korn*" community in Kansas who was lecturing me on the workings of Chicago while we were tramping its streets late one night, "it's funny. All of the people I know who care about the city and who are working to make it better come from small towns and farms. That was even true for the early sociologists at the University of Chicago who invented urban sociology."

Even if charity can be sustained, I am not convinced that it will do more good than harm in the long run. It has always been an inconvenience to be poor. Despite Grandpa's offhandedness about delivering a sack of potatoes, I cannot quiet my suspicion that his arrival sometimes led to awkwardness. Surely the belief that God was the source of good was often accompanied by the smug suspicion that God had recognized who deserved the goods and who did not. Paternalism and a shamefaced acquiescence to it were besetting sins of even the holiest of places.

Modern progress has guaranteed that it is no longer a mere inconvenience to be poor. What it now means is, "You have failed." You were supposed to be a competent individual. You were supposed to be sufficiently rational and efficient to produce abundantly. You were supposed to be able to harmonize the different facets of your life, to balance your checkbooks, to preserve a healthy body and psyche, and to keep your insurance premiums paid in full to meet the catastrophes that are now labeled "acts of God." It gets harder to receive, at least until we become totally demoralized.

Now it is just as terrible to give, for the act of giving has become a sign of separateness. Not only is my success the result of an individualism that isolates me, it is also the result of a competitiveness that makes my conscience uneasy. Is it not true that my success comes at the price of another's failure? Does not my larger operation doom several smaller ones? Surely, we have learned by now that, both here at home and in the third world, poverty is one of the prices we pay for the prosperity of the corporate world.

Here at home, part of the battle against inflation is waged upon the backs of that increasing underclass which can only get the growing number of jobs that are so rationalized and simplified that only a minimum wage needs to be offered to those who have to do them. Who can understand this and still bear to face them daily? Then we move even farther from the inner city. We are less likely to be aware that the battle against inflation also implies that a certain percentage of the able and educated must be unemployed (or, to be euphemistic, "between jobs") to dissuade the employed from pressing for higher wages.

Before Marj and I moved to a gated condominium to escape the burdens of tending to an older home in an "interesting" part of town, I became grateful for the rationalized institutions that have taken over charity. When people came to the door to ask for work or money for food, I usually gave them two or three dollars and sometimes made them a sack lunch before happily sending them to LOVE, Inc., a para-church agency in Fresno that is supposed to know how to help such people since what they really need goes beyond the loose-change charity that can be offered by otherwise unknown non-neighbors.

I know that what I have described is not the whole truth. I know that many do continue to "freely give and freely receive." I believe that even the often-harried agents of charitable organizations are able to respond to yet another request in the spirit of gracious mutuality. After moving, I seldom met a beggar. Yet only two days before first writing this paragraph, someone with all the marks of one of the "undeserving poor" accosted me at a gasoline pump. His speech was slightly slurred. He was slovenly dressed, was pierced in more places than his ears, and a large red-orange tattoo marched boldly across his forehead.

When my hand reached for my pocket, I remembered that I did not have the two or three ones I sought and that the smallest bill I had was a five. He received it with surprise, smoothed it out, and said, softly, "You are a Christian, aren't you?" I said, "Yes," wondering why it was not enough for him to think that I was simply a fellow human being. I sensed neither guile nor belligerence in him and was happy, later, to hope that something of the older meaning of mutuality had remained in me in spite of the fact that, as usual, I had had to remind myself to look him fully in the eye and smile. Within the last handful of years, many at street corners with signs asking for money have appeared.

It seems to me that it is harder to remember what "mutual aid" once meant. We do not have deacons, as such, in the Mennonite congregation to which we belong, and most of us are prosperous. But we do have a deacon's fund, and the funds do disappear. We trust the two or three who are authorized to dispense them. Perhaps another one or two know who receives how much. We do share deeply and sometimes openly in each other's spiritual and physical ills, but we are relieved that our own congregation's monetary mutual aid operates in almost ghostly silence.

One result is that we now talk much of "stewardship." But that word has also changed. Once it referred to being a steward of all the bountiful gifts of God that benefitted both us and others. There was no clear distinction between the godly worth of what was kept and what was given away. To improve the village and to find new land for sons and daughters was as much the extension of the kingdom of God on earth as it was the personal use of the gifts of God.

Now, both time and money have divided into sacred and profane functions. "Sacred" money is that given in charity and for the support of those in full-time Christian service. That which is kept is profane. Now the question becomes how much ought to be given in order to justify the amount one keeps. Now, "stewardship" becomes a question of the tithe, which reinforces the feeling that our money is our own, whether to give or to keep.

The deeper problem is that even our teaching that we are to be generous gives us no way to solve, or even to understand, the root problem. Having accepted the legitimacy of abstraction, we have accepted an artificial division between the sacred and the profane, thus delivering over to the profane almost all of what we do and have and are. In so doing, we deprive our work and our goods of intrinsic sacramental purpose.

FROM TOWN CHARITY TO CITY WELFARE—AND INSURANCE

Worse yet, charities themselves, in their great variety, tend to mimic the abstractness they seek to counter. Each of them focuses on an abstracted need with a specialized expertise that its agents apply to aspects of the lives of selected portions of the needy population. Our best efforts to alleviate the needs of people are themselves models of the abstractive processes that help to create those needs.

The ancient function of the deacons to make sure that aid was appropriate and flowed from all to all must devolve upon state and federal governments. Only they had the right and the capacity to look to the secularized *Halig* of a nation of cities and towns. Charities continue, but now nations must stand above its competing institutions to limit the progress of each in order to secure the harmony of the entire commonwealth.

Both mutual aid and charities, therefore, yield to welfare, if only to fit them into a larger picture. It is true that the array of charitable organizations that has been formed since the Industrial Revolution has been effective enough that some still hope that another "thousand points of light" will solve our social problems without a massive increase in state-sponsored welfare.

It remains to be seen whether the communal idealists of faith-based and other Non-Government Organizations (NGOs), funded by either the government or by massive foundations left behind to immortalize the charitable intentions of their founders, can be more effective than state-run welfare. Even if they are, they, too, will have ceased to resemble either communal mutuality or charity. They, too, will gradually take on the spirit and methods of institutionalized welfare.

What results when modern states and the NGOs that must increasingly become their servants and accept the burden of seeking the welfare of abstracted citizens are massive and specialized bureaucracies? Unfortunately, these can become so rigid and turf-bound that "clients" can seldom be addressed in the context of each one's unique set of needs. Nor can any legislator even imagine how to forge abstracted policies that weave a personal *Halig*.

In the absence of the "sense of the common" of empowered deacons, we are left with the administrative competence of hired functionaries hampered by the growing sets of rules they live by, rules that were invented to prevent corruption and the actual unfairness of arbitrary favoritism but that also prevent the legalistically perceived unfairness of creative common sense.

Similar logics afflict the attempts of the successful to protect themselves against failure. Their chosen providers are insurance companies that live by actuarial tables. Not least of the problems that have grown alongside this way to spread among a greater population the costs of devastating "acts of God" has to do with their effects on the expectations and morals of those who buy insurance.

Typically, the Amish have mostly refused to accept insurance or even Social Security. They have agreed to help each other to mitigate the effects of disaster while schooling themselves to accept whatever God may bring as part of the normal risks of life. Those of us who have accepted a more abstracted life in town and city are aware that some risks have become too great. Then insurance is accepted even if it is neither mutual aid nor charity. It is merely a prudent calculation to spread the costs of those possible disasters that would be too great to permit us to rebound financially.

Unfortunately, calculated self-interest also contains its inner logic. In time, insurance ceased to be seen as protection from destitution due to the accidents that are normal in life. Then people demanded that it restore the prosperity that preceded the disaster. In time, those who have been denied the realistic common sense and the mutual care that genuine community once offered learn to exploit apparent or real tragedy as a way of making their fortunes.

Since actuarial tables automatically adjust to these moral realities, the fourth stage of this logic dictates that the time must come when paying the premiums is the disaster. Indeed, this is already happening. Our condominium board was recently informed that the risk and cost of suits are now so great that many companies refuse liability coverage to our sorts of associations. The tree trimmers we hired many years ago had to pay sixty-five cents for Workers Compensation for every dollar they paid in wages. Many now pay large amounts each month for medical insurance.

What has been said so far is that there was a logic that governed traditional communities. At their best, they were outposts of the kingdom of God. At their worst, they became stagnant prisons of the human spirit. There are also logics of modernity, the logics of abstracted functions and ideas. In the end, progress produces individuals who lose common sense. Even the successful can no longer imagine what a concrete *Halig* might be like. Even if they can, the drive to look out for a now abstracted "number one" erodes the will to seek it.

That same logic moves us from mutual aid to charity to welfare and to insurance. If the abstracting spirit of our age continues, mutual aid may not survive long into the twenty-first century. If charity, except as peripheral benefactions, survives longer, it will increasingly mimic bureaucratic and specialized modes of modernity and might sometimes produce more harm than good. Even welfare and insurance can collapse of their own weight.

MEDICINE—A CASE STUDY

Medical insurance also suffers from the ironies that bedevil other forms of insurance. Indeed, the shifts in health care delivery systems in this century clearly illustrate the promise inherent in town and city as well as the inevitable complications that arise from abstractive progress.

In older concrete communities, the "country doc" was obliged by his sense of the *Halig* of the whole to treat the poor for the price of a chicken or a sack of potatoes or perhaps nothing at all. *Korn* did not have a regular doctor. For some years, Corn had Doc Crowder, whom I remember as a chiropractor whose skills were successfully extended to officiating at human births and tending to many of the typical wounds and illnesses that were normal to farming, to growing up, and to animals.

Corn also had the Schlichtings, a family that transmitted an old-world tradition of "the touch." Doc Fred moved from the farm to Corn and developed a reputation for setting bones. People drove from surrounding states to take advantage of his skill. I needed only to walk down a short block to set two broken bones in an arm when I fell out of a tree. Doctors sometimes referred to him the messed up bones they feared to set by hand but which might not require operations. In turn, he had the good sense to refer to them the conditions that he knew were beyond his skill.

Well, most of the time. During the first summer I worked for Klause, I developed a severe case of athlete's foot. A swollen, viscous blister enclosed each toe of both feet. Uncle Klause cut off the tops of my shoes and I hobbled to the chores of the *Hof*. On Saturday my father took me to Doc Fred. This was outside his specialty, but he was willing to try. He took a scalpel, sliced off all the blistered skin around the toes, and upended a bottle of rubbing alcohol over my screaming toes. In a week or two the blisters were back.

Lithographs of old-fashioned country docs also illustrate the limited nature of their skills. They were often pictured sitting in a rural or village home beside a bed. Those who saw the picture, perhaps in *The Saturday Evening Post*, knew that the patient was seriously ill, because only then would "Doc" be called. He was dressed in a black suit, and a black leather bag with black handles sat on the floor near his feet. His body was bent forward and his eyes stared somberly beyond the floor into the earth that might soon receive the body of the person lying on the bed. The eyes of the patient looked upward, beyond the ceiling, toward a hoped-for vision of departed loved ones coming to welcome another to their eternal home.

No one in the room, not even the doctor, focused on the black bag at his feet. That was the pathetic symbol of how little could be done. Additional tools for first aid and more bottles and vials were in the doctor's home office, but the grieving family knew that there had been no point in taking the patient there, for that bag would contain the few instruments and the bottle or two of medicines that "Doc" might think helpful to this kind of illness.

When I was young, such a doctor could aid recovery from lesser diseases, especially those normal to children. He could skillfully patch up wounds and even extract inflamed tonsils and appendixes. He practiced a tacitly accepted ad hoc form of "insurance" that permitted him to "tax" the richer with a larger fee so that he could survive and even prosper. Of course, many people died who could now be cured, but the system was roughly fair.

It helped that daily work and homegrown food produced tough bodies. It was also true that those who were born with diseases and deformities much less often survived long enough to transmit their ills to the next generation. If they did survive, they were unlikely to attract a spouse. Though this "health care system" helped the gene pool to limit the number of the physically defective to a "natural" minimum, even the most *Halig* concrete communities suffered much heartbreak.

But the community revered the old country doc as much for his ministry to the dying as for his ability to deal with lesser ills. The old lithograph revealed that he was also a priest, one who officiated at the sacred rituals of birthing and dying. The country doc and the country cleric expressed the community's mutuality and did so in the full knowledge that the wonders of life were enclosed in the greater mysteries of that from which we came and that to which we went.

The country doc was the "deacon" who assisted at the birth of a new nexus of processes, mitigated the effects of the less than fatal vicissitudes that were its lot, and presided at the separation of that physical set from the social and spiritual relationships that could not be thought to be so quickly mended. The country doc was a priest because he ministered importantly to the *Halig* of the whole.

Fortunately, for my re-blistered toes, progress had brought early modern medicine to the towns around us. I was then taken to Cordell where the doctors possessed resources that could not be brought to us and could not even be housed in their own homes. Medical science was powerfully enriching the art of medicine. This doctor not only had a proper office downtown above a dry goods store, he also had an operating room and a room of shiny new machines as well as several rooms for recovering patients.

He studied my feet and decided to experiment with his latest scientific toy. He stuck my feet under his new X-ray machine and baked them for as long as he guessed was necessary. The treatment didn't hurt at all and I was completely cured. Irony remains when I occasionally remembered to worry about the long-range effect of all those roentgens, in addition to those I got later from sticking my feet into the flouroscopes that revealed the fascinating structures of my toes. For at least a brief period, every up-to-date shoe store acquired those to help fit shoes.

The modern town doctor no longer appeared in a black suit sitting prayerfully beside a dying patient. Now he was probably coatless, pictured in the kind of white shirt appropriate to any scientist and bending over a patient strapped onto an operating table almost engulfed in some enormous machine. Now the doctor looked directly at the patient, who gratefully looked up at this now more secular priest who served a mysterious science that empowered him to solve the mysteries of the body. This doctor had the authority of the abstracted knowledge that could deliver health. I think it was during high school that I had my only other bout with athlete's foot. All I required now was a daily dusting with a wonderful powder developed by pharmacologists. I remain grateful.

Just months before retiring, I encountered the advanced technologies of an up-to-date modern hospital in a modern city. Now, as in contemporary cartoons in *The Cortlandt Forum*, the patient was again lying in a bed. In the cartoons a small clutch of doctors in white gowns stand at the foot of the bed, ignoring the patient who looks anxiously at them. With medical charts in hand, they are wisecracking with each other about the symptoms or, perhaps, the coming bill. They also study the charts and the monitors that hold the wavy lines and numbers that quantify the patient's symptoms. There is more than one doctor because each of them has specialized in one of the abstract systems of which the patient's body is composed.

Since this is a spare and comic cartoon rather than a richly drawn old lithograph, it is clear that death is not a real option. Even in contemporary television medical shows, whose need for drama demands an omnipresent grim reaper, doctors exist as those who have dedicated themselves to the science of cheating death, not as a priesthood that presides over its arrival and departure. Therefore, the concrete patient disappears behind the monitors and charts and consulting specialists almost as completely as has God and the greater *Halig*.

What I encountered was more like the TV dramas. I was surrounded by nearly a half-dozen doctors and a dozen or more nurses and specialized medical technicians who had been summoned on the instant by a clanging Code Blue. As in the cartoons, almost no one was looking at the patient who had just had the beginning of a heart attack and whose heart rate and blood pressure were crashing. They were all looking at the monitors that were displaying the numbers. Only I, inappropriately, attempted to lighten the mood with a wisecrack.

My timing had been very fortunate. In anticipation of impending retirement, I had decided to begin to take care of my body. Within a week or two at the gym, I noticed a slight pressure when doing vigorous workouts. Not many sessions later, the pressure seemed to be a bit greater, so I showered, dressed, and drove to the nearby Kaiser-Permanente hospital where my cardiologist wife was on duty. She turned me over to an internist who decided to keep me overnight "just in case," despite a not very ominous EKG. A nurse appeared to put needles in my arm—again "just in case." She had almost finished when the monitor to which I was already attached triggered the alarm.

Thanks to the tubes connected to my veins, they could immediately inject atropine to stimulate my heart muscle, fluids to raise my blood pressure, and tPA to dissolve the clot in my artery (at well over a thousand dollars a shot). The drama was heightened, of course, because they all knew that the cardiologist in charge was my wife. And she was probably not the only one who uttered prayers when my numbers began to decline a second time. In any case, both of us were grateful for all the sciences and technologies that had helped those present to respond to my abstracted numbers. Neither the medicine of the village nor of the town could have known how to save my life. Despite the dramatics, I suffered only minor damage to my heart.

More than ever, I exult in the real progress of the medical sciences. I am also very aware of the high costs of that progress. Few of us can afford to pay the bills that could quickly mount in an extended illness that calls for "heroic" measures. Therefore, medical insurance has become essential to protect ourselves from possible destitution, at which point we could join the already destitute who are granted the form of government assistance that is a mixture of both "welfare" and "insurance."

But now health insurance is also becoming hostage to the progress of the medical specialties, which may well learn how to do more for the sick than can be paid for. Meanwhile, modern conditions for living and working create new diseases and deformities that call for the invention of newer subspecialties with increasingly expensive procedures.

At the same time, few of us are developing the common sense and the uncommon will to adopt the life style changes that would strengthen our bodies and our immune systems in order to improve our individual health. Even if many of us did so, it is not certain that fitter bodies and healthy diets could long delay a health care crisis. What is good for our bodies during most of our lives may devastate our pocketbooks as we near death.

For example, the time may come when almost entire populations suffer diabetes or other endemic diseases. Here, too, progress ironically guarantees that more people must become diseased and deformed. Marj, my cardiologist wife, has long been acutely aware that scientific medical progress becomes ever more successful at treating patients "retail" while sometimes contributing to the factors that increase disease and deformity "wholesale." She was convinced that lifestyle changes were as important in the prevention of heart disease as were dramatic surgical interventions after its arrival.

She also knew that most cardiologists were granted little time or incentive to convince patients who were eager to receive the latest interventions but reluctant to change bad habits and to trust that less dramatic medical management could be safer and more effective in selected cases. For years she shared the art and craft of cardiology with interns and residents with whom she cared for the indigents who mostly used the local county teaching hospital.

For the last ten years of her career, she followed a colleague to Kaiser-Permanente, which had been encouraging its doctors to follow similar ideals. Within the week that I began to write this section, she showed me a report presented by the National Committee on Quality Assurance that praised the Kaiser Permanente Northern California (KPNC) system for so significantly reducing death from heart disease among its three million members that it was no longer the leading cause of death in this population. It was, actually, "more than 30 percent lower" than in the general population. Moreover, "the mortality rates from heart attacks [treated] at KPNC hospitals are up to 50 percent lower than at similar hospitals."[2]

Now, more than a dozen years after writing this "case study," my readers will recognize that The Affordable Health Care Act has created a new crisis. Though I am enormously grateful that the miracle of modern medicine has since enabled me to survive a more severe threat, I know that I am not competent to suggest answers.

Although I am very happy to be on the good side of these statistics, I do not cite this either to praise my wife or Kaiser-Permanente. I do so to heighten the ironies that must be recognized. Yes, the heart program had saved money in the short term and had prolonged its patients' lives; but that also could threaten the continued financial health of Kaiser-Permanente.

---

2. From the minutes of the board of directors meeting of Kaiser Permanente Northern California on June 12, 2003.

Deaths from heart attacks are often quick and unexpected. Such deaths are cheap for HMOs and government welfare programs.

The prevention of these deaths, from a financial point of view, guarantees that more of their clients will live to contract the very expensive forms of death that come with cancer, diabetes, dementia, and other lingering diseases. Most of the medical expenses in an average lifetime come in the final years of life. The greater the success of medical science, the more people will age to endure those final months and the longer those months must stretch beyond a mere two years. If *all* fatal diseases became miraculously and cheaply curable, it would take enormous communal resources to allow the entire population to die of old age.

The longer it takes us to die, the more expensive dying becomes. The logic seems inevitable: either the system collapses or we agree that after a certain age, or after given stages of a disease, the system must withdraw its resources except to make possible a quicker, more comfortable death. Since government-subsidized medical care, whether or not fully socialized, is a tax-based form of insurance, it, too, must discover that some things cannot be paid for.

Then our society will deliberately decide who must be allowed to die sooner rather than later. The marketplace has made such decisions in the past, of course; but earlier stages of the process could mask that "rationing" by providing charity-based medical facilities for those who could reach them. Medical ethical dilemmas are already horrendous. If my logic is right, they will become worse, as will the dilemmas that arise wherever the progress of abstracting technologies reach their apotheosis.

I conclude this chapter with the admission that I am neither a sociologist nor an economist. I trek along the paths rationally dictated by my abstractive models and my proverbial images and metaphors. I am also, I think, a modern with the gift of a memory of an earlier era of ad hoc mutual aid and an imagination stimulated by the study of ancient history. I have learned that the logic of continual "progress" in finite environments leads to economic and ecological and moral crises.

As cultural historians have noticed, societies formed of concrete primary communities often became archaic and stultifying, producing hell instead of *Halig*. They also could last for a very long time. Earlier abstracting civilizations became prosperous and progressive and freeing, at least for the small elite who enslaved the rest. These also tended to die more quickly. As I earlier noted, ensuing "dark ages" could be surmounted more quickly than I now think likely.

Excursus D
The Strange Rarity of Sacred *in the English Translations of the Bible*

THIS EXCURSUS REFLECTS UPON what I had heard from my *Korn* elders about the change in the meaning of time and labor and the sharing of scarce resources between the era of the Great Depression and Dust Bowl and the prosperity enjoyed during and since World War II. I said that changes had resulted from theological and worldview shifts stimulated by the technological revolution and the higher prices received for their produce during and after the war. I had described in earlier chapters the broader consequences of the modern abstractive processes, but in chapter 6 I traced concrete *village* mutuality, to *town* charity, and to *city* welfare.

For our elders there had been no clear distinction between the worth of what was kept and what had freely been given away. To improve the village and to find new land for heirs had been as much the extension of the kingdom of God on earth as was the personal use of the gifts of God. But by the twentieth century, both time and money had been divided into sacred and profane, or even new and modern *secular* functions.

Sacred money is what we charitably give to help the poor whom God loves and what we give to support those in full-time Christian service. Apparently, their time is now more sacred than is the time the rest of us work to support ourselves and others. For us, *stewardship* has become a question of the tithe, and this reinforced the feeling that money we inherit or earn is our own whether to give away or to keep. Our energies are not so much extensions of the energy of a God-with-us that is also part of God's free gifts. To move from my bewilderment to the astonishment accompanying my attempts to interpret the premodern and modern understanding of what is sacred, I address the history of the word's use.

Why does *sacred* almost never occur in English translations of the Bible? Since the Greek word *hagios* (ἅγιος) begins with a vowel, it must always have a *breathing* over that vowel. This beginning mark resembles the initial single quotation mark. In translations this is noted by putting an "h" in front of the vowel. If the single ending quotation mark appears, as ἄγω (the verb to *lead* or *bring*), this *smooth* breathing mark shows that the vowel would not begin with an "h" sound. Since the second mark over the initial "alpha" of the Greek word is an accent mark, its first syllable is stressed, instead of the English word's stress on the second syllable.

The adjective form of the Greek word *hagios* (ἅγιος) describes that which is *"dedicated to God, holy, sacred."*[1] The massive Liddell and Scott *Greek-English Lexicon* says that the adjective is used of "what is devoted to the *gods . . . sacred, holy"* and when used of persons, *"holy, pure."*[2]

But when I went to *Cruden's Complete Concordance,* listing all the words used in the King James translation and the Revised Version entirely referenced in Zondervan's 1949 edition, I found no use of *sacred* in either translation.[3] The two Greek-English lexicons mentioned in the previous paragraph are the sources most used by English translators and interpreters and their reversal of *sacred* and *holy* shows that these are equally favored. Moreover, nothing in the two-and-a-half columns of derivatives of *sacre,* an ancient root of the word *sacred,* meaning "to set apart, consecrate," listed in the second edition of *Webster's Deluxe Unabridged Dictionary* departs from its positive religious significance.[4] In other words, the history of *sacred* had always made its use appropriate in canonic translations.

Though James Strong's *Exhaustive Concordance of the Bible,* Part One, also had no entry for *sacred,* his Part Two abstracts and compares selected concepts rather than concentrating on specific words, thus allowing greater freedom for biblical scholars to notice which biblical passages might be relevant. His massive compilation compares older authorized English and American versions with contemporary revisions. In that section,[5] he notes that *sacred* was once used to speak of temple offerings.[6] Though 2 Tim 3:15 uses *sacred* in a heading for that passage, the text itself again uses *holy* to describe the scriptural texts.

1. Arndt and Gingrich, *Greek-English Lexicon,* 9.
2. Liddell and Scott, *Greek-English Lexicon,* 811.
3. Cruden, *Complete Concordance,* 556.
4. Webster, *Unabridged Dictionary,* 1593–94.
5. Strong, *Exhaustive Concordance,* 179.
6. 1 Cor 9:13.

The editors of *Harpers Topical Concordance,* published by Harper and Row, decided when *sacred* presumably equally or better indicates the concept of the Hebrew or Greek word for what is holy was used in texts of the Old and New Testament. When the editors of *Harpers Topical* sought biblical passages using the most recent meaning of *secular* that specified what was neither holy or unholy nor sacred or profane, they cited eighteen passages. Each of the twenty-seven passages which they said illustrated these concepts was appropriately chosen. Since presumably none of the biblical writers had heard of the modern concept of the secular, I continue to marvel that recent English-speaking biblical translators have never—or perhaps very rarely—used *sacred*. For that matter, recent interpreters of biblical texts regularly avoid *sacred*.

I also think that we can learn something important when the editors of *Harper's Topical Concordance* list twice as many biblical passages that illustrate the modern concept of *secularism* as they list illustrating *sacredness*. The objective rhetoric of *facticity* and of ideological certainties diminishes our capacity to read and interpret canonic texts.

For seven of the nine passages where they recognized the concept of *sacredness*, they continued to use *holy* when citing the biblical translation. One passage used *sanctify* and the prayer Jesus taught his disciples told them that God's name should be *hallowed*, a derivation from *Hal* (*Halig, holy*). Though their selection of texts and their "weighting" of the number of texts seemed accidental, they remain appropriately illustrative. It was also clear that their contextual specificity would never justify using *secularism* in the doubled number of those biblical passages, though I suspect that doubling hints of its importance for modern peoples.

Polytheistic Greeks never used *hagios* to speak of what is negative. That the earlier Greeks who had migrated east into India used the adverbial form of that word to become the Sanskrit word for *sacrifice* (that which is "dedicated to God"), testifies to the apparently universal premodern understanding of what is positively *sacred, holy*.

I return to the remarkable reluctance of biblical translators and interpreters to use *sacred* and to prefer *holy* despite centuries of agreement that both terms are equally appropriate. I hope to learn from others who better understand the history of these words. Surely it is trivial to suppose that the rough mark above the Greek word's initial *alpha* vowel shows that it was aspirated and that *hagios* suggested *holy*.

I have so far supposed that like my *Korn* elders, biblical translators and interpreters have, "instinctively," intuited that ancient peoples approved the positive concept of sacredness and holiness and abhorred the negative consequences of disorder and evil wickedness. Surely, they possessed that "common sense." Though somewhat desperately, I have resorted to the conjecture that the modern invention of *secularism* as another antonym of *sacredness* as an "other than the holy," whose consequences can be either positive or negative, was a category essentially alien to premodern theologies and worldviews. Therefore, *sacred*, perhaps illogically, was avoided. But then an ancient abhorrence of the concept of secularism has to be explained. Could they have consciously rejected the concept of contemporary understandings of the concept of what is secular? That, too, seems to me to have been unlikely.

I return to what I had learned from my *Korn* elders and suggest that they and the long line of their elders had not consciously *rejected* the option of secularism. They had not needed it because they had other ways to evaluate what was "other than"—order or disorder, goodness or badness—and I close this excursus with an argument that might justify what I have surmised.

I begin by noting that the original meaning of *saeculum* had included what belonged to an age, or of an age, or of a generation over an extended period of time. Thus, the French *siecle* names a one-hundred-year period, a century. Ancient Egyptian mythology said that the phoenix was a *secular* bird symbolizing immortality. Their *mythos* said that they lived for five hundred years, burst into flames, and revived from their ashes to again live five hundred years. In time, Latins added *worldly* to its definition of the *temporal*. I refer readers to the second edition of *Webster's Deluxe Unabridged Dictionary* published in New York by Simon and Schuster. Like the nearly thirty-volume *Oxford English Dictionary*, this massive single volume also illustrates the changes in the history of their use in addition to defining words.

After General Constantine became emperor of the Empire that became Christendom's Holy Roman Empire, bishops ordained clerics who served "in the world" as priests organizing churches and dispensing the sacraments. Derivatives of *saeculum* distinguished these holy orders from orders sequestered "out of the world" dedicated to prayer and reflection. Both orders were sacred, holy. *Saeculum* did not yet separate the holy from the secular in the modern sense of that word. Until the twentieth century, church historians could describe even bishops as important secular magistrates!

Ancient heirs of Abraham had understood that presumptuous eating of the "tree of the knowledge of good and evil" had disordered the garden of Eden. But Gen 3 describes an exile from Eden that was actually a blessing rather than a punishment. Had they remained in Eden and eaten of the "tree of life," they would have been condemned to live forever with the consequences of their presumption.

I return to my *Korn* elders who wrestled with and related to each other, the *presences* of the soil and what grew in it, the farm animals, the elements of nature, and the *Presence* of God to secure the *Halig* of the whole. They also deeply understood that what they were responsible for and could do, though necessary, could never by itself achieve the wholeness and holiness they sought. And yet, their experience of the Creator's loving and enabling *Presence* had freed them to become grateful to be faithful coworkers in a cosmic quest for an eschatological fulfillment that in its *time* would progress toward the new heaven and earth.

Through time, they had also inherited a series of insights of sages, prophets, and saints along with misinterpretations of the nature of "what-is." Concrete and complex humans capable of becoming enlightened, must also recognize their intermediate location in the cosmos. They experience neither the "beginning" nor the "end" of "time" or of "space." They are both "of the earth" and "of the heavens." And so, they develop worldviews that typically emphasize either a "top-down" or "bottom-up" strategy. In hierarchical, patriarchal "top-down" cultures, it then became possible to emphasize either the aggressive forcefulness of males (the Latin word for a male was *vir* plus *tue*, the root of a word indicating the ideal character or excellence of, in this compound word, a *virile* male). On the other hand, one's patriarchal "top-down" worldview could stress a father's love and nurturing carefulness.

So also, in time, Hebrews and Christ-followers developed a third worldview option, one that emphasized the loving and nurturing of mothers for their children. Of course, both male and female parents could always move between "male" aggressive strategies, "female" responsive categories, or mixtures of passive/aggressive strategies. Especially after Constantine's aggressive co-option of early Christ-followers, the ensuing Christendom developed *haireses* favoring differing strategies.

My Anabaptist-Mennonite heritage and my local church accepts a third worldview and theological option that emphasizes God's transcendence of male/female characteristics and categories and accepts the call to image God as implying that individual Christ-followers also transcend simplistic "top-down" and "bottom-up" identities and strategies. We agree, I hope, that only God can rightly judge any concrete individual's heart, though we are called to a "warfare" that avoids aggressive or passive/aggressive strategies to follow as faithfully and wisely as possible cooperation with the God-with-us, modeled and taught by Jesus of Galilee.

Chapter 10 expresses gratitude that contemporary humanists, philosophers, and scientists, if I rightly interpret some of their leading figures, have made possible the ending of the so-called wars between the humanities and the "hard" sciences and between *faith* and *science*. Chapter 11 addresses the more difficult challenge of correcting the consequences of technology's emphasis upon "I-It," objective interpretational strategies for reaching certainties that makes it difficult for contemporaries to understand our interrelational existence ("I-Thou," to return to Martin Buber's insightful book). In Chapter 12, the writer recounts his harrowing journey home again, expressing his gratitude for safety.

CHAPTER 7

Mutual Nurture of *Halig*

CHAPTER FIVE INTRODUCED THE three positions of the dancers who wove the patterns of the ethos and the *Geist* of *Korn* that illustrated the three aspects of the work of *Halig*. They stood upright or knelt in contact with the earth they tilled and upon which they moved and built. In that chapter I began with "feet upon the ground," emphasizing both the *presences* of the natural elements and of the animals who shared the labor upon which our lives depended and who also entered into the substance of our life together. The fourth chapter focused on the second position of the dance when hands stretched out to touch each other and to share the privilege of giving each other the physical, moral, and social support needed during the years of pioneering, of surviving the great ecological crises of the Dust Bowl years, and of a national depression. *Mutuality* made it possible to survive the changes, the *mutability*, of those desperate years.

To survive and to thrive, they built up the spiritual resources supporting communal fulfillment. In this chapter I focus on our institutions. When Uncle Ed helped his neighbor, both were enhancing the *Halig* that defined and exalted each of its members. Each personal *Geist* uniquely incarnated the larger all-grown-together *Geist* of *Korn*. I propose *mutual nurture* to name ways in which individuals and institutions supported each other's quests for personal *Halig* and the community's quest for its *Halig presence*, its incarnation of a "Holy Spirit."

WITH ARMS POISED TO SWEEP UPWARDS IN THE FEAR OF GOD

The last short phrase of the title translates *Gottesfurcht*, their word for the reverent awe of God whose last syllable can literally translate as *fear*. When taken alone by ancients and elders confronting God, their awe often edged toward dread. And, indeed, the calling or *mission* to image God[1] that closes the account of the creation of the cosmos, should lead those deeply aware that, like the creatures over whom they are to be God's stewards, they retain so much creatureliness that they cannot "succeed" unless supported. In the context of a natural, mysteriously complex ecology of natural forces that even wishes and prayers cannot control, can any human not shudder when hearing the call to seek the wholeness of "what-is"?

My elders so often mentioned *Gottesfurcht* and *Gelassenheit* together that I have thought them to express their pious awe of God and their intention to be faithful. I do not know Hebrew well enough to know how Hebrews expressed it, but when they combined *Gottesfurcht* with *Gelassenheit*, the phrase expressed their awe and wonder of God and freed them to accept gratefully the high calling of humans to image God while "tilling" their gardens as Adam and Eve and their heirs had been called and gifted to work at in the garden of Eden.

When my elders read the passage in Gen 1 that followed the six-day creative work of God, they, too, had been freed to accept that challenge. Like Adam and Eve, they might fail and even be cast out of their "gardens," but, also like Adam and Eve, they, too, journeyed from Eden guided and enabled to seek new lands to till and to do so as those still imaging God.

In other words, when combined by my elders in *Korn*, Oklahoma, the German words *Gottesfurcht* and *Gelassenheit* were not literally interpreted to express *fear* of God. They evoked awe at the grandeur and mystery of the creation and of their calling. They had also been freed from the dreadful compulsion of having to guarantee that somehow their creaturely efforts had to guarantee the productiveness of their "gardens" and the "very good" of their immediate and larger ecologies.

My father had helped me to understand this phrase when I had long ago asked about it, and I had again been pondering it when writing my meditations about my heritage. Two days before rewriting these paragraphs, on October 15, 2023, while listening on Zoom to the Sunday worship service from my apartment at the senior retirement facility where I live, our

---

1. Gen 1:26–31.

senior pastor's homily from the Gospel of Luke[2] helped me to understand that I was hearing a phrase that interpreted *Gelassenheit*.

The young girl Mary of Nazareth heard that she was to give birth to a son she was to name Jesus and that this one would so image God that "he will be called Son of the Most High" and will be given "the throne of his ancestor David" and "of his kingdom there will be no end." Luke wrote his Gospel in Greek, and I do not know how the Aramaic version of Hebrew she would best have understood and would normally have used, expressed her simple response, "let it be with me according to your word."[3] As expressed, a long paragraph later in the wonderful *Magnificat* that Luke appropriately attributed to Mary, I was, for the first time hearing a grateful celebration of what my elders as simply evoked when combining *Gelassenheit* ("let it be") with *Gottesfurcht*.

That Sunday afternoon I reread Gen 1 and 2 in the context of Pastor Audrey's opening "confession" that she, apparently modestly, often hides her skills. For example, when it would have been appropriate to help someone with a cooking problem, she had not wanted to reveal her mastery of that skill. Since "the man and his wife were both naked, and not ashamed,"[4] Adam and Eve might have been astounded during the discussion group after the homily when that theme for a while dominated the dialogue.

Who could not read the story of creation and not be awed? And how can that awe not turn into stupefying dread when reading that mere humans are called to steward our ecologies? Should we even dare to get out of bed most mornings?

When I reread Gen 1 and 2, I wondered whether Adam and Eve ever encountered the temptation to avoid their responsibilities and hide their skills when they heard that they were to till the earth, that is, to manage its ecology, and to name all living creatures. In that context, naming implied determining their character and even when to determine their fate, as in giving them "everything that has the breath of life . . . for food." After all, they had just been warned of the deadly consequences of eating of the fruit "of the tree of the knowledge of good and evil."

And what about my *Korn* elders? Those who tilled the soil have always learned that though their careful and diligent toil was a necessary condition for securing bountiful harvests, even their best efforts could never guarantee success. Rains came or they did not. Pests and blight were often beyond their control. Wonderfully maturing fields might get hailed out just before

2. Luke 1:26–38.
3. Luke 1:38.
4. Gen 2:25.

the harvest could be finished. In short, the *necessary* conditions they could manage were not, by themselves, *sufficient* conditions for success.

Often, in my ethnic tradition, and most meaningfully, diligence and skillful management had been experienced as a sacramental participation in the creative joy of partnering with God and this was the earthly fulfillment that foretold an eschatological fulfillment. While singing "This world is not my home, I'm just a passing through; my burdens I'll lay down, somewhere beyond the blue," they could often remain grateful during the depression years and the dust bowls they endured. And when grieving or rejoicing, they shared their efforts and their emotions with each other. I now return to my meditations on my odd awe at what I was learning in *Korn*.

Small as it was, the boundaries of *Korn* and peoples were too large, and even too scary, to be embraced immediately. Four smaller communities welcomed the explorations of the child who ventured beyond the boundaries of the womb from which it came. The father and mother and siblings that welcomed it to their *Hof* or corner of the village provided the simplest and most basic primary group for mutual nurture. Mediating between the family and the larger *Korn* were its schools and clans and churches.

Most families belonged to clans whose members were normally scattered throughout the community. The clan comprised the kin who enlarged the boundaries of our families and who furnished allies whenever large groups gathered, as on Saturday nights on the streets and alleys of *Korn* or on Sunday mornings on the churchyard. These kin provided entrée to the other spaces of *Korn* and protection from the other clans. Rivalries could be fierce. My father remembered that when he was young it was not safe for a boy from Bessie to venture into *Korn*'s *village* without protective convoy.

Both the school and the clan were integrating and separating in their own ways. The school district formed a nurturing small society that expressed its distinct identity and its geographic sense of place in rivalries with the other school-centered districts. The church that towered over the center of the village had more congregants than the four country churches combined; but each of them had both clustered and scattered members.

THE FAMILIES OF *KORN*

The bounded but richly furnished world of the *Hof* or village stimulated the infant to explore its space and to interact with its inhabitants. Animals and homemade toys submitted to its actions and manipulations while parents and older siblings provided a range of models for its desire to master more complex skills. Each child competed with siblings for its share of goodies and honor as well as for parental favor. Each child also became a contributing member to the *Halig* of the family's *Geist* and to the prosperity of the *Hof* in ways appropriate to its maturation. *Korn* families provided both a sense of security and an adequate grant of freedom for expanding explorations and they positively encouraged their children's aspirations.

It was true, of course, that a few parents were too restrictive and some others demanded too much of their children, and every generation included those who became angry with their parents. It was also true that the personal aspects of that anger were inextricably mixed with the attempt to come to terms with the larger ethos that the parents represented. Rage and bitterness were sometimes great. A few walked away still nursing their wrath.

But the lack of a clear boundary between the family and the community allowed reconciliation to emerge at unexpected points. Clans and schools and churches were such natural extensions of the family that they could reinforce the authority of the home while providing safety valves for releasing the potential pressures inherent in its structure. Moreover, the ritual passages of graduation, baptism, and marriage "officially" transformed the son or daughter into the "brother" or "sister" of all the other adults, changing the dynamics of their relationships and pushing even heavy-handed parents to accept their own children as their peers.

Just as the mutual aid of a concrete society made more or less ad hoc provisions for some to be at least minimally employed and housed and clothed and fed, so also its mutual nurture created an ethos for all its members. *Korn* provided the children of inadequate parents with a variety of role models and of caring adults. Because all created the ethos for all, the children of the marginal had not been significantly disadvantaged, minimizing the number of deviants and failures.

Until I began to speak English at age four, I addressed all the older men and women as *Onkel* and *Tante*. Even later, I took for granted that all of them saw themselves as my extended family, as at least honorary aunts and uncles. I knew also that they would protect and admonish me should that be necessary, and I hoped very much that they would not report misbehavior to my parents, for then my punishment would also have to atone for the embarrassment that I had caused the family. Just as all taught our common languages, so all reinforced the common ethos and instilled respect for God and for our common *Geist*.

THE SCHOOLS OF *KORN*

The village also had its grade school, and it was larger than the surrounding country schools that had already begun to disappear when I enrolled. For two of the four years I attended, one teacher taught two classes in the same room. By my seventh grade, our class was large enough to have a room and teacher of its own. It would have been a bit larger, but one or more country schools remained. Years later, *Korn* had to consolidate with Colony, a village about six miles east. The year I taught there, *Korn* had two small high schools and no grade school. In 2023 its Academy moved northwest of Clinton and no schools remain.

Gatherings of neighbors, attendance at special programs, and festive picnics provided children an almost seamless transition to the larger boundary and more complex "communities" of the schools. Here children interacted daily with up to a handful of their age-mates, developing with them the competitive and cooperative skills that similar development allows. At the same time, they continued to be stimulated by the older children they admired and sometimes feared. Older students were assigned to drill them in the skills that the teacher would introduce but had no time to perfect.

Those who quickly mastered the day's assignment were not always fobbed off with boring repetitions of already mastered lessons. They were free to pay attention to the recitations of the more advanced as well as to review what they had learned while listening to the lessons for the younger, thus growing naturally and confidently into more complex materials. Even younger girls might be recruited by the oldest students to make up teams for lunch-time games. The boundaries of their imaginations were not constrained by the narrow perspectives of age-graded peer groups.

The curriculum was limited, but the environment encouraged depth of comprehension and allowed time to explore individual interests. The setting and the curriculum were large enough to challenge and small enough to reassure them that mastery was within their grasp. When teachers were petty tyrants, the students sometimes managed to coalesce against them until the teacher fled or was dismissed. Dismissal did not always happen soon enough. A friend of mine attended a one-room school in a Mennonite community north of us. His red-haired Irish schoolmarm's moral fault was a fiery temper, and he ruefully remembered, "I got a lickin' every day."

Each school district imitated most of the aspects of the entire community, yet each had also its own distinctive web and ethos and *Geist*. Having grasped its patterns and embodied its character, the children graduated into the life of the concreteness of the larger *Korn*. They were also being introduced to the three basic abstractions that more clearly marked the world beyond *Korn*. Every morning they had left their homes to join a secondary society (the primary school and its graded classes) that drilled them into the intellectual skills they need in the town and the city. After eight years, they joined the graduates from the other districts, expecting older comrades from their own school to protect them from bullying rivals and smooth their entry into the high school or the academy. Now they were ready to extend their explorations to *Korn*'s farthest border and beyond.

These small schools that helped the growing children move comfortably into the larger space of *Korn* also inspired them to strive for personal excellence in competition with their schoolmates for the honors that the schools dispensed, but their most spirited competitions required them to cooperate with these mates when pitted against the other schools in the larger space of *Korn* and then against the schools of the entire county.

The Greenfield school, several miles northwest of Corn, had enough large families to build a brick, two-room school. Despite that district's recognition of my father's promise, the members of their Board hesitated to hire him to teach the four upper grades and run the school. He did not play any instrument and had given few signs of musical talent. How could he lead their little "orchestra"? Surely, he would not be able to train the chorus to best the school taught by the musically talented Esther Bartel. My father chuckled when he much later told me how Greenfield had won the county-wide competition that year. "I knew that I couldn't match her musically, but I took care to find out what the judges wanted, and I gave it to them." The parents were ecstatic.

Though the citizens of *Korn* were smugly sure that their *Geist* was better than those of the surrounding "English," they remained anxious to assuage an underlying suspicion of their old-fashioned foreignness by winning musical competitions. These victories helped assure their status, at least in their own eyes. Music was *Korn*'s first competitive sport, one of the chosen fields on which *Korn* defined its worth over-against the rest of Washita County and the citizens of Oklahoma. I was not musically gifted and I could not raise prize farm animals, but I did my part to represent Corn by twice winning the "timely topic" contest at the county 4-H competitions.

The neighboring communities also tested their merit in athletics, but the early *Korn* settlers feared that competitive sports were worldly. The oldest son of the evangelist and educator who became the Academy's strictest disciplinarian told me how deeply he had envied the neighboring DeFehr boys, who were allowed a basketball goal in their backyard and who played—in cutoff overalls—on Sunday! By the time we moved to *Korn*, the community's "secular" high school had begun to compete in baseball and basketball.

When I was in the sixth or seventh grade, our pride reached its apotheosis. Coached by our class's teacher, the team reached the state basketball finals. The event is still discussed. Nearly sixty years later I heard a *Korn* expatriate mention "the year we won the championship." The score was very close but at the end the team from Oklahoma City's largest high school scored the winning basket. That was the year that the rest of the state realized that Corn was on its map. After that Corn expected to be competitive with neighboring towns and villages. The grandson of one of the Franz boys on its legendary basketball team became a defensive back in the National Football League. Even the Academy competes in multiple sports in its own league. Though small, its girl's academic team, a few years ago, won a state championship.

THE CLANS OF *KORN*

Another set of small societies bridged our families and the larger *Korn*. Most of us could claim the identity and the protection of an extended family. Though a primary group, clans did not have a common boundary and they were also parts of other clans. My close kin, who might extend to third and, even, fourth cousins, were dispersed throughout the spaces of *Korn*. Beyond its borders, they were scattered from Oklahoma to South Dakota and had emigrated west as far as California. Linked clans formed the larger tribe that was "our kind" of Mennonites.

In South Dakota and California, my mother's Kleinsasser clan was a significant part of the tribe known as "Prairie Hutters." In Corn, I belonged to the "Schmidt, Wiebe, Wiens" clan. Around 1870 a still young Schmidt widow in Crimea with several children was maneuvered into wedding a landless bachelor Wiens, to whom she bore two sons. They emigrated from Russia to central Kansas but did not achieve prosperity. It is said that when the oldest of the later sons asked permission to marry his beloved, his future father-in-law reacted with loud dismay: "What? My daughter marry into those low-down Wienses?" In fact, my grandfather by then had managed the still rare feat of earning a high school degree, but rival clans do not easily let personal merit override well-known familial *Geists*. Ever since learning this bit of family lore, I have been convinced that every person needs a clan and that every clan should be able to trace back to at least one skeleton in the closet. My great-grandfather did not have the dubious reputation of a horse thief, but I have learned to be content with petty notoriety.

By the second decade of the twentieth century, my great-grandfather had abandoned my great-grandmother and had gone to Bessie, where his youngest son had moved his general store from Shelly, which withered after the original Mennonite settlers built their school and church on the present site of Corn. Most of the rest of the Schmidt-Wiens children had taken turns keeping their mother for a month at a time. By the end of the thirties, when we moved to Corn from Cordell, my father's parents and siblings had all moved to California or Kansas, but I was happy to have two dozen or more half-second cousins among several Schmidt families and from the Dicks, Funks, Reimers, and Penners whose mothers had been Schmidts.

Since members of clans had necessarily to marry into other clans, we were linked out and farther out into the world. Though we traveled a lot, we did not dream of special trips to resorts or to amusement parks. We went to visit scattered members of our clans. Along the way we might stop at national parks and important historic sites. We were all likely to have cousins or second cousins somewhere who did exotic things and who stimulated our ambition to be equally daring. Relatives were both nearby allies and early windows into a rich and complicated world beyond *Korn*.

I was too young when we left *Korn* to be fully aware of our place in the pecking order of the clans of *Korn*. That was important knowledge, for church and community politics were, significantly, a matter of clan politics. I am sure that we were not among the most powerful family groups, but we could point with pride to one of my father's half-cousins who had become the president of a Bible institute in Nebraska. My father and one of his brothers-in-law (who loosely linked us to the important Vogt clan) were denominational leaders. Some of us remained poor, but scandals were rare. Whether or not we were important, there were enough of us to grant a sense of identity beyond the family, to furnish a measure of protection for each other beyond our immediate turf, and, eventually, to provide a platform for important contributions to the *Halig* of *Korn*.

Several times during my boyhood, the Schmidt/Wiebe/Wiens clan gathered for a grand picnic in pastures along the banks of the Washita River. There was a program with speeches and songs and recitations, but what I remember were the tables of food, the intergenerational games, and the swings—especially the swings. Both of them were long ropes hung from a stout arching branch of a huge cottonwood above a large patch of cleared ground. One of them, with a knot tied about head-high, dangled near the edge of the river's bank. We children then grabbed the rope above the knot and ran sideways until our curved path returned us to the edge of the bank.

There we kicked off, completing a semicircle out over the river and about six feet above it. We were scared, but hardly any of us were scared enough to refuse our turn. The men had taken care to make it less dangerous than it appeared to be. The places they picked carried us over shallow water that flowed above a foot or more of soft red mud. Cousin Elda fell off one year, emerging soaked and muddy but unharmed.

In later life, the swings became a metaphor for me of the importance to us of concrete communities—and of the terror and thrill of transcending them. The other swing illustrated the message best. My best guess is that about eighty feet of fairly new and stout rope was tied to a lofty branch and that half or more of it stretched out along the ground. Those being swung jumped onto a short, strong branch that was stuck through a loop three feet above the ground, gripped the rope in front of them, and made sure to keep their feet in front of the rope that stretched behind them along the ground.

A half-dozen of the strongest and fastest men lined up at the end of the rope and began to pull in unison, paying strict attention to the orders of the one who was in charge of gauging how far and how fast to run back and forth until momentum was gained for a final sprint. Just before the rope became taut, the leader shouted and all the men jerked hard and immediately let go. The timing had to be exactly right so that the swinger was smoothly catapulted dizzyingly high.

On the first arc, my hands were frozen to the rope and my stomach knotted painfully. By the second arc, it became possible to begin to breathe and become aware of the anxious faces of the assembled *Tantes*. After that, as "the cat died," the roaring of the wind in my ears subsided enough that I could hear the rope sinuously lashing back and forth along the ground through the grass and dry leaves.

Of course, our first turns were limited to swings that were judged appropriate to our age and experience and courage. Our last swing might be so high that the rope was nearly enough parallel to the branch from which it hung to develop a bit of slack and we felt the jerk of its return to tautness. If I were now an elder at such a picnic, I think I would join the anxious aunts and veto maximum efforts. My friend Adam Ewert has described a version of the swing that combined the styles we used. They had no branch to sit on, simply grasping a knot while the others pulled. They put the rope away forever when an unskilled boy did not let go in time and nearly killed his brother, who was unable to hang on.

Beyond solicitous aunts, intergenerational ball games, and our traditional "soul foods," those picnics gave us the thrill of an adventure that included altered consciousness and moments of transcendence. However high and far we soared above them, those who remained on the ground welcomed us back—and would continue to acknowledge us during the rhythms of our future lives. Those of us who knew a *Hof* and neighborhood, a rural or village school, a clan and tribe, and the *Geist* of a concrete community are indeed privileged to "know where we came from," to have been prepared to reach beyond them—and to know that our returns would be welcomed.

THE CHURCHES OF *KORN*

Beyond the *Hof* and the schools and our clans were our churches. As smaller versions of the *Geist* of *Korn*, they also fostered a sense of security through familiar rituals while also challenging our imaginations through telling and retelling exotic stories of the ancient Hebrews and early Christians. Even my small country church on the wrong side of the river encouraged a higher culture. During some summers, we children were gathered to study High German. Always we were encouraged to love music and to play an instrument.

If country schools were our "conservatories" of music, it was the church that became a concert stage. Congregational singing was a major sacrament of our churches. To join the choir was almost a rite of passage. A Sunday concert by the Tabor College choir, led by the legendary Prof. Richert, was a major congregational event. One year our small country church scheduled a well-attended week of evening meetings with Prof. Richert to improve our knowledge of musical notation and to extend our acquaintance with better hymnody. Families with musical talent taught themselves to play guitars and other instruments.

My mother was so distressed that I had difficulty carrying a tune that she set me on the piano bench and made me sing the melody lines she pounded out while harmonizing the alto. I wish I could apologize to the piano teacher in Cordell for the heavy onion aura I occasionally trailed with me from the large hamburgers I bought at Tony's with the dimes that were my bribe for enduring her lessons. For *Korn*, four-part harmony may have superseded cleanliness in the quest for godliness.

During almost every Easter season the entire student body of the Academy, seldom more than one hundred, sang Handel's "Hallelujah Chorus" in the large Corn church. Mennonite congregations scattered over western Oklahoma met annually for a singing convention, often in large tents erected for the crowd that attended. Each of the church choirs took its turn on stage, torn, no doubt, between an unacknowledged desire to showcase its excellence and the official intention of glorifying God. The Academy still exults in the "firsts" that are consistently won in state competitions by its students.

"Growing up" seems especially to have occupied my imagination while in church. My present memories of the service become vivid about the time

I started school, when boys were allowed to sit with each other in the first or second row of pews on the men's side of the church. I can still capture the feeling of turning around and kneeling with the entire congregation during the time of prayers, when I could check my growth by resting my stomach and chest along the seat and rejoice when my head could reach the bottom of the backrest. Then I would sneak envious glances at the taller boys, whose bodies angled upward until their heads could rest on the top of the pew.

Some of the teenagers could see over its top, but then their faces might be only inches from the faces of the oldest men, who knelt facing forward because they were too stiff to turn around. Then the lads hunched down again. It seems to me that at about that age some of them avoided church until they repented of "backsliding," got baptized and married, and returned to sit in the back pews where young wives had recently been allowed to join their husbands. The mature men sat in the middle rows until, with old age, they moved directly behind us boys to better hear the preachers and to keep wary eyes on us.

Clearly, there were patterns to follow in growing old. Even during services that had nothing designed for us, and especially when they had been conducted entirely in High German, we were learning that adults had privileges that we might eventually grow to enjoy. We also knew that some adults were accorded special attention. Some were admired because they had managed their *Hofs* well. Some were also able to express our common wisdom and ideals in fitting and gracious words. These became community leaders. We boys admired our fathers. Our fathers admired leaders like H. H. Flaming. A missionary on furlough was another sort of hero, one like us who had returned from exotic places to show pictures and tell stories that fired our imaginations while reassuring us of the rightness of our ethos.

The churches added services designed for youth, probably during the adolescence of our parents. Every other Sunday evening we had "Christian Endeavor," in English. Each year a chairman, vice-chairman, and secretary were formally elected from among the high school youth. After some obligatory hymns, the chairman and secretary marched solemnly to the front and sat behind a small table beside the pulpit. After the chairman called the meeting to order, the secretary read the minutes of the previous meeting and called for whatever additions or corrections were required. Each act in the variety show that followed was carefully announced. Poems were recited and short speeches were delivered. Duets, trios, and quartets showed that we could sing in parts.

Almost always one of the Brown children was called on to present the entire family, instruments in hand, to perform popular Gospel songs. Often there were competitions: Bible knowledge quizzes, Bible verse memorization contests (the last one standing won), and "sword drills" (won by the one who most quickly found and read a verse whose chapter and verse number had been called out). The most dreaded moment came at the end when one of the officers announced who of us would be responsible for what sort of presentation at the next meeting.

Spontaneity could also happen amidst the formality. Near the end of the meeting all were invited to come forward to "do their thing." My Aunt Betty regaled our clan with the story of the time she and a friend marched to the platform of their country South Dakota church to sing and act out the chores of the week, "This is the way we wash our clothes, wash our clothes, wash our clothes," was the refrain for Monday. Throughout the program even the most "old world" elders beamed in approval that we were being granted the opportunity to perform in public, to learn oratory and music, and to practice Robert's Rules of Order in anticipation of our later participation in a larger world of politics and culture. They knew that *town* and *city* waited for us. Indeed, they had always been present in our small *village*.

THE CONTRADICTIONS OF CONCRETENESS

I have been describing a social context for growing up that was based on aspiration. In the family, church, clan, and school, as for *Korn* as a whole, we were always growing "into the shoes" of those who were older or wiser than we. We, in turn, were models for those younger ones who were practicing the excellences we had attained. The significant social groups of *Korn* were organized both horizontally and vertically. It was a community that helped us to define ourselves by its heroes as much as by our peers.

Children could not be expected to understand what constituted the excellence of an educator like Prof. Duerksen or of a spiritual guru like H. H. Flaming. But they did know that their parents and other adults deeply respected them. Meanwhile they aspired to imitate their older brothers and sisters and their younger uncles and aunts who, in turn, followed the patterns being enacted by those above them who were beginning to grasp yet greater virtue.

Corn's ladder of aspiration led gradually and naturally to a vision that trancended *Korn*. Those youth who best learned what *Korn* taught did not have to flee in despair or disgust at a "glass ceiling." They could aspire to leave and then return to help enrich its *Halig*. With *Korn*'s blessing they could dedicate themselves to go elsewhere in mission to those who presumably did not have so rich a heritage. The seeds of town and city that are inherent in every village had been so watered and fed that already my generation's parents had aspired to "town" while still preserving concreteness for their children, enough concreteness, at least, for me to make it a key to my version of its meaning.

There is, however, a fundamental contradiction built into the constitution of a concrete ethos and its ladder of aspiration. To the extent that a community becomes wholly concrete, it curves in upon itself, making an idol of its achievements. Then its vision of excellence reaches its limit in the partial merits of its leaders and no further transcendence becomes thinkable.

Competitiveness also has its built-in contradiction. Initially it spurs ambition to excel, which leads to the search for new methods to triumph over one's peers. Those who wished to jump the highest eagerly switched from the "scissors kick" to the "roll," only to be bested by those who first mastered the "Fosbury Flop." On the other hand, the goal of the communal competition for power is to become the superior who subordinates the others, thwarting rivals and limiting competitiveness to "harmless" pursuits, like athletics and music. Both aspiration and competition can lead to the perverse pride that produces stagnation, and those communities who cannot imagine improvement stagnate.

It is probably true that many primary communities in history tended to be limited by leaders who had been content to stagnate at the bare level of enduring common sense that permitted them to maintain their communities and their authority within them. Talented and ambitious youth had to leave to find contexts for further maturation. Most villages tended to become intellectually and spiritually comatose. Our word *coma* is derived from *kōmē*. This was the old Greek word for *village*.

Korn also had its share of those who distrusted transcendence and who were either fearful of the world beyond their boundaries or so convinced of the righteousness of its peculiar *Geist* that they wanted to make their ethos absolute and to draw our boundaries more tightly about us. There were periods when their voices were influential. My father told me later that one of the women in our congregation ceased to give for missions when she learned that those in Congo were not being taught to pray in German. One of my father's colleagues told me that the two of them sometimes discussed what it was about *Korn* that inspired its youth to reach out with ambition and in mission to the world and they had wondered why periods of expansive outreach in villages like *Korn* were often followed by periods when they again closed in upon themselves.

Pride of place has always a double face. Gratitude for the virtue of *Korn*'s *Geist* could quickly slide into the idolatrous pride of those who were sure that God agreed and loved us better than God loved others. Each time

I praise *Korn*, I feel driven to notice a darker side. But, in truth, the *Korn* I knew often rose to goodness. For that matter, the worst evils are often the result of distortions of the greatest goods.

I am grateful that that is not the *Korn* I remember. Perhaps I was fortunate to have been abstracted before I wanted to leave; or, more likely, I was fortunate in how my parents mediated its several moods to me. What I remember is that *Korn* itself both nurtured my sense of myself and gave me the impetus to catapult beyond it. At least a few escaped its nascent claustrophobia by replacing many of the elements of that ethos with surprising new ones in a rebellion that never achieved transcendence. They merely delivered themselves over to the expectations of different kinds of communities.

When I returned to Corn to teach, I learned that many who had never left it physically or who had gone and then returned had achieved transcendence in their hearts and imaginations while continuing to cherish the home place. There were also some who had borrowed a strident mix of old paranoias and new abstractions that they were recommending to the rest of the community as a final definition of perfection.

The families, schools, clans, and churches complemented each other to prepare us to fit into the complex larger web of Corn. With many of my friends, I also learned very early that our community expected us to seek education beyond its boundaries. We also learned that the expanding trajectories of clan and tribe and people extended around the globe, marking our larger identities over against the geographic identities of county, state, nation, and world into which we would also grow. The children who grew up in the *Korn* I knew were expected to embrace larger loyalties. And, though some were not taught as well as others, some of us were prepared to resist captivity to the tyrannous claims of any one of them.

We children did have "best friends" who were our own age, but we were never limited to the mindset of our age-mates. Our growing sense of who we were was held within the embrace of small and then slightly larger groups who both cherished us and expected us to grow beyond them since they, too, were subsets of larger communities. Meanwhile, we were always striving to imitate those just older than we who had already mastered the skills that we were learning. Even our toys were tokens of our aspiration to grow into the status and activities of our fathers as we imitated them in our play with homemade versions of their implements and tools.

KORN AS A COMMUNITY OF DISCIPLINE

No one assumed that aspiration and competition, by themselves, were adequate motives for virtue. All of the ancient Mediterranean societies that combined to give rise to modern Western civilization assumed that infants need external training. The classical Greeks used the same word for training infants that they used for training dogs or horses. As philosophers insisted, it is the most spirited and strongest animals that become the worst if they are not strictly disciplined into the traits that allow the achievement of the potential excellence desired by their owners.

How much more must human infants be guided to act in accordance with virtues they might not naturally seek if left to their own devices. The habits inculcated by early training were an indispensable foundation for an adult's ability to choose freely the continuing disciplines that led to excellence. (I use virtue and excellence as roughly synonymous for what is both morally and nonmorally admirable.)

Discipline into appropriate human responses began almost at birth. Morning and evening chores on the *Hof* together with one's parents provided perhaps the most effective formation of significant skills and attitudes that the growing child would need. Though wearisome, chores made mutuality real. Working at the same tasks as their parents, they, too, contributed to the prosperity and *Halig* of the *Hof*. Weeks of labor in the fields brought strength and taught endurance. We learned that life does not always have to make sense, but still, one must finish the row. Participation in a family-run store or shop in the village or town was also an effective preparation for the future. Those of us who grew up in the village were farmed out to the *Hofs* and fields of others.

The parents of *Korn* also assumed that both positive and negative inducements must be used to ready children for the greater power of internal aspiration. *Korn* made rich, and sometimes distorting, use of both rewards and punishments. As soon as an infant attains a social consciousness, it responds happily to affirmation. The approbation of those who are most important to one is a powerful reason to perform those actions and to develop those character traits for which one is being praised. Since "a little bit of sugar makes the medicine go down," a judicious use of "goodies" can also encourage the continued practice of virtues.

Of course, the quick use of praise can cheapen it, distorting a child's estimate of what has actually been attained. I understood quite early that praise for trivial accomplishment was embarrassing. How could I trust a flatterer to recognize real merit? Too lavish use of goodies confuses a child's growing understanding of more intrinsic motives for right actions. Their overuse can quickly teach that it is better to seem good than to be good and that goodies are the real goals of our efforts. I suspect that *Korn* was often too hard on children and that some of my friends could have profited from a bit more praise and a few more "goodies."

Negatively, punishments were also used to keep us on the straight and narrow path of goodness. The pains that naturally and quickly accompany some wrong actions are powerful moral teachers. However, most physical punishments that children receive, like "goodies," are also external to the nature of the actions and, therefore, can teach them to hide their flaws rather than to mend them. Then shame and pain can teach them to calculate more devious, and apparently easier, routes to the "goodies."

Open public shaming and half-covert gossiping are especially dangerous modes of discipline. Marj had grown up in a community that was much more tolerant of moral lapses than was *Korn*, and she dreaded moving to a Mennonite milieu because she had seen too much of the damage that gossip had done during the brief times that she lived in Mennonite enclaves. I tried to convince her that that was not the whole story, to lessen her fear of moving to Fresno so that I could teach at a Mennonite college. Gossip, I claimed, includes a community's attempt to uphold its ideals by disapproving of transgressions against them. Gossip was that part of the web of defining talk that was evil to the extent that it condemned persons instead of actions and saddled them with negative judgments rather than with ultimately redeeming affirmations.

Gossip, in its fullest sense, originally stood for something more significant than idle chatter. The word comes from the Old English *godsibb* ("God-relative"), the one who is designated the godparent at a child's baptism. Dictionaries still list "companion," "close friend," and "sponsor" as secondary meanings. A *godsibb* was obligated to surround growing children with words and deeds designed to shape a godly character. Perhaps, like some modern grandparents, they interacted too little with their wards and talked too much to others about them.

It remains true that the web of talk that defines the *Geist* of a concrete community will also help to shape the social nexus of each person who participates in that relational web. It may be difficult for moderns whose self is complicated by participation in many separated secondary webs to appreciate how importantly one's sense of oneself depends upon ongoing conversations.

My brother and I discovered how significant that web was to our mother and how importantly we figured in its talk during an afternoon discussion that began with a belligerent "I can't understand Doug's lifestyle." Jake, the South Dakota Prairie *Hutter* she had married several years after our father died, took turns with Doug and Marj and me to try to explain a passion for adventure that included rock climbing (including an ascent of El Capitan), kayaking turbulent mountain rivers (as well as a one-thousand-mile paddle from Seattle to Glacier Bay, Alaska), and that had taken him on several arctic expeditions.

A trek around Denali was featured in the National Parks Centennial edition of the *National Geographic* (July 1979).[5] The discussion ended when she concluded, "I still don't understand it." And then, glaring at me, "For that matter, I don't understand either of my sons." After a short silence, she softened, and added, "But I have to say this. There was never a time that I couldn't go to church and not hold my head up."

"Gossip," I also told Marj, "is the community's left-handed tribute to the importance of those being criticized. Our significance extends as widely as the circle of those who gossip about us." That sounded hollow when we discovered, after arriving in Fresno, that a hot rumor had made the rounds that Marj had fled to my parents in Kansas two months earlier because I had become a hippie in the mountains of Colorado. In fact, she had gone to stop an unwise exploratory surgery on my dying father, and I remained behind because I had agreed to teach a weeklong adult class for a Mennonite church in Denver.

It was true that I had given cause for suspicions. In 1969 we had holed up in a shack in the Rocky Mountains for a winter and spring so that I could complete a first draft of my dissertation. I was also almost the only person I knew in our churchly tribe who sported a beard. Worse yet, I had written a long analysis for our denomination's magazine that had proved controversial. What is important to know is that relatively healthy communities contain checks and balances. A couple of months later I learned that an important denominational leader, recently appointed the president of our seminary, had been so incensed that for two days he had driven around tracking the rumor to its supposed source and then delivering a stiff rebuke.

Marj and I had also known friends and acquaintances who were not "restored to fellowship" in their congregations until they had publicly confessed the indiscretion that had hastened their nuptials. Yes, sexual sins seemed to be singled out while more serious character flaws were often ignored; and yes, those sessions were profoundly difficult. Those of us who were their friends were usually distressed that this shaming was demanded. I suppose that some did learn from this to postpone intimacy until marriage, or at least to be more careful to prevent conception. (After all, even

---

5. Gillette, "Continent's Highest Peak," 66–79.

hypocrisy has its use as a down payment on the future practice of the virtue that is being acknowledged.) Some were stigmatized for life.

There was also a more positive effect, though unhealthy communities might never discover it. After confession, suspicion and gossip could end. Now everyone knew the basic facts of the case. Everyone knew that everyone else knew that they knew. After a while the painfully reconciled ones might be given important tasks in their communities and in their churches. I hope that my failure to remember *Korn*'s "illegitimates" means that there were few.

More importantly, I hope that my forgetfulness is a sign that *Korn* could move beyond judgment. With continued erosion of concreteness, these sessions before a congregation's mature ones do not happen and gossip remains covert. Nor are completely tolerant cultures preferable. Cultures that easily take moral failure for granted are unable to foster excellence and, by that rejection of their responsibility to stand for virtue, produce a much more demoralizing pain.

I suffered a few spankings while growing up, and usually I assented to their rough justice. I remember begging my mother to get it over with, fearing that Dad's hand would be heavier. Unfortunately, some in our community must have been abusive. I was later told that my father was vigorously reprimanded by some of the women in our country church for having taken me out of the service for spanking three times one Sunday morning when I was especially restless. Perhaps, as one of the pastors, he was trying to set an example how to maintain a sense of the sacred. Perhaps he was just embarrassed and upset.

What surprises me most is that those women could be as bold as our seminary president and dare to accuse a pastor of even that mild a form of "child abuse." The punishment must have been effective. Though it did not teach me to pay attention, it may have channeled my restlessness into mind games. Perhaps that was the lesson Dad intended me to learn. More likely, those parishioners led my father to suspect that he had created more of a disturbance than had I. In fact, I received very few spankings growing up, and, with one exception, none of them had done more than sting a bit.

I accept the use of judicious external rewards and punishments though I suspect that they are also testimonies to our failure to work out more creative ways to make them unnecessary. I, too, am a parent, and I know that I used anxious gruffness and a bit of instant pain a time or two to teach my children not to run into the street in the city where we lived. I also tried to use praise sparingly enough to make its use significant, while tacitly agreeing to let Marj be more effusive. Between us, I hoped we struck the right balance. We also sparingly used goodies as bribes to secure the behavior we wanted. I know I often failed.

One of our children once climaxed several days of defiant behavior by goading me until I lost it. The spanking was quite mild, and I repented immediately. What shocked me was its effect. That child became immediately sweet and obviously happy—for days. I finally concluded that I had been maneuvered into administering atonement for a troubled conscience. Over a year or so, the sequence was repeated, perhaps two or three times, permitting me to discover that the paddling needed only to be symbolic to achieve the desired effect. The other child responded entirely differently, and I ceased to use that method of discipline.

Those who have experienced little of an older concreteness will likely be distressed or amused by these confessions and will be appalled by my insistence that an active conscience can be a fortunate acquisition. There are false forms of guilt, and guilt itself is always experienced negatively, but a proper sense of guilt is a natural counterpart to an appropriate sense of accomplishment experienced by maturing persons in organized cultures of aspiration. Having admired a heritage experienced as a chain of excellence elicited the desire to be a faithful representative of that tradition.

It is entirely natural, however, that one can grow tired and despondent during those long plateaus during which new skills are quietly developing a "second self" that is waiting to reveal itself as powerfully one's own. Then one yearns again to enjoy past masteries and one is tempted to become addicted to their repetitive performance. One may even come to yearn for the rest that is implied in succumbing to pleasures that are sufficiently intense to bring temporary forgetfulness of strenuous but not-yet-successful efforts to master the trait or skill that is sought.

Then the suitable pleasures that accompany the proper use of food or drink or sex or games or work or parties become sought for their own sake; and then even subconscious states, like those experienced during the stupefaction of a daily rat race, or in an orgy or a mob, or in alcohol or drugs, become apparent goods and serious addictions.

"Backsliding," of course, does not have to be so dramatic to be real; and then true guilt is needed to repent. It consists in the recognition that one has not yet fully become the self that has already been adopted in anticipation. It is one's emotional response to the fact that one is betraying oneself. To the extent that one's significant community embodies an aspiration to that higher self, such guilt will include the sense of having betrayed the larger *Geist* that also is one's own, whether or not that community is aware of what is happening. True guilt is the recognition that one has betrayed oneself as well as the larger community that anticipates one's triumphs.

Such guilt testifies to the wish for continued progress, provided there is a way to accept pardon and forgiveness. Then it is important that one's immediate heroes, and a community's spiritual guides, stand by to support the aspirant. They can warn against false guilt, pointing to their own experiences to reassure the one struggling with discouragement. They can point out that self-criticism is itself an affirmation that an ideal has been internalized, if only, so far, as the power to judge departures from it. At this point genuine humility is the recognition of one's own real but partial excellence and is a sense of ownership of one's worthy aspirations.

Here also lies a subtle danger. Instead of accepting one's concrete self with honest humility, one can so wholly identify with one's abstracted judging self that one moves outward in the premature conviction of virtue reached, presuming to snatch motes out of the eyes of others while ignoring the plank that obscures one's own vision. Or one can continue to judge aspects of one's now fragmented self in the presumption of representing the voice of God and the vote of the community.

Unfortunately, I think that Corn worked more self-consciously at raising the sense of guilt and granting the grace of forgiveness during ritually dramatic revival meetings and other church occasions than in one-on-one soul tending. Equally unfortunately, ritual expressions of judgment and grace could reinforce the presumption that mere ritual had given one a legitimate platform for judging oneself and others.

Some have suffered all their lives from the shaming that accompanied their own or their family's failures as well as from the guilt with which they were saddled. Some have even assumed that the God bequeathed them was as judgmental as their concrete communities had all too often been. On the other hand, that negativity was the other side of their high ideals for us. I also know that grace was often real.

I have described the families, schools, clans, and churches of *Korn* as designed to nurture its citizens, and especially its children, toward the excellence that was dreamed of by its *Geist*. I also argued that those nurturing structures reduced the number of deviants and failures. With the last chapter of Hebrews in mind, they would have said that they were building an earthly camp that was designed to emulate the institutions of an earthly kingdom of God for a small set of God's pilgrim people. If they had become aware of the claim that their children had mostly flourished, they would have rejoiced that, once again, "all other [good] things" are added to those who "seek first the kingdom of God." They would also have remembered those who did not fulfill their promise and would have repented their failure to nurture them better.

But it was not just our community's sages and saints who contributed to our mutual nurture. Each of us sensed, somehow, that everyone contributed to the *Halig* of the whole. Ferd, the intellectually and physically disabled man who showed up at recess at a two-room country school to play with the children also played his part, if only by good-naturedly menacing the little children who good-naturedly enjoyed pretending to be scared. He, too, was cherished, even when the butt of jokes perpetrated by naughty boys.

The community that cherished Ferd must also acknowledge us. That was a comfort during the growing-up process of forming a realistic estimate of our own place in relation to the abilities of others and coming to prize our own significance to the health of the whole. I knew that my athletic ranking was nearer the slightly crippled at the bottom than to the stars who acknowledged our scale of abilities when acting as team captains taking turns selecting players for their teams from the eager candidates before them.

From the usual pool of ten or twelve available boys in my Corn grade school classes, I knew that I would never make a basketball team and that I would be chosen ninth or out of luck for a noon-hour game of baseball. I also knew that on the continua established in the classroom, I would be nearer the top. On the very important scale of social skills, I may have come almost to the middle.

I later knew where I had come from. Thanks to the common ethos of that concrete village, I also had a realistic sense of my place within it. And I had learned that it was desirable to become an adult. I was quite sure that adults tended to like me and that they would welcome me and my peers to their ranks. I puzzled for a while after the popular young lady in Saigon expressed envy for my rootedness. I knew that I was near the edge of inner chaos at the time. "Yes, she's right," I finally concluded. "I do know where I come from. I come from *Korn*. I may become a drunken bum. But, still, I will be a drunken bum from *Korn*. I may not want to go there, and they will not want me to stay; but it will remain true that they will have to acknowledge me." And I was strangely comforted. Of course, I did not seriously think that I would be an utter failure. I had become confident that there would be a place for me.

CHAPTER 8

The City as a Kaleidoscope of Peer Groups

Groups of gatherers and hunters and then farmers and shepherds clustered in small villages made it possible for humans to survive and to develop the fundamental institutions for family, clan, and tribal societies. At the end of the Ice Age in Western Europe, the well-watered savannas of what is now south-eastern Turkey extended the domestication of plants and animals. The annual rising and ebbing of the Nile River, scattered lush oases, and seasonal rains around the Mediterranean also made small settlements possible.

Only the development of larger social groups and their institutions made cities, and civilizations possible. Human bodies also had to be domesticated to construct dams and canals to harness rivers. To build the great cities that emerged around the Mediterranean Sea required rulers and armies of soldiers, priests, and administrators.

The abstractive genius of early civilizations had so focused human energy that utopian dreams had been evoked. In the last four hundred years of Western history, educators, scientists, explorers, entrepreneurs, rulers, and bureaucrats built a modern civilization incomprehensible to earlier gurus and elders. Cultural and scientific knowledge and technological prowess has produced many physical and material blessings.

This chapter, however, describes the unfortunate side effects that follow when great civilizations fail to focus on the ONE great thing. Though I will speak of increasing disorder and of an apparent increase in the number of failures and deviants, I do not wish to imply that many modern children will become deviants or failures. In fact, a significant number will continue to gain some experience of concreteness and will build on that foundation. Since Adam and Eve were expelled from "Eden," versions of my mythical

Korn have endured, even if only in vestigial forms. A primeval anticipation of *shalom* persists.

I called *Korn* a *village* because it contained enough concreteness that the ideal of *Halig, shalom*, could be cherished. *City* is my metaphor for the "ideal" of progressive abstractness. Every actual community is a mixture of these pure types. I have used *town* to name those places that seek the progress of abstractness while retaining a memory of the features of concreteness. In this strict sense, *Korn* was a *village* that was also a *town* reaching toward *city*, though that word is literally appropriate only for large metropolitan areas.[1] Of course, ethnic ghettoes and other city neighborhoods may retain strong characteristics of *village*. For that matter, even workplaces and other specialized settings try to incorporate aspects of concreteness. In my life, places like Cordell and Clinton and Weatherford more clearly typified *town* on the seamless continuum of waning concreteness that stretches from *Korn* to Los Angeles .

For example, I assume that everyone is a mixture of the "pure" states of extroversion and introversion. Yet the nature of that mix permits me to apply one word or the other to my acquaintances without having always to qualify the extent to which it does not apply, and I can point to some that are happily poised between extremes. All are free to reinterpret what is an ideal mix of introversion and extroversion and to imagine a town, even one large enough to be called a city, that could be a healthier community to grow up in than was my actual Corn.

THE CITY AND ITS NUCLEAR FAMILIES

Does it take a village to raise a child? When describing the schools of *Korn*, I started by emphasizing how naturally the nurture of the *Hofs* merged into the nurturing of the children in the larger settings of the village. Each family, school, clan, and congregation shaped a tonus that served a *Geist* that was a model of the larger ethos and tonus and *Geist* of *Korn*, which itself was a member of yet larger tribes and peoples. But now *Hofs* and village neighborhoods have mostly disappeared; and something else, the modern nuclear family has become so standard that it is hard for us to remember that this is something new. It is true that isolated nuclear families existed on the edges of ancient cultures. These were the heavily disadvantaged ones without significant clans or fellow citizens to protect them against exploitation. In the

---

1. The Greek word for *village*, *kōmē*, was secondarily used for those who lived in quarters or districts of *towns* or *cities*. Liddell and Scott, *Greek-English Lexicon*, 1018.

older world, isolated individuals and nuclear families were usually failures and often deviants.

Both sides of the vigorous debate about the role of villages for children have, I think, missed something important. On the one hand, the nuclear family has become the vestigial remnant of the village, now asked to do the cultural job that was once done in all the units of smaller concrete places. Now it is almost the last setting for knitting together the basic functions of life. It is supposed to be a refuge from our daily race among the many specialized societies that challenge and distract us. It is the only bounded space within which a tiny primary community can seek wholeness that is defined by maturing qualities rather than by the progress of mostly quantitative "bottom lines." In this respect, the family has become more important than ever. In the absence of small schools, nearby clans, parish churches, and a village, the nuclear family has been asked to guarantee that its children will have the moral excellences and spiritual character that are necessary even for abstracted modern states and corporations.

On the other hand, this would-be-village attains a very limited concreteness. Most of the significant daily functions of its members now take place in abstracted secondary societies (childcare centers, workplaces, malls, clubs, schools). A home is the setting for only some of the important aspects of life. In fact, the normal modern child seldom experiences a concrete, basic, bounded, primary society that is sufficiently like an ideal village to be able to construct an adequate image of its own or a larger communal *Halig*.

Many of us find a circle of friends, a congregation, an ethnic identity, and even a workplace that continue to bear some of the gifts of the village. And, therefore, many will continue to receive attenuated versions of those gifts. Perhaps children are their most important creators. I have admitted that I am astonished at the skill by which children work at evoking some concreteness in city and suburban neighborhoods that would otherwise seem to adults to be little more than an accidental collection of individual families.

It is also true that many parents have become more deliberate about creating a rich environment for their children. My mother worried that our demanding jobs would make us inadequate parents. So did we. During several years, in fact, one or both of us arranged less than full-time contracts so that we could limit the amount of babysitting our children enjoyed; and so Marj was pleased when my visiting mother commented one day, "You know, you spend more time deliberately doing things with your children than I ever did with mine. Somehow, I was almost always doing other things." That was true, but it was not the whole truth. In a more concrete community those "other things" tacitly included us.

I do not believe, however, that the shrunken space that is the nuclear family adequately replaces an entire village and its intermediate institutions. Though unable to construct significant aspects of a concrete life, it is asked to carry out the nurturing functions that had once been built into an entire community. In fact, a nuclear family, even when gathered in its home, increasingly takes on the features of other secondary societies. Inevitably it takes on aspects of the abstractions to which it is supposed to be the antidote.

Modern children live with increasing abstractness. None learn the full satisfaction of working together with their parents and siblings to create the entire unit's material and spiritual *Halig*. Therefore, the child's experience of mutuality is mostly limited to the nurture that it receives. It is true that older children care for younger siblings and can participate in household chores and that these provide opportunities for significant training, but this is not the full mutuality implicit in quickly becoming a contributor to the family as a significant unit of production.

The inner dynamics of the family and the relations of adults and children are profoundly changed within the new nuclear family. Both in the home and at ritual events like school and clan picnics, there were precious occasions when *Korn* adults played with children, but no one would have dreamed that parents should intend to become their pals. Communities of aspiration more often achieved mutuality by pulling the children "up" into the activities of adults than by encouraging adults to join the play of children. Children were expected to imitate their parents. Adults who reveled in youthful activities would have been considered childish.

Because nuclear families are no longer concrete parts of a larger social concretion, they can no longer assume that their children will just grow up. They must invest heavily in time and funds to help their children attain the moral and intellectual skills that will help them to achieve respectable "upward mobility." This focus on children as children also prepares them to feel entitled to the attention and the goodies of the larger society that must appear to revolve around them. Of course, many of them understand that they will have to work hard to master the tools of their chosen trades, but they can hardly conceive the fundamental transformations of their expectations that are required to rise to more profound *Halig*.

When advising entering students, I was sometimes saddened that so many of them seemed to be entirely assured of what they would become. They did not want to be mentored, but they did want to know how most efficiently to get required courses out of the way. They also wanted to know how quickly they could begin to take classes in their chosen major field. My pleas to allow for the possibility that we might be able to help them to rethink their goals seemed to me to fall on deaf ears. Young moderns now take for granted that they "arrive" as completed persons sometime before college. It made sense to me that every child does want to "become big" and that this happens physically during high school. When I mentioned this to a small-town school principal, he nodded appreciatively at the notion that adolescents now shift from aspiration to personal elevations to horizontal expectations of fame and goodies at the cultural level already achieved. He suggested that I was too optimistic. He thought that this shift more often happened during junior high.

When *Korn*'s adults failed to keep an appropriate balance between their children's needs and their own, they more often sinned by demanding too much, insisting on too much work and forbidding at least some amusements for no better reason than that ungodly *Englisha* appeared to enjoy them. I have already mentioned my father's frustration when asked to quit school and turn over his earnings to his parents until age twenty-one. Anger against parents could grow into rebellion that was inextricably mixed with rejection of the larger ethos that the parents represented. As insisted earlier, there were also resources that fostered reconciliation.

Now, however, parents neither represent nor are supported by a concrete village. And now rebellion becomes a personal and family tragedy. Is it only apparently paradoxical that, on the whole, parents and their children now appear to be better friends than they were in more traditional cultures? Some even aspire to become pals. Both sides sense the increased fragility of the family in a world that is losing the institutions that once reinforced its efforts. The family has become too precious to risk its fundamental disruption and it is often too impotent to justify overt rebellion. One contemporary solution for adolescents is to restrict familial interactions to those aspects of life that can be conducted with reasonable amiability and even tenderness. Tensions are defused by diffusing critical aspects of character formation to secondary associations.

Both the parents and their children live with a variety of peer groups that they do not share with each other. The "they" over against which identity is forged becomes increasingly vague, as do possible targets for rage. All too often the anger comes to be expressed as depression that is focused on the only quasi-concrete target that remains: oneself. When anger becomes too great to be contained, abstracted individuals disfigure or even destroy themselves. When they lash out at others, their targets may be other authority figures or strangers. In extreme cases, adolescents who are on reasonably good terms with their parents have been known to shoot randomly at schoolmates.

The modern child can develop a "common sense" of the ethos of its home, but this comprehension cannot include all the basic components of even the simplest sort of complete life. Nor does the ethos of the home receive automatic affirmation among other homes or settings. In *Korn* the basic values taught in the home were also taught in other homes as well as by the school, the clan, the church, and the entire community and so they automatically came to be seen as objective, as "the way things are." In the city, home truths are more and more seen to be specific to each home, and are perceived to be relative truths. "But Mommie, Carla's parents let her do that." Therefore, "when with the Romans, do as the Romans." Even religiously and morally conservative nuclear families that seek to build traditional values into their home life tacitly prepare their children to adapt to other settings with very different value systems. When grown, morally pluralistic adults may, without apparent unease, try to reproduce the ethos of their parental homes within their own nuclear families.

A host of unexpected consequences must accompany every fundamental shift in the character of families and communities, even if these shifts do not immediately produce large numbers of deviants and failures. Indeed, the most able and "virtuous" modern young adults are also those who are so busy developing their own potential goods along with the progress of the abstracted functions they serve that they are likely to decide not to have children, at least not until the biological clock induces some to bear one or two.

A modern advanced culture like ours now faces the enormous irony that the best of our youth fail to reproduce themselves, thus requiring immigrants from third world and other more concrete cultures to invigorate our culture and economy and to maintain the power implicit in the size of our populations. At the same time, we must transform these immigrants into citizens who embody and preserve the excellences of our way of life; and this means that immigrants soon acquire the ethos of those they were imported to replace. In time this leads to subsequent waves of less advantaged immigrants who then contribute children to the ranks of the successfully abstracted as well as to the growing indigenous underclass of our own "fourth world" of deviants and failures.

Though driven to defend the choices that my wife and I have made and to be grateful that our children are creating healthy families, I agree with those who insist that too many of our children are becoming deviants and failures. Of course, I am not so quick as they to blame parents, since I do not believe that families were ever designed to do so much of the job of nurturing children. Even if it could be true that it does not take a village to raise a child, it is becoming clear that it does take something like the village to maintain and nurture a larger ethos within which the family can healthily raise the child.

THE CITY AND ITS SCHOOLS

In the absence of primary communities to support and supplement the efforts of nuclear families, we turn to important secondary societies to nurture our children. We then look to charitable groups, to churches, and especially to public schools. The modern school has become the hospital of choice for what is thought to ail our children.

Schools did not exist in societies more concrete, and more primitive, than *Korn*. Then children simply learned adult skills in the direct apprenticeship that consists of the imitation of the adults of their band or village. Many of the earliest of the settlements in the American new world founded simple schools for their children, since the kind of world they envisioned required skills that might not be taught at home. Ivy League colleges for advanced education quickly appeared. But all of these were shaped to complete the *Halig* of homes and villages that aspired to a new kind of democratic excellence.

During the nineteenth century, state departments of education were set up to organize public elementary and secondary education as well as land grant colleges. This public school system was organized to prepare the children of both natives and immigrants for the emerging Industrial Revolution and was itself consciously molded in the image of the new factories. State bureaus assumed control of rural and village schools that already existed and began to impose *progressive* technologies onto classrooms.

By then the American frontier was filling up, and many villages died as those with better locations became small towns. When iron tracks inched their way across the prairies, towns along the railroads prospered although they began almost immediately to lose their autonomy as new corporations in the cities determined the flow of traffic and the prices of the wood and coal and produce that the hinterlands produced. Then once-thriving towns could wither. When technology and distant factories added tractors to their plows and cultivators, progressive farmers could buy out their slower neighbors. Even with more land these farmers no longer needed many "hands" on their farms, and families grew smaller.

When automobiles and buses appeared, not even the fierce loyalty of rural people to their country schools could save them. State Departments of Education argued vigorously that only larger schools could afford to provide the one grade per room per teacher that was the desired setting for the new standardized textbooks and rationally thought-out methods for teaching an "enriched" curriculum. Most expensive of all were the tellingly named "Industrial Arts" classes that were demanded. How could mere farmers stand in the way of the progress that could teach their children to understand better the increasingly complicated machines that the few children that remained on the land would be operating and that others of their children would be building in far-off factories?

Like the villages and the towns, families and country schools were losing their power to shape their own turfs. Consolidation had the cachet of modernity. The children of Greenfield, near the end of WWII, were among the last to walk to the end of the driveway to board buses that carried country children to the school in *Korn*. Then politicians and educators set their sights on closing many of these consolidated schools in favor of still larger schools in larger towns. The village of *Korn* now has more inhabitants than when I lived there, but it has no school.

A child who left a *Hof* to walk to Greenfield knew that this school was a manageable extension of the life it already knew. Several dozen schoolmates would challenge the social skills brought from home, but the little scholar would not need to fear anonymity among hundreds. Anticipation shaped by aspiration was more dominant than fear, unless the teacher was a tyrant.

The combined students of two country one-room schools, like the one I visited a few miles away with a church friend, might have fit into any classroom of the school I attended in Cordell for four years. Jefferson School had a single room and a teacher for each of its grades. Although it did not yet have a kindergarten, I assume that the school was considered up-to-date. I do not have records for my first two years, but there were thirty-seven students in the third-year class picture and thirty in the picture taken of my fourth-grade class.

Even Jefferson was not a natural extension of our home. It replicated the structure of abstracted institutions; and, like early modern factories, it sought the efficiencies of size and of rationalized procedures. It, too, had its bottom line. It was created to provide competent workers for the specialized workplaces of our new "new world." But the schools of Cordell still received children from surrounding *Hofs* and provided them with teachers who remembered well the village.

I suppose that many "town" schools continue to remember greater concreteness while teaching for a "city" future. And it is clear that, as in older country schools, the basics continue to be "readin' and 'ritin' and 'rithmetic," even if not "taught with the aid of a teacher's stick," to perhaps misquote the old ditty. I edited this paragraph at the end of the first week of July 2023 and perhaps within the week our daily paper reported, again, that literacy had decreased for the 2022–2023 school year. I have become aware that a surprising number of American adults do not master these basic skills.

Meanwhile, technological and social progress continues, and every major technological advance comes with yet another abstracted symbol system that has to be learned by those who want to be successful. Like modern assembly lines, more and more, faster and faster is demanded. Our daughter's husband came to Fresno with a PhD in chemistry to teach at Fresno Pacific University. For many years he researched how to teach all levels of teachers to master the skills needed in S.T.E.M and other disciplines. I take this shift in his interests to be a sign of the times.

Schools are under enormous pressure to reduce the number of failures by again emphasizing "basics." Specialists are hired for those who have learning difficulties. As is typical of an abstracting society, every new problem elicits a new set of experts to specialize in that problem. As these learn more, they inevitably discover more and more neural and social disabilities that make learning difficult and then spin off sets of increasingly exotic sub-specialties to address these special students. We rejoiced that the kindergarten child of a friend of ours received the attention of enough specialists that he virtually had the personal attention of the equivalent of a full-time teacher. The decorum of a normal classroom could not survive his *presence*, but he could already carry subtraction across numerous digits and read at a second or third grade level.

At the other extreme, more conventionally gifted students are offered advanced courses in specialized magnet schools. The high school son of another of our acquaintances has been feted as a finalist in one of the most prestigious science competitions in America, and his researches have already been touted as possibly contributing to improved treatments of HIV/AIDS. A number of years ago two teenagers, who had both spent a few years in our small congregation while they were growing up, happened to visit on the same Sunday. Since I knew about their interests, I was able to introduce them to each other as two who had already decided to seek PhDs in Theoretical Topology, an arcane sub-discipline of mathematics. Obviously, some quite young students are capable of mastering very advanced symbol systems and will become very successful in their specialized niches in advancing sciences.

When I think of the public schools of Fresno, I remember to be pleased at the education and the personal attention that my children received from our local schools despite a significant influx of the children of non-English speaking immigrants. A long tradition of competent administration and a cadre of idealistic teachers in our local elementary school served us well. We were also aware that the ethos of the school was changing. I am sure that our children's teachers had never been taught that some of the designers of public education well over a hundred years ago had intended it to aim at patriotic mediocrity. If they did know, they were happy to be subversives who "undermined" the original design by nurturing the children in their care and encouraging them to aim at excellence.

Somehow, the increasingly harried teachers that I know continue to nurture and teach their pupils and to help many of them to move on to high school and to college and to successful careers. Although some are being salvaged who would formerly have been failures and the very best students are doing spectacularly well, experienced teachers sense that something profound has happened to make their job more difficult and that the system is failing a great number of students who no longer aspire to excellence. There literally are not enough funds to hire increasing numbers of specialists to work with the most needy students, to hire better trained teachers for the very gifted, and to give personal attention to "normal" students while adding more and more administrators and clerks to administer all the subspecialties and to report all the data demanded by state and federal bureaus—as well as to test and test and test in order to produce the quantified bottom lines demanded by politicians, entrepreneurs, and corporations. I suspect all that testing makes it more difficult to teach well and to learn well.[2]

I have also been amazed to discover the enormous number of things that schools now have to do that were once taken care of in the normal course of life in more concrete communities. Now there are feeding

---

1. Readers interested in obtaining a more balanced account of what motivated important business leaders to support taxation for free public education may find additional information at the Center on Education Policy (CEP) located in the Graduate School of Education and Human Development at the George Washington University. Its brief eight-page "History and Evolution of Public Education in the US" seems to me to be a balanced guide to available information. The writers address the motives that stimulated the long effort to achieve a free system of public education and mention the racial, ethnic, class, and other prejudices that had to be overcome to teach all the nation's children.

However, the stress and difficulty of persuading voters to support the higher taxes resented by all classes of citizens and the fact that the wealthier classes would have to make up for the unwillingness and actual inability of the poor and of wage earners to pay what was often thought to be their "fair share" of the costs, led the proponents of free public schools to stress the advantage of a disciplined working class willing to endure the monotony of mechanical routines on the assembly lines. After all, they would be educated in schools structured like these rationalized systems.

To highlight the prejudices and motives and arguments that ensued, I recommend readers access another document titled "Historical Timeline of Public Education in the US" (see bibliography under Race Forward). This document lists thirty-four items illustrating what influenced some key voting blocks to support free public school systems for everyone.

programs to help undernourished children to thrive and to be able to attend to the lessons. Recess is no longer a time to relax and to decide which games to play with each other. Teachers are asked to make sure that children who go home to watch television learn how to play games and get vigorous exercise. We were vaccinated at school, but now schools must constantly be on the lookout for a long list of health problems. We also had overactive brats, but most of them learned to settle down and the rest dropped out or were tolerated until they could move farther west. Now teams of social workers and psychologists are attached to school systems to diagnose and treat a host of newly defined developmental and emotional abnormalities. Of course, citizenship was also a goal of country schools. But with the discovery that homes were "failing" and that immigrants continued to need to absorb the nation's *Geist*, specialists set to work to produce curriculums to teach "values."

I do not need to continue the critical litanies that create pressure for administrators and teachers to do more and more while buildings crumble and large numbers of children come to school from homes whose parents are ill prepared to model for them the competencies demanded by a progressive society. Since the larger political community believes that too many families are incapable of doing the functions once handled by primary communities, it is deciding, piecemeal, to add very expensive programs to do the tasks that the entire primary community had formerly done ad hoc and on the cheap.

Of course, the larger political community and its schools now recognize learning disabilities and know how to create specialized programs to address them. Unfortunately, our abstracting culture is baffled by a growing number of students who are neither "nerds" nor "morons" but who are content to resist their teachers' attempts to help them to develop skills and attitudes they will need to become "all that they can be." Immanuel Kant urged college professors to ignore the "idiots" (whom he assumed to be not worth the effort) and the small number who are "geniuses" (who would normally do very well without special help). We should, however, agree with him that it is profoundly important to "teach to the middle," especially at the elementary and secondary levels, both because they are the ones who can profit greatly from our efforts and because their moral and intellectual elevation is basic to the development of a more excellent society.

So far as I know, Kant did not think about the possibility that there could be a large and growing number of "the middle" who show no interest in aspiring to greater virtues. We must now wonder why it is that increasing numbers of children from all social classes in our technologically advanced society are not anxious to advance beyond the level of maturity that is fully attainable by a junior high "teenybopper" or a high school "jock." This is not a problem that can easily be solved by spending more money or creating yet another cadre of specialists.

In fact, children have always sought best friends at least close to their own age, but in small concrete communities their "set" normally encompassed a wide range of ages and interests and types of character. In keeping with the demand of abstracting societies that "birds of a feather must flock together," town schools assumed that age was the most important criterion for educational readiness. In the city, educators have noted that similarity of age is not similarity of intelligence and interests, and in keeping with the modern demand for efficiency there is a call for groupings that will more accurately put children with others like themselves. Since readiness for reading may be quite different than for arithmetic, large schools can attempt more complicated ways to sort out like with like.

However, even "special" students need the range of models and the comforting continuity of a normal classroom. Among these complicating and even contradictory problems is the fact that young children should live with older ones to satisfy their desire to "grow big."

Our daughter was fairly content in school until about the fourth grade when she began to complain that she had no real friends. When pressed to explain, she finally blurted out, "There isn't anyone like me. I've looked everywhere, even in other grades." I am confident that no Greenfield child ever said anything like that. They certainly complained when other children would be mean to them, and they surely had a best friend, perhaps elsewhere in the community; but the several dozen children in country schools were as much a fact of life as the weather. This was the collection of unique individuals with whom one had to make one's peace. This group called for them to find their place while aspiring to become like the more mature ones. It also gave them realistic spectrums for the discovery of their place in the community.

To our request for further explanation what it meant for someone to be "like me," she finally offered, "they all watch soaps. When I come home I still like to watch cartoons with John." Puzzled that this was all we got, I went to the school, looked around, and understood what she meant. Already, in the fourth grade, the girls used rouge and lipstick, showed off their budding breasts, and dressed like the slightly older "teenyboppers" who imitated popular rock starlets. Linda was still a girl, and I was very happy that some of the genes I had contributed to her may have slowed her physical maturation.

These girls, like children from earlier times, still aspired to grow up to be like admired older children. Unfortunately, the older ones they admired were not intermediate steps in a hierarchy of increasing excellence. When these girls became teenagers, many of them had reached the "opaque glass ceiling" that defined their aspiration. The older girls they knew, and their mothers, were also watching soap operas and listening to pop divas.

Until then, I had been glad that our children were growing up in a culturally mixed and "interesting" older part of town. The school was also serving other racial and ethnic immigrant groups, and I assumed that this experience would encourage them to develop friendships among a variety of economic and cultural classes and help them to be comfortable with other groups. But I discovered that if our children, whose church community still embodied a ladder of aspiration, met only a narrow subset of the class structures within other ethnic groups, they might well become convinced that none of "them" were "like us." If ethnics who shared our children's classrooms had been separated from their own cultural ladders of excellence, disproportionately representing their own culture's deviants and failures, then nearness might increase prejudice rather than prevent it.

Fortunately, the sabbatical we took during her sixth-grade year took us to New Haven, where we lived in a country setting whose school profited from the presence of a sprinkling of the families of business owners, professionals, and Yale professors. There, thanks also to a brand new full-leg cast necessitated by too high a jump on the trip East, she became an instant member of a group of a half-dozen girls who were enough "like her." Both of our children were later accepted to magnet schools that they had chosen and were happy to find others like themselves in settings that included peers from different groups and classes and ethnicities that also aspired to develop their potential.

Modern elementary schools are far too large and too abstractly structured to serve the deepest need of children for settings sufficiently concrete to prepare them for a larger world by both building on the familiar ethos of a family and offering the variety of embodied maturities and virtues that stimulate their aspiration to develop the character and skills of an ascending scale of heroes. Neither of these needs is well served in larger public schools, even in those that are doing an admirable job of teaching academic "basics." I suspect that the need for a smaller concreteness partly explains the growth of home schooling, sometimes at the cost of perpetuating an impoverished one. No doubt the need for the stimulation of a range of peer groups accounts for the loose banding of these parents to create a variety of larger settings.

It is surely relevant that the modern predilection for grouping like with like led early modern administrators to create separate junior high schools to address the special developmental issues of early teens. This has also become the time for cliques to form around specific constellations of styles and attitudes. Now the gathering of like with like reinforces a sameness of dress and dreams within cliques belligerently posturing themselves over against all other social constellations.

After high school these cliques will break up, and their members move into a kaleidoscopic variety of other peer groups. Meanwhile, educators who emerge from increasingly specialized departments of education in universities continue to struggle with the built-in contradictions that are the result of fully developed abstractions. As in other fields, they try to cure the ills of abstraction with the tools developed from ever more sophisticated abstractions, while classroom teachers who earnestly attempt to apply the common sense that grows out of real experience grow increasingly cynical of these sorts of solutions after they have been adapted into technological fixes like "No Child Left Behind" by politicians exploiting the dismay of anxious voters.

THE CITY AND ITS PEER GROUPS

Unfortunately, larger proportions of our citizens no longer create cultures that comprehend the worldview that aspires to *shalom* or of the disciplines needed to sustain their quest for it. When like choose to be with like, they are, in principle, content to define themselves to fit the culture and the status of the group. To seek to "outgrow" the group is taken to be snobbery. In principle, an "in group" cannot recognize the hero who embodies excellences that they have not already claimed for themselves. Too many junior high and high school students have already joined the peer groups, gangs, or cliques that display the style that their members suppose will satisfy them forever.

Instead of admiring heroes who embody a set of higher virtues, too many adult peer groups continue to form the fan clubs of celebrities modeling a given style. For each of these popular "styles," celebrities define the specific aptitudes and attitudes their fans admire and they are careful not to offend by revealing the virtues and the long disciplines that might actually have lifted them beyond the image they have crafted to ensure their fame. What celebrities give their fans is the conviction that the world approves of what they have already become and that it is not desirable to seek anything more. "Love yourselves and love me for projecting the image you have chosen for yourselves. I am essentially like you, and the world has responded by showering me with fame and riches and sensual experiences. Are not these the 'goodies' that validate our lives?" Indeed, the coarser the style that is adopted, the more likely it is that its "poets" project mockery or actual hatred of more elevated decencies.

I have insisted, of course, that no actual civilization can escape some level of concreteness. If it could, then even cliques and peer groups would fragment into the isolation of self-enclosed individuals who are no longer able to form a social self that is a nexus of relationships to others. Some of the outlaws of earlier epochs remind us that it has always been possible to become a sociopath who encounters others only as objects to be used as one sees fit.

However, many observers admit that their numbers are increasing. I cite the fact that never have we jailed so many people, but I do not know whether there are actually more criminals than in the past or whether a culture fearful of its own "progress" has chosen to define more behaviors to be criminal and to incarcerate those who commit them for longer periods. Nor do I know whether there are more of the isolates whom I hear muttering to themselves on city streets or whether previous generations, either fearful of seeing themselves in the emotionally distracted or charitably deciding to care for them, locked them into mental hospitals. However, I am less concerned with those at the extremes than I am with the moral and emotional brittleness of increasing numbers of "normals" that seem to have become trapped in the egocentric cocoons spawned by sped-up modernity. For example, I have heard college deans insist that it has become harder for students to tolerate dormitory roommates.

In any case, it remains true that almost all of us continue to seek out those "like us" who share the tastes and behaviors that define the level of relative virtue we have chosen. Lawyers and doctors and engineers and others who are mostly defined by their professional status often prefer to mingle with each other and to talk about their vocations. Those whose jobs do not capture their full attention cluster into groups that form around selected avocations. It is difficult to imagine a "goodie" that might not become a collectible with a fan club that exists to unite those who share that passion. An astounding variety of activities, from sports lovers to RVers to quilters to gourmands to square dancers, allow an equal number of associations to form around enjoyment of those activities.

The goal of all this devotion to goodies and experiences cannot be summarized solely by the mottos "he who dies with the most toys wins" and "been there—done that." In fact, most of these devotions cannot be pursued by isolated individuals. Things and activities are the magnets that allow us to find and cluster around the "like us" who replace the clans and tribes and ethnicities of our more concrete pasts and which now objectify and validate the identities we choose for ourselves. They also remind us of three things.

Even adolescents who seem to be wholly defined by the style of their peer groups and their chosen celebrities are likely to shift their allegiances to these "adult" pursuits. None of these shifts require them to renounce the quest for wealth, fame, or sensual experiences; though what is required to achieve these goodies can induce a significant number to endure the discipline needed to prepare for a well-paid job or profession. Finally, how many of these pursuits and their accompanying associations seek *Halig*?

If peer groups reject elevation can they comprehend the saving uses of honest guilt? Competition remains as a goad for fame and goods and sensual success on their chosen playing fields. Those who do not successfully mask their possible ambition for better things and nobler attitudes will be ridiculed, but those who are caught out when they cheat in competitions for fame and wealth and sensory pleasures seem seldom to exhibit guilt because they "know" that it was not wrong to seek these goodies and that the goals appear to justify the means used to attain them.

Therefore drugs to enhance athletic ability, date rape pills, and dishonest ways to increase one's wealth are not guilt-producing transgressions. And when adepts fail to observe the sensibilities of those whom they wish to impress, they do not confess their "sins." They only express regret that someone has chosen to feel offended at something they have done or said. In a world that loses the mutuality of genuine relationships, more and more identify with products, keeping designers' names on clothes, drinking "cultic" brands of beers, flaunting tattoos, and wearing the iconic symbols of athletic teams that display the characteristics they admire.

For some moderns, even shame has almost died. Never having known a clan or tribe with old world traditions or a culture that demands excellence and that rewards aspirants with recognition for actual virtues, they dare to flaunt the degradation endemic in groups of deviants and failures. Then even notoriety counts as fame, as with those who are willing to appear on TV shows to defend their worst behavior during confrontations with those they have abused and cheated. Then they can preen before their envious peers while cherishing their fifteen minutes of fame offered by a disapproving larger public. For them, it is not shameful to be deviant.

Paul and other followers of Jesus recognized that among these prodigal children were those who became willing to question their errors and sins and to accept the good news of a waiting Father and to come home. How many modern prodigals become the penitents whom Jesus said were the first to seek the kingdom of heaven?

Saul of Tarsus was not a prodigal son, and he and other apostles could appeal to righteous pagans to consider the good news he preached. Like Paul, these also would have to endure the culture shock of rethinking their prime errors and primal presumptions that had been built into "top-down" civilizations. Like these, perhaps a majority of modern adults still belong to a "moral majority," or sets of intellectual elites, or to religious denominations who know that they do not belong to the fan clubs I described above. These still seek what is right, true, and holy. I have also sought to discover what is right, true, and holy. And I have discovered, with Paul, that I also had to go through culture shock to be transformed.

Indeed, how different was Paul or a seriously right-minded pagan or I from our more "prodigal" siblings? I argue that those of us who have "graduated" from primitive, proverbial cultures might continue to display the mindsets, and even, sometimes, the advanced addictions of those whom Paul described as "slaves of sin and death." As "enlightened," of course, our addictions may be very subtle. It is very hard to admit that we may have to repent of our virtues, of what we prize as honorable, or even of our "certainties."

In the preface to this book, I spoke of delegates to political conventions who had lost the mindset of proverbial villages seeking wisdom and the patience to wait for the wise to guide them through genuine perplexities. Increasing numbers of these delegates become political ideologues, followers of ideological *haireses* whose celebrities are those who best master the art of explaining the systematized rationality (the *ratio scientiae*) of ideologues catering to a given political or ethical orthodoxy.

That those proclaiming accepted certainties might also be functional demagogues is resisted even when they should have recognized their similarity to members of other parties countering them with opposed certainties and even members of their own "sect" touting different versions of their own "heresy." Intellectual academics, serious moralists, and those adopting systematized theologies often adopt the same "style" until they recognize that they are limited and finite mortals who dare not presume to the powers of omniscience or of omnipotence.

With Paul, I know that to judge the *hearts* of others or to presume to master the organization of concrete ecological wholes is forever beyond us. Though our gifts make it possible to increase our knowledge of the workings of the cosmos, we must learn to marvel that our progress presents us with greater mysteries. In short, theologians, philosophers, moralists, scientists, and statesmen must seek the primeval gifts of patience and await guidance when confronting hard cases.

CHAPTER 9

The City and Its Congregations

THE OLD ENGLISH WORD *chirche* was translated from *kyrios*, a Greek word for God, the "Lord." The possessive ending to this word implied that something belonged to God. A temple implies *God's house*, the spiritual and tangible center for a concrete people of God who lived in a local area.

By the middle of the twentieth century, a Baptist church had joined the Mennonite churches that were themselves divided into two Mennonite denominations. Yet, by setting and heritage, a sense of unity under God tended to overcome the divisions that lurk even when brothers and sisters and cousins live together. Probably almost all these *Korn* "Baptists" were ethnically Germanic, still Mennonite, and part of the *Korn* clan.

Now, even rural Christians commonly use the term *congregation* for those who assemble in a given place to worship. The original Latin *congregare* was used of herds of animals and flocks of birds. That flocks will be "of a feather" could be taken for granted, but I suspect few Christian "flocks" accepting that word have been aware of its derivation. Of course, this word has for centuries added sacred connotations.

CONGREGATIONS IN ABSTRACTED CITIES

Congregare also implies the three levels of abstraction that characterize modern life. Nuclear families and individuals that have been abstracted from primary communities now gather from anywhere and everywhere in the city to join with others like themselves to form secondary societies that concentrate on the now abstracted religious aspects of life. These aspects are now mostly irrelevant to the other specialized functions of daily life, like the workplace, the mall, and the club. Unless closely connected to older concrete communities, city dwellers are less and less able to imagine a sacred canopy hovering over "God's space," as implied in the original meaning of *church*, and so it becomes fitting to think of their edifices as *worship centers* to name the abstracted function that centered this flock's beliefs and lives.

The word *worship* is linked to *worth* which, like *honor*, can be ascribed beyond earthly ideals and humans to what is sacred. Only a dictionary whose entries are chosen for nonlinguistic reasons, like the *Oxford Classical Dictionary* will add *household* to *worship*.[1] Its entry explains that the hearths of primitive houses were the original "worship centers." Meals were prepared in its fireplace, which was closely associated with its patron spirit or deity that, like its hearth, centered the home.

Meals began with placing some food on its floor to be shared by its deity. Ancient Greeks named it *Hestia* and Latins called *Vesta*. After the shared meal was eaten and the table was cleared, they poured some wine on the floor, originally dirt packed thickly enough to keep water from entering, to share with household divinities. In Athens, these wine offerings were separately offered to the great Zeus, to heroes, and to Zeus *Soter*. Like Zeus *Ktesios*, this deified *Soter* (savior) "is hardly more than a deified store-jar in origin."[2]

Religious groups meet in worship centers because being "of a flock" implies thinking alike, it was appropriate for early modern congregations to define themselves by theological abstractions or by specific practices like modes of baptism. In any case, important practices are chosen because they emphasize doctrinal differences between *denominations*, a word that had not carried any religious meaning. This was especially true of *Protestants*, another word without inherent sacred significance.

Though driven to the city, modern Christians may be so fearful of it that they try to freeze their earlier ethos and thought, often producing a caricature of the religious character of their past concreteness by concentrating on specific beliefs and practices. These congregations are often more rigid and narrow than the churches they left behind.

Contemporary pluralism has led congregations that are more comfortable with the city to minimize their original insistence on theological orthodoxy in favor of the rational calculations of what is required to demonstrate "seeker friendliness." I now briefly point out that the same dynamics that are at work among other abstracted peer groups tend to shape contemporary congregations, and I especially concentrate on their growing inability to form effective communities of aspiration.

---

1. Rose, *Oxford Classical Dictionary*, 960–61.
2. Rose, *Oxford Classical Dictionary*, 960.

In the world of my grandparents, concrete communities did not give a great deal of attention to organizing the activities of children beyond the creation of local schools. Instead, the children and youth were included in the life and work of the entire community in such a way that their own ambitions were caught up in a larger communal aspiration for *Halig*. As the three abstractions of progress eroded the older institutions of mutual nurture, it became important to become very deliberate about the way in which children were growing up.

Because not yet aware of the ironies of progress, they were thrilled by the promise of higher education and of technology to contribute to their personal and collective *Halig*. I could still sense that my parents were serving both themselves and a larger cause when they concentrated on applying modern pedagogical theory to our rearing. Even the new medical theories that called for mothers to switch from breastfeeding on demand to bottle-feeding on a rigid schedule permitted them to celebrate the presumed promise of becoming modern parents. Though it is a fact that I distinctly remember the shocked gossip about a young mother who left the Sunday morning service to bottle-feed her infant in the basement instead of discreetly nursing her in the pews. How much more was Sunday School a way to practice the patterns of progress they were learning—and all for the greater glory of God.

Because my parents' attention to me was a by-product of their attention to God and of their own developing competence in town culture, their acts did not make them the center of my childish world. Rather, their attention still mostly lifted me into their enlarging one. They seldom stooped to my level to become pals. They raised me to theirs so that, before God, I could become their equal. I learned more than the information and the moral rules they wanted me to learn.

Though they did not consciously intend it, I learned to expect the unexpected, to wish to grow beyond the place I stood, and to live in awe of and trust a God who brings larger visions. The absolute lay above and beyond me, not in ways of life so fixed that they could be taken for granted. Not all were so fortunate. Some of my parents' generation were so caught up by the lure of economic and cultural progress or by their devotion to a "higher cause" that they made one or the other of these an idol and sacrificed their children to it.

The abstracted life of the city makes it more important than ever to pay special attention to our children. At the same time, it fundamentally changes the actual nature and effects of that attention. Most of my childhood friends have eagerly embraced the city; we have explored and appropriated its promise. But we still have so strong a memory of the village that some of us unconsciously assume that the complexity of the city is a natural addition to our knowledge of where we come from.

Our children or grandchildren, however, begin with the city; they are growing up with Babel, surrounded by such a multitude of cultural and institutional languages that none of them becomes a true mother tongue. In the city, the world presents itself to children as separable packets of experiences, coming as if from different universes. And they receive only glimpses of many of the packages. For example, many have little sense of what parents do at their jobs. What they learn is that each aspect of life has its own place and its own content. All "truths" come in sets that are relative to their contexts. To survive, one must learn to adapt to the shape of each context. Because they do not grow up experiencing all of the basics that makes a culture work, they do not develop the full common sense that guides the putting together of the disparate aspects of life. Each of them increasingly becomes the more or less insulated center of consciousness that must order the egos of others and the egoisms of abstracted institutions to meet their own perceived needs. By junior high or high school, as discussed earlier, the only apparent solution to the loneliness inherent in such a dangerous world is to join a peer group, to subordinate our individuality to its collective style, and to present a united front to outsiders.

Town and city congregations have become so intensely aware that their children are in danger that they have concentrated on three ways to assist their nurture. The first way is to attempt directly to strengthen the authority and competence of the nuclear family. So massive is this effort that large stadiums have been filled with men eager to learn how to be fathers from football coaches, sports celebrities, and even preachers. It can be argued that Christian psychologists have replaced theologians and evangelists as the primary shapers of Christian identity for many contemporary congregations.

The second way is to admit, albeit tacitly, that the nuclear family is too fragile to succeed at this task and to shape congregational programs to take on the job of nurturing children. The third way is to try to create a positive context for religious and moral values by writing laws and shaping state and national policies in the hope that politics can help to change the cultural climate of a "progressive" nation.

The common denominator of these contemporary approaches is the belief that specialized, and therefore abstracted, secondary institutions and programs can develop the expertise and channel the energies that correct the problems that have been created by the progress of modern abstractions in the first place. Almost all of them, even those attempted by congregations, deliberately focus upon what they perceive to be the needs of children and youth rather than upon reconstructing enough of a *Halig* concreteness into which children could naturally be included as aspirants to increasing Christlikeness. Good as the content of these programs may be, children receive them as additions to the normal stream of separable packets of experience that they are learning to enjoy or to endure.

Finally, because each congregation tends to attract its own species of the likeminded, it creates a less expansive ethos than was true of older churches, and each *congregation* molds its children to fit the *Geist* of its immediate "flock." I grew up with the enlarging awareness of clan and tribal identity. Modern congregations ask us to identify with those who share our set of ideological abstractions.

"Christian education" is one packet among many others and is, often, among the least of these, for it comes in brief time periods linked by no discernible thread. Under these circumstances it may not matter much that our teaching purports to carry ultimate truths and sure moral standards. Nor should it comfort us much if we have "good" children. It may be that children are truly learning goodness. Or it may be that they are learning to adapt to the expectations of our church packets just as they are learning to adjust to other contexts. The deeper learning that accompanies all these packages may be merely the trick of learning to be adaptable to one's contexts.

If this is the case, it does not help much to insist on "our" truths or to assert them more earnestly and more often. They still remain one set over against other sets. "Train up children in the way that they should go; and when they are old, they will not depart from it."[3] But this maxim better fits communities concrete enough to reinforce a common ethos. If "the medium is the message,"[4] as Canadian philosopher Marshall McLuhan pointed out a long time ago, then obedience to the content of our message is not necessarily principled. If character is shaped also by the medium, then a person's later adaptation to peer groups that horrify us does not always mean that there has been a fundamental change of character. The ability to make such shifts may indeed be the deepest learning we bequeath our children.

A second major problem with deliberate attempts to create programs for children is that, too often, our stance as adults is falsified. We live in a world with many secondary associations and their abstracted functions. When we turn to our children in our congregations, we do not aim to help them to understand and to cope with our larger world in any concrete sense. We concentrate, instead, on those abstracted religious beliefs and practices

---

3. Prov 22:6.
4 McLuhan, "Medium is the Message," 20.

that fit the ideology of our particular flock. We especially try to inculcate the moral "values" that fit the ethos of this flock but which we can only hope will be applied to all the other societies into which the children will be delivered as they grow up.

Finally, we water down even this narrowed understanding of what is real to what we imagine will suit their present comprehensions. We set up age-graded programs to educate them, to entertain them, to socialize them to each other, and to discipline them. Even when appropriate, our intentions to condescend to their levels too often forget how traditional cultures tacitly lifted its young into maturity though less obviously focusing on them.

When children and youth experience adults who have made it their vocation or avocation to fit into the world of the child, they can too quickly assume that the true citizens of our congregations *are* the children. The world has been cut to their dimensions, and they have then become its all-important center. Indeed, the adults in churches that focus on this condescension can lose their desire to mature more fully into the image of God—and become childish. Perhaps parents trying too hard to be pals and churches too eagerly trying to be "appropriate" inspire the special mistrust and even arrogance some claim to perceive in modern youth.

"Welcome those who are weak in faith." But Paul adds that this advice does not include welcoming them to "quarreling over opinions."[5] In this passage he was not thinking of children, though it also applies to them. In my first chapter, I admitted the sin of pretending to fall asleep to hear what I then would have called "doubtful disputations" as in the KJV. Though still a child, it was important for me to know that they did occur and that such disputations were important. Those who are mature and wise must engage in them to guide those who are still "weak" and to correct adults who succumb to weakness.

It remains important for children to admire those who are strong in the faith and those whose wisdom they yearn to learn. It is especially important to encounter those whose lives are so mysteriously joyful and meaningful that a child would want to grow up for very envy of that blessed status. Yes, we must continue to pay attention to our youth, but let us not forget that they need those who model what they, too, must want to become.

THE CONTRADICTIONS OF ABSTRACTNESS

So far, I have rarely used the word *ideal* to name what is worthy of being desired, as in an "ideal" combination of traits that contribute to a blessed

---

5. Rom 14:1.

life. Nor have I used the term *idealist* to name those philosophers that assert the more or less independent reality of ideas beyond a physical world.

I have most often used the word to point to a "pure state" of a given condition, like the "ideal" introvert or extrovert who would exhibit only the one quality or the other. Either of these conditions would be highly undesirable. It is in this sense that I have spoken of an "ideal" village as one that was so concrete that its members could neither desire nor imagine any sort of redeeming liberation from the bounds of its geography or ethos. Such a village would indeed deserve English words, like *coma* and *comedy* that have been derived from *kōmē*, the ancient Greek word for "village."

Such a place would procure what it needed from its own territory, especially its food. In fact, the root of the word *kōmē* named a "bundle of hay," and we honor its meaning as food in *com*estibles. Such a community would also be so completely curved in upon itself that change from within would be almost impossible, thus earning its reputation as existing in a *coma* and as *comatose*. Finally, its normal efforts to break out of its stupor would take the form of low *com*edy, as in the periodic drunken ribaldry and ritualized satirical accusations that release tensions though changing nothing.

There is no "ideal" village of this type, though too many yearn for that. Nor could anyone live in the kind of city in which wholly egocentric individuals moved among purely functional settings governed by rationalized recipes presumably revealing certainty. Yet modern "progress" has brought many of us near enough to such a condition that increasing numbers now suffer the debilitating consequences I have been describing. Young people are especially affected by our culture's erosion of the natural ladders of aspiration toward mature adulthood that remained possible in the towns that developed during early modern eras.

It is true, however, that abstraction stimulates people to yearn again for concreteness. Few employees are content to concentrate only on the functions they are hired to perform. Many spontaneously reach out to each other to build a friendly and supportive ethos in their work place and to encourage mutual aid for personal crises and mutual nurture for each other's ambitions. Competitively driven middle managers, clerical workers jammed into a warren of cubicles, and production workers on noisy assembly lines instinctively seek to create an ethos that supports a distinctive *Geist* in their workplace that contributes to the personal and communal *Halig* they continue to desire.

Managers prize those employees whose gregariousness spreads good cheer among their colleagues and whose chatter creates a web that inspires the sentiments of kinship, energy to improve its functioning, and loyalty to the total institution. Large institutions may create a department wholly dedicated to the creation of such morale and may spend significant amounts of money on picnics, competitions, and community service projects that involve both the employees and their families. Even companies that cynically exploit their employees demonstrate the importance of the yearning for mutuality by promoting at least the illusion of a corporate nurture that isn't merely exploitative.

Though also the products of abstraction, houses that line a city's streets are not allowed to remain isolated havens for nuclear families. Whether motivated by village memories or by our children's search for nearby playmates or by the fear of intruders, many of us work at transforming what appear to be rows of separated houses into neighborhoods. Over-the-fence chats give rise to friendships that link others around the block and across the street into surrogate "kin," some of whom may organize neighborhood watches and then celebrate their increasing concreteness in block parties, even if there are no suitable cottonwood trees for hanging daring swings.

Schools, of course, have never been limited to their strictly educative functions. Though so large that they can no longer be considered neighborhood schools, they now are asked to take on many functions that were once handled by families and by communities as a whole. And, so, effective schools try to become a center for activities that appear to have little to do with teaching and learning the "basics" but which create an ethos that stimulate both.

Though I was sure that I did not have time to become active in PTA or to assist classroom teachers, I did at least once find myself setting up (or was it tearing down?) carnival booths. And I admired friends of ours who poured energy and money into organizing "Winter Guard," a drill team squad that stimulated pride and discipline in a group of girls in a high school with a high dropout rate that was then going through a period of low morale.

I have already mentioned the way very disparate individuals cluster around interests and avocations to form groups of the likeminded, many of which include additional family members to form something that resembles a clan, which itself is linked to other "clans" in larger "tribes." Indeed, one cannot flee to a bar for solitary solace without discovering habitués who are anxious either to exclude or to embrace.

My wife and I became very interested in contemporary attempts to design living spaces that offer some of the advantages of a village. Shortly after retirement we moved into a settlement of thirty-four units that features beautiful landscaping, a swimming pool, a jacuzzi, and a clubhouse that allowed us to host larger numbers than can fit into a home. Though almost ideal for those retired members who are content to escape typically harried routines, we wished at times for the sounds of children at play. We also felt slightly guilty for the locked gates that screened us from a noisy world "out there."

Earlier in our lives we made several attempts to convince friends to form a cohousing community. Typically, these are variations on planned unit developments that gather twenty or more families into an area that is arranged to provide safety for children while allowing them to play freely across back yards. Common buildings often contain guest rooms available to visitors, spaces for shared tools and crafts, and recreational equipment. Many have a kitchen and dining hall, and members take turns preparing weekday evening meals. Careful attention goes into planning for the luxuries offered by public spaces while making sure that each home and its yard offer private spaces. Their goal is to shape spaces that naturally evoke neighborliness without compelling it. The popularity of such units in northern Europe and, now, in the USA testify to the desire for building some of the assets of the village into the city.

Modern congregations have very strong reasons to seek increasing concreteness. Every serious religion seeks to reconcile all aspects of life to its understanding of the fundamental nature of what is real and what is supremely important. Though many conventionally religious people are content to limit servicing the "spiritual" aspect of their lives to more or less weekly worship settings, many people who are frightened by the abstraction in their lives are attracted strongly to congregations that demand much more. A large majority of congregations in North America remain small enough to offer intense fellowship and to require participation in almost all of their activities.

Large seeker-friendly congregations balance the appeal of charismatic leaders and orchestrated worship assemblies by dividing their members into smaller groups for discipline, teaching, and fellowship. Largeness permits them to provide a wide mix of settings, from large rallies to small, intense settings for mutual care. Very large congregations may also add gymnasiums, exercise rooms, bowling alleys, and restaurants so that more and more of the normally separated functions of life can be concentrated on their campus.

Though it is possible that such a congregation may begin by cultivating a carefully defined species of birds of a feather that flock to a pastor who combines the qualities of a hero and a celebrity, their subsequent growth may begin to attract different kinds of seekers. Within the lifetime of a gifted leader, they may approach the richer variety of styles and gifts that characterize actual tribes and small towns. For such a congregation to grow into a *church* would depend on its ability to transcend its initial abstractness by creating increasingly concrete institutions that incarnate its *Halig Geist*.

FOUR CHALLENGES TO BECOMING A COUNTER-CULTURAL OUTPOST

At least four challenges would have to be met for it to become a counter-cultural outpost of the kingdom of God. The first is to survive the passing of the founding leader and to continue its maturation by finding pastors who are defined by wise statesmanship in the building of a people, subordinating popularizing and naturally divisive charismas to serve the greater *Halig*. The second is the challenge of countering the abstracting effects of age-grading and interest-specific ministries so that the children of the congregation will identify more with small and, then, larger groups that are sufficiently mixed to incite aspiration to mature spirituality. The third challenge is to retain enough of these children and grandchildren to increase the richness of experience and the variety of gifts that are necessary to keep the congregation from the coma that would result from fixating idolatrously upon any given level of its early vision.

Finally, it would truly become a concrete church if it could establish the sense of at least a porous spatial boundary around itself so that it could minister to the needs of a larger community that it partially defines and so that it could model a *Halig* evoked by its sense of a sacred canopy. I am convinced that a civilization that can survive its own abstractive progress requires the construction of something like concretely *Halig* villages within the city. And, although I think that I could not survive within the still too abstracted ethos of some mega-congregations, I have begun to hope that some of them are growing toward concrete holiness.

People are created with complementary drives to link concretely with others as well as to pull apart. In the past, the embrace of a tribe or a village could become as cloying as its exclusions would become destructive. Then those that had been happy to flee the village for the autonomous individualism promised by the city responded to a counter-pull toward concreteness, building aspects of it into each of the many secondary associations to which they belonged, only to discover that each institution wanted to absorb more of their attention into its quasi-concreteness.

GRATITUDE FOR *KORN'S* HALIG AND THE QUEST FOR THE CITY NOT MADE WITH HANDS

I have long felt that most of my *Korn* generation were wonderfully blessed. Many of us experienced enough healthy concreteness that we have been able to live off its human and spiritual "concreteness-capital" while adding the intellectual and cultural breadth of the city. We maintain a psychic balance despite juggling the demands of a multitude of functions. I have one large load of guilt. The children whose lives we have touched have mostly begun with the city in which we ended. But I fear that we have lived off our concrete capital, paying little attention to maintaining and creating social contexts that could have passed it on as part of their birthright.

I think we also have one huge frustration. Many of us have handled fairly well the series of functions that have made up the round of our days. But it is the nature of a village to absorb almost all of one's attention. And we have been damned by our inability to figure out how to juggle the demands of the many would-be-more-or-less-concrete-villages to which we belong.

One answer is to pour our energies into one of the functions that make up our lives. Since we have to live and it is honorable to provide both the necessities and the goodies for our families, the workplace often becomes the magnet around which we center. That we are then called *workaholics* obscures the possibility that what drives us then is neither the love of work nor the aspiration to climb an institutional ladder nor the desire to provide more goodies for our families. These motives may be justifications that serve, and mask, a deeper urge to simplify our lives, to create a dominant center that orders competing claims to our attention. Ironically, it would then be the case that workaholics are those who are too "lazy" to do the more strenuous multitasking that is needed for building the *Halig* of a more complete life.

Another answer is to focus on one's home and family. Then one must limit the demands of the workplace to those legitimate functions that one is paid to perform, and perhaps even to cheat on these, while refusing to become more than minimally involved in any other functions that do not pertain to the life of one's "shrunken village." To do this while employed requires a talent that earns a secure and adequate salary and implies a refusal to aspire to advancement within the institution. Of course, this choice works best if one has skills that permit one to be self-employed. Ironically, even those who then busy themselves with creating a rich cultural and intellectual environment for their families would likely be thought to lack ambition. Unless the family as a whole can become a mutual unit of production that serves a larger cause than its own satisfactions, it is likely that its members will become a peer group focused on the immediate interests of the children rather than on inspiring them to transcend the stages of their growth.

If higher states of consciousness do not guide the quest for wholeness, then lower states will impose their own addictive disciplines upon the self. More than four hundred years before Jesus, Plato explained in books VIII and IX of his *Republic* why the children of workaholics reject that "productive" way to unify their lives and "democratically" allow all of their many desires for goodies and pleasurable experiences to express themselves in turn.[6] No doubt it is possible to enjoy surfing from one desire to another and to revel in mastering the techniques of pleasure appropriate to each without worrying about coherence or larger meaning.

Plato allowed that such a culture was more esthetically attractive than other types, but he also presciently insisted that the democratic pursuit of goodies and pleasurable experiences produces an inner anarchy that almost always leads to the despotic dominance of one of the passions. What Plato called the despotic state of the self has now been named *addiction*. A culture that loses the aspiration to *Halig* will produce wholesale addictions, and the worst of those addictions will be those that serve the most powerful of now distorted desires. He also insisted that such cultures give themselves over to be ruled by tyrants.

Since religious cults have always revealed the fault lines that exist beneath the cultures within which they arise, it is understandable that contemporary people react to them with a fascination tinged with the horror that comes from a half-conscious recognition of their own need for a guru to impose order on their souls. A son of a family linked by marriage to our Kleinsasser clan joined a cult-like group led by an effective radio preacher that grew into the tens of thousands, and he became a leading teacher among them. His parents and siblings also joined, shaping their identities around a distinctive set of doctrines that included some genuine insights, as far as I could tell.

Though not as extreme as the Davidians of Waco, Texas, or the followers of Jim Jones, they fashioned a tight moral and religious ethos that included the rejection of popular Christian holidays and strictly limited the contacts of the faithful with the families of their birth. A direct member of our clan and his family joined a similar "Christian clique" that also tried to develop a "tribal" sense that threatened to withdraw them from us.

As is often the case, the maturation of this group led to larger understandings and revealed inner tensions that ultimately led to divisions and to

---

6. Bloom and Kirsch, *Republic of Plato*, bks. 8 and 9.

the gradual move of many, perhaps most, of the members into more mainline congregations. The maturity and graciousness this family exhibited when they left the sectarian group was, for me, a testimony that the group they joined had also been marked by mutual nurture. One could wish that all our posterity would become as *Halig*.

I have been told that the first family I mentioned has also moved out of their cult, though some have emerged with psychic scars. My stepfather's cousin was not so fortunate. He was one of the hundreds who drank the poisoned punch at Jonestown.

I assume that those who join religious cults are among the best of those who search for communal discipline and identity. They retain a memory of transcending *Halig*, are profoundly aware of our culture's loss of spiritual depth, and are willing to bear the cost of stretching toward their aspirations.

More alarming are the myriads who know neither where they come from nor have mentors who stimulate higher aspirations. Just as there are always hosts of adults who make it their business to make a buck, catering to the passions of the immature, so also contemporary culture is full of petty tyrants willing to impose a host of petty disciplines on those who need the security of even dysfunctional groups to fashion their identities. Pre-adolescent males cluster around gang leaders and cliques of girls are manipulated by their "queen bees." Nativists and racists form secretive organizations. Anxious citizens parrot the views and styles of their chosen political ideologues.

Like many of my comrades from an older *Korn*, the "great generation" that matured during World War II were fortunate to come out of the Great Depression with a recognition of the need for mutual aid, a commitment to mutual nurture, and with a strong aspiration to fulfill our nation's promise. But now too many who inherited their mantle grow defensive and afraid, for we wish to guard the town we willed to create and we do not understand the anomic city that we unwittingly made possible. Too few of us find our purest joys in self-liberating communion with God and with each other, transcending the fragments of ourselves in a higher vision.

We come closest to singleness of self in regression to earlier states, reverting to the physical and the sensate and to the things that possess us. Our purest sentiments are discovered in a nostalgic recovery of our childish innocence as we vicariously relive it through our children. Disneyland was built by and for adults who turned to cartoon fantasies after losing the capacity for visions.

Our children become the vehicle for the recovery of our lost meaning when we groom them to justify our creations by gratefully inheriting them. In so doing we destroy their innocence and we rob them of the one joy that should be supremely theirs: the joy of becoming a man or a woman who cooperate with others to build a *Halig* community. It is both tragedy and simple justice that they turn upon us. The only option apparent to increasing numbers of them is to accept the world we have offered and to die or to smash it in the hope that a real one will emerge. Some imagine that negation of the adult world is the beginning of creation and the subculture of the youthful pack emerges.

I first wrote a version of the preceding two paragraphs more than thirty years ago under the impress of both countercultural anger and "hippie" idealism. Now I am nostalgic for the students I had during that era. They could be very angry, but they also intended to build a more wholesome world. They still had a sense of community, both as mutual aid and mutual nurture. Now I fear that the upwardly mobile segment of our youthful population has increasingly lost the memory of concreteness that could inform a more profound idealism. The alternative to rage, for many, is an acceptance of the quest for goodies, whether as sensations or of things, as opiates against a profound boredom. Though preparing to join an affluent class, even they listen with apparent approval to those who chant the deeper, more scatological, rage of those who live on our meaner streets.

When I spoke of our schools, I claimed that increasingly complex symbol systems (and this includes all the concepts and words and formulae of abstract specialties) make it more difficult for "average" people to succeed. There is, however, a deeper reason that recruits from all classes might form a larger underclass of deviants and failures. Abstracting societies demand that birds of a feather flock together. Refugees and exiles from primary societies form secondary societies. Living patterns follow suit. The rich live with the rich. Large blocks of houses are filled by those who have reached whatever level of affluence allows them to be able to afford the asking price for that development. They are designed for those of similar ages and life styles and with similar numbers of children of similar ages.

But no one wants to live next to deviants and failures, who must now "choose" each other. Unfortunately, like also breeds like. Their children now grow up without the range of models and "Dutch uncles" that older concrete communities provided. Unnecessarily large numbers of them become deviants and failures. Even if the schools that serve these communities attract good teachers and are adequately financed, they are handicapped by the fact that the homes from which the children come do not fit into smaller primary groups that model aspiration to excellence. Nor is there a sufficient sprinkling of children with higher expectations to show the way. Well before I retired from college teaching, I began each semester hoping that enough of the students in my classes would become so interested in the subjects I taught that they would call the best out of the other students and inspire me to be a better teacher.

Meanwhile the children of the successful also grow up with a narrow range of models, an inadequate grasp of the basics of their culture, and a lack of common sense. One can recognize an "advantaged" community as a place where "merely average" children and even potential "late bloomers" think of themselves as failures because they do not get into the segregated tracks which are the pride of ambitious schools with "enriched" curricula. Though they could have been successful had they been allowed to define themselves over against a representative slice of their peers, many of these also drift into the various rings of a large city's slums, victims of the typecasting of an abstracted world unless they are allowed to remain parasites of wealthy parents. Then their "straight-A" siblings may enter a very selective college and begin to bring down their expectations for themselves since now everyone around them was also a "straight-A," and they begin to think of themselves as average.

BEYOND PEER GROUPS AND *CONGREGARE*: THE QUEST FOR CONCRETE *HALIG* IN THE CITY

Every way of constructing a society produces a certain percentage of deviants and failures. Life regularly arranges itself along continua that take the shape of bell curves. Geniuses, at one extreme, match idiots at the other. The brother of an Olympic athlete may have been born with disabilities. Some people, who are neither geniuses nor athletes, have the gift of making things work; and they succeed at almost everything they do. On the other hand, people with nothing obviously wrong may have been blocked by external circumstances or may simply not have had what it takes to do well at anything.

Modernity makes possible all sorts of progress. It now turns out that this "progress" can become part of the external circumstances that breed failures and deviants, perhaps at an exponentially increasing rate. Neither the new underclass nor any of the successful classes are able to teach what the village taught, the ability to conceive of the *Halig* of a concrete whole and the aspiration and the common sense to work toward that beauty. It is true that forms of mutual aid and mutual nurture continue to be invented, but they are fragile plants in a hostile environment. It is also true that charity and high ideals, however significant, can rarely address increasingly mutant structures.

Now states build massive prison systems and welfare institutions to deal with the problems that small communities could sometimes solve or at least contain in quiet ad hoc ways. In keeping with the spirit that created both the need and the institutions, all the efforts to solve the crises created by abstraction result in more abstractions. Every new need calls forth a new specialty and a new discipline of more esoteric abstractions, each of them dedicated to solving "retail" the problems that progress creates "wholesale." Of course, the rate of failure cannot forever grow. If ways are not found to turn it around, there will come a breaking point when an entire culture is destroyed as surely by its human as by its material waste products.

We are not the first great civilization to achieve the kind of abstracting progress that I have described. In fact, civilization itself is a product of individuals who rise above their narrow contexts to form specialized groups that focus on the progressive development of basic functions. Our civilization, however, has been the first to destroy the concrete agricultural villages that have always been the essential material and spiritual basis out of which a higher culture could arise.

In the past, the benefits and the ills of "modernity" were experienced by a small elite. When such civilizations collapsed, the great majority of the population suffered the losses inflicted by marauding armies and robber bands, but their rural institutions remained and could recover to become the foundation for the emergence of yet another higher culture. In the modern West there are no longer such self-subsistent hinterlands.

We are left with the task of creating the kind of social institutions that are sufficiently concrete to build an ethos of mutual aid and mutual nurture and yet are sufficiently abstract to foster the arts and sciences that bring the goods we can legitimately desire and the experiences that can rightly enrich our lives. But, above all, we shall have to learn to regain our focus on "the one great thing," our *Halig*.

CHAPTER 10

Faith, Time, and Science

AFTER MY MEDITATIONS ON *Korn* and my comparison of that concrete heritage with the abstracted life of contemporary heirs of late-modern cities, I ask readers to think that the progress we rightly celebrate also brings unexpected negative consequences. Added spaces, places, and experiences enrich our lives, but squeezing them all in so changes the tempo of our lives that we grow weary of the daily rat race. I remember the shock experienced by the farmers on the central Kansas churchyard when I suggested that they now worked harder than had their elders when I challenged them to compare the rhythm of their lives before so many "labor-saving" machines had been invented.

Beyond the subtle consequences of a complex and hurried life upon our harried psyches, this chapter and the next asks readers to consider this thesis: *Many of our elders and we have succumbed to heretical forms of modernisms whether or not stoutly resisting an interpretation of evolution denying the existence of a creator of the cosmos.* The next chapter adds that *whether or not they or we insist on a supposedly biblically based orthodoxy, we have modernized our interpretation of canonic texts.*

I conclude this introduction by now offering an ironic apology for now shifting from storytelling meditations to a more abstract analysis of worldview shifts to tell a complex story of Western attempts to explain the formation of the cosmos and to interpret ancient texts.

The faith, hope, and love filling pilgrims escaping from what had been presumed to be "paradises" did not need to demand supposed ideological certainties or to trust sophisticated complexities while keeping the open hearts of the childlike whom Jesus said would enter the kingdom of God.[1]

---

1. Mark 10:15.

They sought radical transformation rather than "bottom-up" levels of linear evolution that continues to mentor those who seek to imitate God.[2]

In the first three chapters of this book, I described the processes of abstraction that emerged in the progress of families, clans, villages, cities, and civilizations and that institutionalized sociopolitical practices along with natural physical forces experienced as active *presences* granted at least quasi-divine status (gods). It is also reasonable for enlightened postmoderns experiencing themselves and other organic concretions to be larger than the mere sum of their parts to ponder what else beyond the concrete organisms and creatures in the cosmos may be larger than the sum of their parts.

In the next chapter I urge that we late moderns need to learn from our elders and from scholars how to interpret ancient biblical texts. Granted the constant experience of disorder among and within its different sets of parts, it has always been rational to question what sort of unity the cosmos might have and how it can be sought. The writer of Hebrews[3] asked his readers to rebuild in the image of a "better country," as in, a "heavenly one." His text described those with whom God covenanted by putting laws into their hearts and minds[4] and adding that, by faith, Abel, Noah, and Abraham worshiped, built an ark, and "set out for a land of promise . . . living in tents" along with heirs and looking for "the city which has foundations."[5]

Speaking of followers of Jesus, the writer urges that the Lord disciplines those whom he loves and calls sons.[6] Those who become followers of Jesus "seek the city which is to come" and is lasting.[7] Indeed, to speak of "the cosmos" is also to question how it can become *Halig*.

AN INTERPRETATION OF EVOLUTIONARY CHANGE THAT COUNTERS EARLIER FORMULATIONS

To return to my opening thesis, I urge that neither the idea of *evolution* nor the nature and methods of science are inherently heretical. To explore this, I summarize Ilya Prigogine's challenging, *The End of Certainty: Time, Chaos, and the New Laws of Nature*.[8] Since I barely understand a few of the simpler

2. Gen 1:26–28.
3. Heb 10–13.
4. Heb 10:13–16.
5. Heb 11:10.
6. Heb 12:4–11.
7. Heb 13:13–14.
8. Prigogine, *End of Certainty*, viii-vix,1–8.

mathematical formulas scientists use to explain the laws of nature and the evolution of the cosmos and since I have not mastered the history and philosophy of science, I await correction and reproof. I ask readers to wrestle with my attempts to interpret the implications of his book that reflects and adds to a radical rethinking of the laws of nature.

It is important to remain aware of what contemporary scientific theorists understand about the history of the cosmos and the principles and processes relevant to that story. As a historian who asks theological and philosophical questions, I read Prof. Prigogine's interpretation of the ancient Greek and of Newtonian physical laws of nature to ask what he and contemporary cosmologists think to be the most promising explanations that account for the origin of the universe and of the changes that have led to what we presently experience.

To convince readers who have decided to read my meditation about growing up in a rural ethnic Mennonite community that it might also be worthwhile to read about possibly significant recent breakthroughs in tracing the evolution of human life, I briefly sketch the remarkable life and mind of one of these theorists.

PROF. ILYA PRIGOGINE'S LIFELONG QUEST TO DISCOVER THE "ARROW OF TIME"

Prof. Prigogine was born into a Jewish family in Moscow during the early turmoil of the revolution of 1917 that led to the triumph of Leninist Bolshevism. The family escaped to Germany and then moved to Belgium, where Ilya grew up. He was so precocious that he could read music before learning to read books, and he says that he spent more time mastering the piano than his other early fascinations with history, archaeology, and philosophy. After enrolling at the Free University of Brussels, he concentrated on chemistry and physics and earned a PhD in 1939, at age twenty-two. I begin by summarizing Prof. Prigogine's introduction, titled "A New Rationality" and his last chapter, "A Narrow Path."[9] Along the way, I include items from the rest of his book and from later responses to his proposals.

His opening passage begins with a quotation from a book published by Karl Popper in 1988. Popper and Prigogine claim that for two thousand years the "dilemma of determinism" (quoting a phrase used by William James[10]) has haunted Western civilizations. On the one hand, science has asserted that "every event can be explained or predicted." On the other hand,

---

9. Prigogine, *End of Certainty*, 183–89.
10. James, *Dilemma of Determinism*, 145.

"common sense attributes to mature and sane human persons ... the ability to choose freely between alternative possibilities of acting."[11]

He notes that this "profound dilemma" connects closely to the meaning of time and that it was "the incorporation of time into the conceptual scheme of Galilean physics that marked the origin of modern science."[12] Unfortunately, from Prof. Prigogine's point of view, neither Isaac Newton nor even recent quantum physics includes "any distinction between past and future." Here, he quotes and later requotes Albert Einstein who declared, "Time is an illusion."[13]

Insisting that in both the physical and social sciences the past and the future must constantly be distinguished, Prof. Prigogine clarifies that what has been denied is "the arrow of time." He makes this *time paradox* "one of the central concerns" of his book.[14] He also points out that the *time paradox* first became clear when Ludwig Boltzmann, a physicist in Vienna in the late nineteenth century, tried to create an evolutionary explanation of physics as Charles Darwin had done for biology.

The physical laws of nature formulated by Isaac Newton were designed to produce *certainties* expressing the *objective* facts of the interactions of unchanging objects. This meant that all changes could, in principle, be reversed. In other words, as Pierre-Simon de Laplace (1749–1827) declared, from its knowledge of the size, shape, direction, and momentum of the world's ultimate particles, an omniscient demon could at any point in time deduce the past or future states of the cosmos.

Of course, the reversibility of atomic interactions and the certainty of physical laws made determinism inevitable only if atoms were absolutely unchangeable. In the nineteenth century, it became obvious that at least a few atomic elements did naturally break up, when undergoing fission. It was also becoming clear that the explanation of something as basic as light required the assumption of waves and not just as photons taken somehow to be like atomic particles.

After Boltzmann "the arrow of time has been relegated to the realm of phenomenology."[15] This theory holds that all human knowledge comes to humans through sense organs. What really might be behind the phenomena the senses translate to us is then unknowable. "We, as imperfect human observers, are responsible for the difference between past and future through

---

11. Prigogine, *End of Certainty*, 1.
12. Prigogine, *End of Certainty*, 1.
13. Prigogine, *End of Certainty*, 1, 58, 165, 187.
14. Prigogine, *End of Certainty*, VIII-VIX;1-8..
15. Prigogine, *End of Certainty*, 2.

the approximations we introduce in our description of nature."[16] Prigogine adds, "This is still the prevailing scientific wisdom." And it is this "wisdom" that he and others refute. This desperate phenomenal "solution" allowed the *certainty* of natural laws at the *price* of insisting that they *and a determined world* could only be asserted of the phenomena revealed to us by our senses. The real world sends data that our senses translate to our conscious awareness, and we live within the world we receive, even if illusory.

Prof. Prigogine cites "the spectacular growth of nonequilibrium physics and the dynamics of unstable systems, beginning with the idea of chaos."[17] This new science uses the mathematical rigor of traditional science to calculate the *approximations* that occur naturally. As opposed to *determinism* which holds that evolution follows rules that allow "only one sequence of future states," the new physics says that a single particle in three-dimensional space has three degrees of freedom.[18]

Prigogine states: "We now know that irreversibility leads to a host of novel phenomena, such as vortex formation, chemical oscillations, and laser light, all illustrating the essential *constructive* role of the arrow of time."[19] The revision of the concept of time suggested "the formulation of the physics of unstable systems. Classical science emphasized order and stability; now, in contrast, we see fluctuation, instability, multiple choices, and limited predictability at all levels of observation."[20] The new laws of nature express "possibilities or probabilities," not certitudes.[21]

But instead of basing this new physics on "states of mind," as in phenomenalism, Prof. Prigogine returns to basing it on "states of the world." Instabilities in nature itself breaks time symmetry, and not the supposedly "creative" role of the observer. In other words, the new laws of nature express actual natural events "that bring an element of radical novelty to the description of nature." To *include* probabilities in the formulation of the basic "laws of physics," frees us from the old classical determinism of Isaac Newton's physics. "The future is no longer determined by the present."[22]

His closing comments admit that "this confronts us with the most difficult questions of all: What are the roots of time? Did time start with the

---

16. Prigogine, *End of Certainty*, 2.
17. Prigogine, *End of Certainty*, 3.
18. Prigogine, *End of Certainty*, 201.
19. Prigogine, *End of Certainty*, 3. Emphasis in original.
20. Prigogine, *End of Certainty*, 3–4.
21. Prigogine, *End of Certainty*, 4.
22. Prigogine, *End of Certainty*, 5–6.

'big bang'? Or does time preexist our universe?"[23] Here he admits the necessity of speculation, though insisting that he does so within "the domain of macroscopic physics, chemistry, and biology. It is the domain in which human existence actually takes place." After all, "how can we conceive of human creativity or ethics in a deterministic world?"[24]

He insists that the "triumph of Newtonian physics in the eighteenth century" led the Western world to separate science from traditional wisdom. He concludes that "we are observing the birth of a new science . . . [that] reflects the complexity of the real world, a science that views us and our creativity as part of a fundamental trend present at all levels of nature."[25] The ethno-religious story I have been telling is part of my affirmation of traditional wisdom.

Prigogine's book is titled *The End of Certainty*. By also reinterpreting the nature of time he is able to avoid resorting to ignorance about a supposed "real" world. The new physics he and many others present uses the mathematics of probabilities to assert that large masses of interacting erratic atoms consistently average out to produce significant probabilities that new processes emerge, some of which cannot be reversed. Thus, the loss of certainty justifies enduring new possibilities, including evolution, free choice, and an ethics requiring humans to exercise responsibility for stewarding the real world we inhabit.

Though *certainty* about any *individual* event or entity can no longer be deduced, human observers have been returned to the world of subjects interacting with each other and, in principle, capable of responsible ethical actions chosen to improve our relationships to other subjects and to improve our ecologies. Of course, lack of omniscience, earthly limitations, and the fact of having been thrown into the world without consciously and intelligently experiencing even our own beginning and end means that humans often err and produce more disorder than the peace and prosperity they desire.

Prof. Prigogine and other scientists and philosophers debate aspects of this new worldview. Those of us who want to assert more, can admit that this new science offers good news. Though no theist should want to claim that it proves the existence of a supernatural Creator, they should recognize that many eminent scientists have rejoined the humanists, historians, philosophers, theologians, social scientists, and all "serious citizens" who seek to heal disordered relationships and who assume that humans can learn

---

23. Prigogine, *End of Certainty*, 6.
24. Prigogine, *End of Certainty*, 6.
25. Prigogine, *End of Certainty*, 7.

from the consequences of action what actually helps to heal our disordered world. They, and we, can repent past mistakes and become open to be guided by common sense, by the rigorous self-correcting arts, and by disciplines that educate us and explore what goes beyond present knowledge. His book never explicitly addresses his Jewish heritage or acknowledges theistic convictions.

To sum up the first part of this introduction to a revised physics, we must acknowledge that science itself depends upon a scientific community dedicated to a process of reproof and correction. This process no longer allows the logic and methods taken to be appropriate to unchangeable bits of matter aggregating to each other to dictate the logic and methods of other domains of knowledge or of their adherents. Moreover, the study of the motions of stellar objects, like the later discoveries of the motions inside individual atoms, reveals complexities that excite awe and wonder.

Indeed, all human probes of the very large macrocosm and a very small microcosm reveal mysteries. Whether zealously *hedgehoggish* or ecstatically *foxy*, those who seek to know discover that creaturely images imply our kinship with the rest of "what-is." Even legitimate and disciplined efforts to eat the fruit of the "tree of knowledge" expels us from the innocence experienced in the supposed "garden of Eden." But, as expressed by my *Korn* elders, *Gottesfurcht* and *Gelassenheit* name the awe and grateful acceptance of what truly *is*. Those aware of their place within this cosmos recognize their need for these attitudes.

Since material natural objects sometimes do irreversibly take on new properties, the new physics that continues to find mathematical expression does so expressing the possibilities and probabilities that occur among large "populations" of interactions. As in the physics of light, of thermodynamics, of gaseous and fluid diffusion, to say nothing of nuclear fission or fusion, statistical *probabilities* that are calculated turn out to be consistently accurate even in applications where the consequences of isolated *individual* interactions cannot be predicted.

What Prof. Prigogine happily accepts is that positivistic physical scientists cannot dictate to the social and human sciences, to the humanities, or to theologians and philosophers the methods and objectivity that had classically been taken to be appropriate to specific domains of knowledge in the natural world and then assumed to be the ideal also for all other domains of knowledge. In other words, the methods and logics applicable to the domains of human interactions must be responsible to the subjectivity that keeps such domains of research responsible. Of course, our rhetoric here must be carefully stipulated. For example, when *subjectivity* connotes the allowance of prejudices, ignorance, or to allow the powerful or the rich or the privileged to dominate, then the search for valid truth has been betrayed.

THE DILEMMA OF DETERMINISM

In the first and longest chapter of his book, Prof. Prigogine sketches the long history of this dilemma beginning with its presumed emergence in Greek philosophy and science as early as the fifth century (BCE). Democritus posited that when the cosmos began to be formed there had always been innumerable, tiny particles which he called *atoms*. This Greek word denies that they could be cut or broken into smaller bits.

These solid, compact, and unmodifiable ultimate elements of all later things differed only in size and shape. His second principle or assumption was that they moved erratically in an "unreal but existent" infinite void. This necessary movement was apparently simply a given, an aspect of a natural law. All complex things in the cosmos emerged from atoms "colliding and interweaving and forming things by aggregation." His encyclopedic knowledge and his writings on virtually all significant topics were so coherent that he was nicknamed *Wisdom*.[26]

Apparently, poverty had led the father of Epicurus to found a school far from Athens to teach sons of richer Greeks the wisdom developed in Athens and elsewhere. While still quite young Epicurus studied with philosophers and attracted students to himself. Early in the fourth century (BCE), he founded what became a famous school in Athens. For nearly four decades, he led "a simple, remote, and hidden life with his students." Later Epicureans revered him.

He taught that, like humans, the "bodies" of the immortal gods were shaped by collections of atoms, but the atoms composing their "bodies" were the finest and most pure and lived in outer space between worlds experiencing perfect blessedness and free of all the disturbances caused by "the great metaphysical and physical powers" that afflict human lives. The ancient Greek word for these "powers" was *daimones* whether good angels or evil demons. Writers of the New Testament broadly referred to them as "principalities and powers."

Having accepted the principles of atoms and their motion in the void of space as taught by Democritus, Epicurus "explained" that the attribute of weight accounted for their motion. Unfortunately, their fall within infinite space implied that their strictly downward motion and equal speed in a

---

26. Cary, *Oxford Classical Dictionary*, 266–67.

vacuum forbade their hooking together to form larger cosmic entities. He could not explain why these falling atoms erratically swerved (the *klinamen*), ultimately creating the great "swirl" allowing them to aggregate and to form the cosmos.

Epicurus also intended to deliver humans from the fear of death, teaching that at death the atoms that make us human scatter and humans are delivered from all disturbances. His ethical ideas sought the pleasure and happiness that frees humans especially from those caused by human desires and passions. His theory of knowledge was also consistently materialistic. The extremely thin atomic "skins" of all aggregated entities break off and stream so swiftly away from them that they cannot be seen. After penetrating sense organs, they jostle the very small atoms of minds/souls that translate what is experienced by the five senses.

His ethics was also rationally constructed from his acceptance of the two fundamental assumptions of Democritus. Envious rivals caricatured his search for a higher form of pleasure by insisting that his goal of pleasure implied, "eat, drink, and be merry," but he counseled withdrawal from public life to seek with the likeminded "the joy of [life's] simple and pure existence."[27] When readers of Prof. Prigogine's book discover that he, too, claims the legacy of Epicurus, they, too, may take seriously that they might need to recapitulate, in some sense, the wisdom and disciplines of the past.

I conclude this apparent approval of the thoroughgoing materialism of Epicurus or of his theory of knowledge, or of his theology or ethics by, ironically, "washing my mouth with soap." The "new physics" and his affirmation of "the arrow of time" that Prof. Prigogine celebrates in his penultimate chapter also fundamentally counters Epicurean physics. What is being celebrated are the ironic consequences of his paradoxical acceptance of the *klinamen*. Epicurus had so much realistic common sense that he asserted irrational and unexplained swerves in the logically steady fall of atoms because it was the only way he could account for entities, things, persons, and even gods and in the mix of order and disorder that are encountered.

How many of us prefer the option of a physics of cause and effect teaching a completely deterministic cosmos denying choice, responsibility, fairness, democracy, or the "evolution" of enlightened sages? Most Western thinkers had for a thousand years accepted canonic texts explaining that a good but fallen creation offered a Creator guiding them to sanctification within this earthly era while offering the eschatological hope of a fulfilled re-creation.

---

27. Cary, *Oxford Classical Dictionary*, 324–25.

Though, for example, options had been offered also by Heraclitus and Parmenides,[28] and though Plato had grappled with this paradox in *The Sophist*, "Greek philosophy was unable to solve the dilemma.... This duality has plagued Western thought ever since."[29]

Prof. Prigogine added that "this debate took a turn in the eighteenth century with the discovery of the 'laws of nature.'"[30] Especially, "Newton's law relating force and acceleration, as in the physics of trajectories which was both deterministic and, more important, time reversible."[31] It also led to the nightmare of the demon posited by Laplace.[32] Many historians have added that "the Christian God as conceived in the seventeenth century as an omnipotent legislator"[33] reinforced this determinism. Prof. Prigogine quotes Gottfried von Leibniz, "In the least of substances, eyes as piercing as those of God could read the whole course of things in the universe"—all of what has been and shall be.[34] Albert Einstein thought that determinism was the only "position compatible with the achievements of science."[35]

Since the nineteenth century many eminent philosophers have grappled with the meaning of time and of human existence. Indeed, beginning with Descartes in the seventeenth century, many brilliant minds have, like Epicurus, resorted to something analogous to the *klinamen*. Often the modern option is dualism. Descartes asserted two fundamental realities, mind and matter. Very recently, Stephen Hawking tried to make time an accident of space in his *Brief History of Time*.[36] Then, realizing that an "arrow of time" was needed to produce intelligent life, he arbitrarily introduced an "anthropic principle," giving "no indication of how the anthropic principle could ever emerge from a static geometrical universe."[37]

Prof. Prigogine ends part I of his second chapter with a paragraph quoting Alfred North Whitehead that the early Greeks have given us both the long attempt to explain everything in nature as logically and necessarily determined *and* "the idea of democracy based on the assumption of human

---

28. Prigogine, *End of Certainty*, 10.
29. Prigogine, *End of Certainty*, 11.
30. Prigogine, *End of Certainty*, 11.
31. Prigogine, *End of Certainty*, 11.
32. Prigogine, *End of Certainty*, 11.
33. Prigogine, *End of Certainty*, 12.
34. Prigogine, *End of Certainty*, 12.
35. Prigogine, *End of Certainty*, 13.
36. Hawking, *Brief History of Time*, 60–65.
37. Prigogine, *End of Certainty*, 11–17.

freedom, creativity, and responsibility."[38] The rest of his book offers the option of a philosophy that harmonizes with a "new physics."

COMPLICATIONS

More complications within the physics of nature are discussed in the second part of his second chapter. In the first part, he emphasizes that the "problems of time and determinism form the dividing line between science and philosophy."[39] They also divide the two cultures described by C. P. Snow: science and the humanities.[40] Prof. Prigogine immediately insists that science "is far from being a monolithic bloc."[41] Nineteenth-century physics both affirmed Newton's deterministic natural law and "an evolutionary description associated with entropy." Evolution and entropy contradict reversibility and determinism.

"It is fair to say that irreversible processes are the rule and reversible processes the exception."[42] The second law of thermodynamics states that for isolated natural systems energy remains constant, but entropy increases. The Greek word *entropy* "simply means *evolution*."[43] Thus, solar radiation and many weather and climate variations cannot be reversed. Newton had emphasized entities in motion, but pendular reversibility is an idealization. Its entropy, friction, guarantees that it will end up at rest unless energy is reapplied. Stirred fluids also come to rest.

Prigogine states, "We have inherited two conflicting views of nature from the nineteenth century: the time-reversible view based on the laws of dynamics and the evolutionary view based on entropy."[44] Of course, *entropy* only implies change within individual systems. Changes within an apple tree may produce a new species of apples. Climate change may mean droughts for some areas and floods for others. But the end of solar radiation inevitably darkens the earth.

The very different quantum mechanics that has emerged since the late nineteenth century also deals with physical nature and does so expressing itself through mathematical idealizations. In the late nineteenth century Ludwig Boltzmann, a physicist in Vienna, realized that Charles Darwin was

38. Prigogine, *End of Certainty*, 17.
39. Prigogine, *End of Certainty*, 17.
40. Snow, *Two Cultures*, 1–21.
41. Prigogine, *End of Certainty*, 17.
42. Prigogine, *End of Certainty*, 18.
43. Prigogine, *End of Certainty*, 19.
44. Prigogine, *End of Certainty*, 19.

redefining life as the result of never-ending change (evolution) and that this "placed becoming at the center of our understanding of nature."[45]

Darwin studied changes in the populations of species when, in changing ecologies, there is a "drift" that causes species' changes. "Correspondingly, Boltzmann argued that we cannot understand the law of thermodynamics, and the spontaneous increase in entropy it predicts, by starting with individual dynamical trajectories; we must begin, instead, with large populations of particles."[46] Global drift would be the result of the large number of particles colliding with each other.[47] Problems in his expression of his hypothesis doomed it.

Prof. Prigogine argues that the world we experience is an "unstable, evolving world" and that the "main reason to discard the banalization of irreversibility is that we can no longer associate the arrow of time only with an increase in disorder. Recent developments in nonequilibrium physics and chemistry point in the other direction. They show unambiguously that the arrow of time is a source of *order*."[48] He then cites reasons from thermal diffusion to show that irreversibility "leads to both order and disorder."[49]

> Whatever the past, there exist at present two types of processes: time-reversible processes, where the application of existing dynamics has proved to be successful (i.e., the motion of the moon in classical mechanics, or the hydrogen atom in quantum mechanics), and irreversible processes like heat conditions, where the asymmetry between past and future is obvious.[50]

From Prof. Prigogine's point of view, the traditional laws of physics "describe an idealized, stable world that is quite different from the unstable, evolving world in which we live."[51] Furthermore, scientists and engineers clearly and precisely direct the machines using mathematical idealizations to achieve the result they want.

The relevant domain of analytical mechanics remains valid for engineers redesigning farm equipment. The relevant domain of developments in quantum mechanics dealing with wave functions, as in laser emissions, involves a newer kind of physics that is also valid and is also mathematically expressed. And if the laws of nature differently complement each other, it

---

45. Prigogine, *End of Certainty*, 19.
46. Prigogine, *End of Certainty*, 20.
47. Prigogine, *End of Certainty*, 20.
48. Prigogine, *End of Certainty*, 26, emphasis in original.
49. Prigogine, *End of Certainty*, 26.
50. Prigogine, *End of Certainty*, 28.
51. Prigogine, *End of Certainty*, 26.

becomes obvious that domain-specific laws cannot be absolutized. Nor can they dictate to the domains of behavior relevant to the social sciences or to the humanities.

In his second chapter, Prof. Prigogine confesses that traditional scientific wisdom and even Newton and Einstein frustrated him, and he could not avoid questioning the "roots of time."[52] Some scientists at the University of Brussels had, since 1870, studied thermodynamics, and in 1946 he had organized the first conference on statistical mechanics and thermodynamics at which he lectured on irreversible thermodynamics and was berated for questioning traditional wisdom. "Throughout my entire life I have encountered hostility to the concept of unidirectional time."[53]

By 1989, Prof. Prigogine and colleagues had demonstrated some processes of thermal diffusion far from equilibrium that made it possible for matter to evolve new properties that became permanent.[54] In a sense, "we can say that matter at equilibrium is 'blind,' but far from equilibrium it begins to 'see.'"[55] The conclusion to his second chapter begins with "The arrow of time plays an essential role in the formation of structures in both the physical sciences and in biology. But we are only at the beginning of our quest."[56] In the last paragraphs of the chapter, Prigogine rejoices that nonequilibrium physics shows that his youthful dream "to contribute to the unification of science and philosophy by resolving the enigma of time"[57] has been realized, since his views are like those expressed by Bergson and Whitehead.

Though his philosophical observations remain fascinating, chapters 3–6 become increasingly technical. He begins chapter 7 stating that "science is a dialogue between mankind and nature, the results of which have become unpredictable. At the beginning of the twentieth century, who would have dreamed of unstable particles, an expanding universe, self-organization, and dissipative structures?"[58]

So long as it had been taken for granted that unchanging material particles formed the world by interacting with each other and aggregating to form all things as determined by laws of nature, all events were reversible, in principle. Therefore, time itself could be ignored while humans actually

52. Prigogine, *End of Certainty*, 30.
53. Prigogine, *End of Certainty*, 62.
54. Prigogine, *End of Certainty*, 64–66.
55. Prigogine, *End of Certainty*, 67.
56. Prigogine, *End of Certainty*, 71.
57. Prigogine, *End of Certainty*, 72.
58. Prigogine, *End of Certainty*, 153.

shaped by time could assert scientific certainties. This "recalls the totalitarian nightmares described by Aldous Huxley, Milan Kundera, and George Orwell."[59] And that is why he welcomed the irrational acceptance of unexplained swerves that allowed Epicurus to embrace common sense and, later, dualists who accepted a nonphysical "substance" also interactively dialoguing with nature.

Of course, Prof. Prigogine more happily accepts the new "laws" of physics relevant to the changing, evolving, actually experienced world that is

> associated with deterministic chaos and nonintegrability. Chance, or probability, is no longer a convenient way of accepting ignorance, but rather part of a new, extended rationality. . . . At the statistical level, we can incorporate instability. The laws of nature, which no longer deal with certitudes but possibilities, overrule the age-old dichotomy between being and becoming. . . . This disorder constitutes the very foundation of the macroscopic systems to which we apply an evolutionary description associated with the second law, the law of increasing entropy.[60]

In his next-to-last chapter (8), Prof. Prigogine states that most scientists assume that time began with the "big bang," but he thinks it more likely that "the birth of the universe was only one event in the history of the entire cosmos, and that we therefore have to ascribe to that so-called 'meta-universe' a time prior to the birth of our own."[61]

That we live in an expanding universe is the standard cosmological model. This model asserts that the universe began at "a point that contains the totality of the energy and matter in the universe. However, this model does not enable us to describe this singularity because the laws of physics cannot be applied to a point corresponding to an infinite density of matter and energy."[62] "Clearly we are at the edge of positive knowledge, even dangerously close to science fiction."[63]

Fortunately, Prof. Prigogine's insistence on the importance of "the arrow of time" both delivers us from determinism and the presumptions of a materialist, positivistic worldview that the logic (and the *logos*) that classical physics assumed had been appropriate for time-reversible processes, like pendular motion, must apply also to all other domains. As he insists,

---

59. Prigogine, *End of Certainty*, 154.
60. Prigogine, *End of Certainty*, 155.
61. Prigogine, *End of Certainty*, 163–64.
62. Prigogine, *End of Certainty*, 164.
63. Prigogine, *End of Certainty*, 166.

neither determinism nor chaotic chance fits all that science observes when surveying natural processes. What philosophers, theologians, humanists, analysts of social institutions, historians, and the rest of us can celebrate is the freedom to discover what appropriately serves the search for truth, justice, beauty, and peace.

On what might have preceded the big bang, he admits that only speculation is possible, but he argues that Einstein's special relativity theory makes it possible "to complete our discussion of cosmology." He also admits that a discussion of gravitation "which first requires a generalization of the space-time interval" will be required.[64] Apparently, he thinks it should comfort readers that the fifteen billion years it had taken for our earth to revolve around the sun from the big bang to the present size of the universe is a relatively small number compared to the ten billion times per second that the electron of a hydrogen atom rotates around its nucleus! Knowing that, this big bang "appears to have no parallel elsewhere in physics."[65]

To put it bluntly, this singular primordial event doesn't even belong to a science that otherwise deals only with classes of events! His very next paragraph admits that many scientists "have been willing to explain this singularity in terms of the 'hand of God,' since it transcends physical rationality."[66] Other scientists have assumed that there are no privileged times or places in the universe and that enough new matter is constantly generated to make up for the amount of matter that expands out of it. This theory asserts a "steady state" universe. Nor can science explain how atoms could continue to be, or ever had, appeared out of nothing! For the big bang, the "first second of life still remains an open question."[67] The ultimate philosophical question remains without an answer: "Why is there something rather than nothing?"[68]

This chapter ends with "Questions concerning the origins of time will probably always be with us. But the idea . . . that time preceded the existence of our universe . . . is becoming more and more plausible."[69] Prigogine's final chapter charts the narrow path "between two conceptions that both lead to alienation: a world ruled by deterministic laws, which leave no place for novelty, and a world ruled by a dice-playing God, where everything is absurd, acausal, and incomprehensible."[70]

64. Prigogine, *End of Certainty*, 166–72.
65. Prigogine, *End of Certainty*, 172–73.
66. Prigogine, *End of Certainty*, 173.
67. Prigogine, *End of Certainty*, 175.
68. Prigogine, *End of Certainty*, 173.
69. Prigogine, *End of Certainty*, 182.
70. Prigogine, *End of Certainty*, 187–88.

Prof. Prigogine uses the phrase "arrow of time" in connection with a "dice-playing God." He respectfully and appropriately clarifies that the narrow path he followed scientifically was between what in the last paragraph of *The End of Certainty* threads between "the dramatic alternatives of blind laws and arbitrary events" that his preceding paragraph characterized as his rejection of "the two alienating images of a deterministic world and an arbitrary world of pure chance."[71]

Theists proclaim an eternal Creator whose trans-cosmic power is the necessary and sufficient cause of any created cosmos, but skeptics rightly point out that even if their hypothesis provides a rational cause, they have, in fact, posited an uncaused power whose existence is as unexplained as is that of any taken-for-granted cosmos.

The options of "blind laws" and "pure chance" have haunted Western science since the fifth century BCE, and Prof. Prigogine's account of that history has been sketched above. I also suggest that this renowned late-twentieth-century scientist and Renaissance man's use of a "dice-playing God" is his ironically appropriate interpretation of Christianity's dalliance with describing God's power with the use of the three omni words: omniscience, omnipresence, and omnipotence. Of course, Prigogine has rejoiced that since Democritus, Western science had the common sense to assert irrational swerves (the *klinamen* of Epicurus) or equally unexplained causes of dual "substances."

I now add to this chapter of *The End of Certainty*, a review of Prof. Prigogine's comments about the Laplace demon whose omniscient knowledge of the character and motions of every atom at any given moment allows the deduction of all its past and future interactions. To counter this devastating, deterministic conclusion, Prigogine knows that he must challenge one of the traditional assumptions of Western science.

Underlying the traditional "laws of nature" accepted by Western science has been the assumption that any cause must produce its inevitable effect upon supposedly unchangeable bits of matter. Of course, it had become obvious to physicists and chemists that light could not merely be explained in terms of photons taken to be bits of matter, that some atoms fission, and that Poincaré resonances, thermodynamic processes, etc., cannot be reduced to the aggregation of bits of matter.

Prof. Prigogine surrendered certainty to regain sanity, and his "arrow of time" had allowed him to acknowledge that time allows us to ponder the choice of our responses. And time had led to irreversible chemical and, eventually, cultural evolutionary processes justifying his freedom to

---

71. Prigogine, *End of Certainty*, 189.

cooperate responsibly with others in a search for knowledge and in the building of a *city*, another metaphor for an enlightened culture that seeks knowledge, and *Halig shalom*.

Again, I do not know whether he acknowledged that he, too, *wrestled* (*yisra*) with the *El*(*ohim*) of Gen 1 and of his Hebrew heritage, I interpret his book to reveal his profound wrestling to understand and to be responsible to what he recognizes to be *real*, and I hope that I rightly interpret his comments about the omniscient demon that Pierre Simon de Laplace, a brilliant French mathematician and aristocratic statesman, invented in the late eighteenth or early nineteenth century to clarify the implications of Isaac Newton's laws of nature—especially "Newton's law relating force and acceleration, which was both deterministic and, more important, time reversible," made it possible for such a demon to be "capable of observing the current state of the universe and predicting its evolution"[72]—despite the fact that, in the twentieth century, Newton's law was superseded by quantum mechanics and Einstein's relativity theory, "determinism and time symmetry—have survived."[73]

Prof. Prigogine adds that "many historians believe that an essential role in this vision of nature was played by the Christian God as conceived in the seventeenth century as an omnipotent legislator. Theology and science agreed."[74] I add that theology and science should agree only to respect the truth and faithfully seek the kinds of evidence appropriate to each.

I appreciate Prof. Prigogine's sly quotation from Joseph Needham whose book *Science and Society in East and West* reports the irony with which "Chinese men of letters greeted the Jesuits' announcements of the triumphs of modern science. For them, the idea that science is governed by simple, knowable laws seemed to be a perfect example of anthropocentric foolishness."[75] Since the Japanese and Chinese had accepted that nature means "what is by itself," to speak of "laws of nature" subjects what must be reverenced to what cannot merely be objectified and ideologically abstracted.

Prof. Prigogine adds a long quotation from Albert Einstein saying that if the moon could contemplate its path around the earth, it would, of course, assume that it had freely chosen to do that and that humans also assume their freedom instead of realizing that human self-love protects them

---

72. Prigogine, *End of Certainty*, 11.
73. Prigogine, *End of Certainty*, 12.
74. Prigogine, *End of Certainty*, 11–12.
75. Prigogine, *End of Certainty*, 12.

"from being regarded as an impotent object in the course of the universe."[76] But Prof. Prigogine counters that, unlike Einstein and those physicists who agree with him, he chooses to agree with philosophers like George Wilhelm Hegel, Edmund Husserl, William James, Henri Bergson, and Alfred North Whitehead that "the central problem of ontology" remains "at the very basis of the meaning of human existence."[77]

Prof. Prigogine quotes Karl Popper to show that the "marvelous success" of modern physics had seemed to confirm Laplace's determinism and has become "the most solid and serious obstacle to our understanding and justifying the nature of human freedom, creativity, and responsibility." Still quoting Popper, "The reality of time and change is the crux of realism."[78] Then quoting Henri Bergson, Prof. Prigogine insists that it is time "that prevents everything from being given at once,"[79] making it "the vehicle of creativity and choice."[80] It is time's existence that proves nature's indeterminism.

In *Dilemma of Determinism* William James[81] had also shown that, to go beyond determinism, it was necessary to go beyond the laws of Newton, Schrödinger, and Einstein upon which mathematics had lent its aura as had also the dominance of the science of evolution.

Several decades of experiments in thermal diffusion paradoxically revealed that "irreversible processes (associated with the arrow of time) are as real as reversible processes described by the fundamental laws of physics." Indeed, "irreversible processes play a fundamental constructive role in nature."[82] These shocking conclusions fundamentally challenged Newtonian physics.[83]

Prof. Prigogine added that it took so long to generalize the new laws of nature that included irreversibility and probability because both the traditional "desire to achieve a quasi-divine point of view in our description of nature" [84] (to preserve determinism) and a new field of mathematics (fractals) had to be developed. "We need a 'divine' point of view to retain the idea of determinism. But no human measurements, no theoretical predictions, can give us initial conditions with infinite precision. It is interesting

---

76. Prigogine, *End of Certainty*, 13.
77. Prigogine, *End of Certainty*, 12–14.
78. Prigogine, *End of Certainty*, 14.
79. Prigogine, *End of Certainty*, 14.
80. Prigogine, *End of Certainty*, 14.
81. James, *Dilemma of Determinism*, 145.
82. Prigogine, *End of Certainty*, 27.
83. Prigogine, *End of Certainty*, 26.
84. Prigogine, *End of Certainty*, 38.

to contemplate what becomes of the Laplace demon in the world of deterministic chaos."[85]

Introducing perhaps Prof. Prigogine's last allusion to the Laplace demon,[86] he insists that *maps* (and I add that ideological "maps" can be added to the scientific maps he implies) "are idealized models that cannot capture time's true continuity."[87] At the end of his fourth chapter, Prof. Prigogine turns to

> more realistic situations of special importance to us [that] will be the non-integrable Poincaré systems, where the break between the individual description (trajectories or wave functions) and the statistical description is even more striking. *For these systems, the Laplace demon is powerless, whether the knowledge of the present is finite or infinite.* The future is no more a given; it becomes a "construction," to use the expression of the French poet Paul Valéry.[88]

What for Prof. Prigogine was "more realistic" made no sense to me until I returned to pages that described "Poincaré resonances."[89] One example I could understand was that when one hears a note being played on a musical instrument, one hears more than that note since its harmonics, its *resonances*, are also heard.[90] Subsequent pages illustrate similarly "diffusive motions" that occur at both microscopic and macroscopic levels in the universe and are indeed "realistic" and incredibly important for scientists to understand.

I have given so much attention in this chapter of my meditations on my heritage to *The End of Certainty* because both the new more realistic laws of physics Prof. Prigogine presents and has helped to develop as well as his philosophic, humanistic, and existentialist appreciation of the limitations experienced by human creatures exhibits so much common sense. It had not led him to the reductionist conclusions of a so-called science that has too often assumed that what made possible so many technological advances, improved medical interventions, cultural enlightenments, and even luxuries validated the conviction that humans were merely objectified automatons at the mercy of deterministic laws. Indeed, the new physics of atomic fission and processes of diffusion should also be greeted with awed

85. Prigogine, *End of Certainty*, 38.
86. Prigogine, *End of Certainty*, 106.
87. Prigogine, *End of Certainty*, 106.
88. Prigogine, *End of Certainty*, 106, author's emphasis.
89. Prigogine, *End of Certainty*, 106, 39–44.
90. Prigogine, *End of Certainty*, 40.

reverence. Every dimension of reality deserves the methods of discovery appropriate to its own domain.

In the last three paragraphs of his last chapter, Prof. Prigogine says that since "arbitrary simplifications" of empirical observations that had been integrated with "theoretical structures" could not overcome common sense objections to the time-paradox, it had been necessary "to introduce new physical concepts, such as deterministic chaos and Poincaré resonances and new mathematical tools to turn these weaknesses into strengths . . . providing fresh insights into the new relationships between the knower and the known."[91] He concludes that following his narrow path "that avoids dramatic alternatives of blind laws and arbitrary events, we discover that a large part of the concrete world around us has until now 'slipped through the meshes of the scientific net.'"[92]

SINCE PROF. PRIGOGINE'S DEATH IN 2003, THIS NEW PHYSICS CONTINUES

I have been given several indications that since his death in 2003, the new perspectives Prof. Prigogine and his colleagues initiated have been extended beyond the natural sciences to the social sciences and to wider human sciences. Thus, a January 2018 issue of a psychological journal included an essay saying that

> Prigogine's ideas are extremely important for the understanding of the perspectives of transformation of psychological science in the twenty-first century from the study of predictability and self-consistency of individuals to the understanding of personality as self-determined and self-organized system that creates a higher order out of uncertainty and chaos.[93]

Debate continues and includes important scientists who sponsor other perspectives. Though the big bang remains the leading contender among global explanations, there is no general consensus. The effort to find a physical explanation for the origin of life also continues, and I end with a report that Jeremy England, an associate professor at the Massachusetts Institute of Technology who, in 2013, had "made waves with a new theory that cast the origin of life as an inevitable outcome of thermodynamics."[94] He had

91. Prigogine, *End of Certainty*, 188–89.
92. Prigogine, *End of Certainty*, 189.
93. Quoted in Leontiev, "Ilya Prigogine," 5–14.
94. Wolchover, "First Support," para. 1.

been conducting computer simulations that other leading experts agreed deserved their attention.

Though the second law of thermodynamics and experience show that when a cup of coffee is placed on a table, it cools to room temperature, Prof. England tested the hypothesis that "for some initial settings, the chemical reaction network in the simulation goes in a wildly different direction: In these cases, it evolves to fixed points far from equilibrium, where it vigorously cycles through reactions . . . harvesting the maximum energy possible from the environment."[95]

Thermodynamic studies done by Prof. Prigogine a half-century earlier and later "fluctuation theories" proposed by others apparently quantified the likelihood that under very special conditions a particular environment might "force-feed" the concentration of energy to overcome entropy and lead to new forms of life that might self-replicate. These had made possible Prof. England's suppositions and his computer simulations, as noted above.

Nancy Wolchover notes that the implications for "real life" computer simulations remain speculative. She also reports that "many biophysicists think something like what England is suggesting may well be at least part of life's story."[96] But whether he identifies the most crucial step depends on identifying "the essence of life," and opinions differ.

Furthermore, the conditions on earth long ago or inside a cell cannot be predicted from initial scientific principles, so to what extent can simplified computer simulations imitate reality? Yet "the networks seemed to become fine-tuned to the landscape . . . to achieve rare states of vigorous chemical activity and extreme forcing four times more often than would be expected. And when they happened, they happened dramatically."[97] Experts suggested simulations that might more closely replicate what could have been true of early tidal pools and volcanic vents, though this requires guesswork.

Others have insisted that even if such fine-tuning is possible, England's thesis is "'necessary but not sufficient' to explain life . . . because it cannot account for what many see as the true hallmark of biological systems: their information-processing capacity."[98] In other words, there are very long and large steps beyond producing simple chemical changes to what bacteria require to move toward what nourishes them and away from poisons. For that matter, reproduction goes beyond the structures allowing survival and

---

95. Wolchover, "First Support," para. 7
96. Wolchover, "First Support," para. 9.
97. Wolchover, "First Support," para. 19.
98. Wolchover, "First Support," para. 21.

what already exists. How do genes enable reproduction that additionally transmits "information" to newborns? And, beyond that, how did humans learn to communicate with each other?

The response of a Harvard chemistry professor who supervised England's undergraduate research clearly implies what I also celebrate. He acknowledged his student's capabilities and carefully defined England's "potentially interesting exercises in nonequilibrium statistical mechanics of simple abstract systems"[99] while also noting that they do not yet have anything to do with biology or the origins of life.

The *Quanta* report by Nancy Wolchover I summarize adds, "Even if England is on the right track about the physics, biologists want more particulars" that would include also a theory how primitive protocells could have evolved "into the first living cells, and how the genetic code arose." "England completely agrees that his findings are mute on such topics."[100] To the basic questions just mentioned, he has admitted that the present evidence is so fragmentary that we are left with "a fraught mess."

Her brief report on Jeremy England's research includes a quotation from Rahul Sarpeshkar, a professor of engineering, physics, and microbiology at Dartmouth University who awaits "concrete physical evidence of these abstract constructs" from experiments "perhaps using biologically relevant chemicals and energy sources such as glucose."[101] She also cites those researchers who acknowledged that England's thesis was "necessary but not sufficient" until further research somehow accounts for the information-processing capacity of life.

Her last brief paragraph returns to Prof. Sarpeshkar: "What Jeremy is showing is that as long as you can harvest energy from your environment, order will spontaneously arise and self-tune.... Living things have gone on to do a lot more than England and Horowitz's chemical reaction network does.... But this is about how did life first arise, perhaps—how do you get order from nothing."[102]

I add that this last paragraph ends with an ultimate philosophical and human question. I have summarized so much of Wolchover's brief report of Prof. England's thesis and simulations so that I can end this chapter by returning to the thesis stated at its beginning to summarize Prof. Prigogine's history of Western science that is the focus of this chapter.

---

99. Wolchover, "First Support," para. 24.
100. Wolchover, "First Support," para. 24.
101. Wolchover, "First Support," para. 21.
102. Wolchover, "First Support," para. 26.

Prof. Prigogine's book recounts the long history of Greco-Roman interpretations that only partly avoided the deterministic implications of their idolatrous interpretations by adopting the arbitrary swerves that Epicurus had accepted or by assuming a logic of causes and events guaranteeing a long sequence of orderings and dis-orderings that necessarily led to endless cosmic eras.

I began this chapter with the observation that Abraham would have known and likely witnessed the New Year's Festivals that had for centuries reenacted essentially the same sequence of creation told in Gen 1. Though the Genesis account canonized many centuries after his death very differently interpreted this sequence, and though our account of the *Enuma Elish* dates from the clay tablets much later discovered in Nineveh, I assume that the sequence reported in Gen 1 represented the Ancient Near Eastern "science" of that long era.

CHAPTER 11

The Need to Question Our Readings of Canonic Texts

In the first nine chapters, I meditated on what I learned from elders whose rural lives had remained in touch with the patterns and attitudes of premodern cultures whose simple tools had amplified the strength of their hands and arms. The legs of horses and oxen had pulled the plows and harrows that they guided to till the soil and the wagons that brought the produce of the fields to their *Hofs* and markets.

Those meditations led me to their work on the soil, with the aid of living creatures, to receive their "daily bread," to share with each other their work and their needs, and to nurture each other's *Halig*, their wholeness and holiness. Their worldviews were shaped by living *presences* because they most intently interacted with living concrete plants, animals, and other humans. In the words of Martin Buber, it was an "I-Thou" world.[1]

The rhetoric of their daily speech, of the revelatory stories told by gifted storytellers, singers, poets, sages, and prophets, like the rhetoric of their deepest meditations, was mythopoetic, as I have described and mostly, so far, imitated. It was also the rhetoric of all canonic sacred texts. Even the four basic elements (air, water, fire, and earth) of the ancient world were presences.

Of course, sand, dirt, rocks, insects, unwanted vegetation in gardens, too much water in fields, too hot or cold air, and unruly fire could be objectified as objectionable—and as if mere *its* to be managed or obliterated. It had always been possible to twist fibers into cloth or nets or ropes and to shatter and to shape rocks into primitive cutting instruments. Trees could become lumber to build shelters and furniture or slimmed into shafts for

---

1. Buber, *I and Thou*, vii–ix.

arrows and spears. In time fire, air, and coal could focus enough heat on metals to shape more sophisticated tools and weapons.

Other living creatures and even humans could be objectified and treated as *its* to be eaten or abused or obliterated rather than as honored *Thous* or, if transhuman, revered or feared divinities. But, more significantly, earth was the living *source* and *nourisher* of their bodies, fluids were the *blood* and air the *breath* of life. Fire was the *essence* of the mind and soul that imaged divinity. As sages, poets, singers, and storytellers knew, to speak truthfully of their experienced world required the poetic rhetoric of images, metaphors, and stories (*mythos*). Indeed, the neutral Greek noun *to poiēma* defines *anything made or done*: 1. *a work, piece of workmanship.* 2. *a poetical work, poem.* 3. *an act, deed.*[2] To emphasize its living, concrete context, I add that from its root *poiē*, the adjective, *poiēros*, was formed: *grassy*.

While meditating about growing up, I realized that during the preceding generation or two my elders had become increasingly aware of technological improvements. The invention of stationery steam-powered threshing machines and internal combustion engines powering self-moving wagons (trucks), automobiles, and tractors were far more powerful than oxen and horses and they gladly purchased them to increase their efficiency. Early modern technocracy so profoundly magnified the force of *it-ness* that they began to lose aspects of their earlier awareness of the life of premodern and of biblical peoples.

In earlier chapters I traced the three levels of abstraction that subtly shifted what had been a concrete living world of subjects, each of whom had a *presence* interacting with other *presences*, and creating complex secondary societies whose institutionalized patterns of behavior functioned like the quasi-*presences* of natural powers and of gods or goddesses, angels or demons. Especially in chapter 10, I traced the history of a long process that led to "laws" of nature and to ideologized sets of rationally systematized axioms, hypotheses, or principles that could be organized into sciences and ideologies from which presumed certainties could be deduced.

Also in chapter 10, I distinguished the mixed consequences of technological progress and among what the various sciences continued to clarify about the generalized rules of the workings of nature, of human nature, and of the institutions established by more or less concrete primary or secondary societies. We now must diligently discern the claimed certainties that conclude the logically organized systematics of ideologists. That ideologists, often insisting they voice "the truth, the whole truth, and nothing but the truth," must regularly debate with the ideologists of complementary and

---

2. Liddell and Scott, *Greek-English Lexicon*, 508.

contradictory ideologies suggests that each, at best, may be relevant to a part of the whole of "what-is."

I hope that chapter 10 truthfully points to the resolution of the "war" that early modern science exacerbated between *faith* and *science*. If I have rightly interpreted Prof. Prigogine's *The End of Certainty*, scientists are obligated to continue to seek to understand what can be discovered to be true about the history of the evolution of life from the evidence revealed by the amazing tools that technology has assembled. His book has shown me that a long history of attempts to argue that concrete, conscious, purposeful *life* has evolved "bottom-up" from the accidental collisions and aggregations of unconscious bits of material elements have, so far, failed. It also seems to me that the late and postmodern physical sciences he reports acknowledges that they, too, like the life sciences, the social sciences, and the humanities, are communal enterprises that seek endless reproof and correction. This chapter goes beyond tracing some of the negative consequences that temper our appreciation for the undoubted advantages brought by progressive civilizations whose sciences and technological innovations have brought enlightenment, improved healthcare, prosperity, and even luxuries and entertainments for many of us. It challenges many of us to relearn how to read canonic texts.

I agree that even if I admit that I think early fundamentalists were right to reject what I have stipulated to be a reductionist "bottom-up" version of evolution, I also admit that remaining fideists have the right to distrust my assumption that theistic versions of evolution can be faithful living options.

In this chapter I summarize Hans Frei's prophetic *Eclipse of Biblical Narrative: A Study in Eighteenth and Nineteenth Century Hermeneutics*. This study shows that how the Bible was read and interpreted during these two centuries dramatically changed. I add illustrations how I think some of my own *Korn* elders and their heirs have become "modernists" while actively intending to resist the spirits of our era.

PROF. HANS FREI'S PROPHETIC CALL TO RETURN TO THE TRADITIONAL READING OF BIBLICAL NARRATIVES

Many biblical texts taught Hebrews and Christians to shape their beliefs about God and their relationships to other humans and to their ecologies. The Psalms became the first source of the church's chanted and sung expressions of praise, confessions, laments, and petitions. The histories that narrated the Creator's accompaniment of the heirs of Adam and Eve from Eden frequently included other literary genres.

Prof. Frei has explained that biblical narratives were strongly read as *realistic* from the Apostolic Age and, though Western Christendom "had never wholly lost"[3] this, it was again emphasized during the Renaissance and Reformation. Preachers and theologians, like Augustine, "had envisioned the real world as formed by the sequence told by the biblical stories."[4] To be read as realistic means that it was about actual history. Prof. Frei introduces his interpretation of such readings by describing their three major elements.

The First Element

To read biblical narratives *literally* assumes that they describe actual historical circumstances. However, that a passage makes best sense at a literal level does not mean "that it is a reliable historic report."[5] What is needed are examples of actual or apparent conflicting accounts of the same event as well as actual revisions to the canonic laws summarized as *Mosaic* on Mt. Sinai. More significant are the continuing debates among biblical writers how to interpret the *meaning* of significant events.

Neither premodern theistic readers nor polytheistic readers thought that these disagreements diminished the authority or truthfulness of their respective canonic texts. The Judaeo-Christian Testaments report both what false prophets and orthodox prophets initiated and interpreted and what those wrestling faithfully with God and each other debated.

In principle, neither the so-called wars between believers and skeptics, between science or faith, or between the humanities and natural sciences that Prof. Prigogine reported would have been debated in sacred texts in proverbial cultures. Earlier elders and even my *Korn* elders still basically knew how to read canonic texts. The eighteenth- and nineteenth-century hermeneutical shifts that Prof. Frei detected reveal the modernistic consequences of recent technological developments that brought much undeniably good news along with equally undeniable bad news. I agree that many of my immediate elders were often belatedly compromising their older biblical worldview because they were later "catching up" with the eighteenth- and nineteenth-century shifts reported by Prof. Frei.

3. Frei, *Narrative*, 1.
4. Frei, *Narrative*, 1.
5. Frei, *Narrative*, 2.

The Second Element

The "real historical world" being interpreted by biblical readers meant that they expected to be able to fit stories together. To be a single story required that there be a *sequence* of stories and literary theorists show that *figuration* was required. This was both a literary and a historical procedure. Stories had to figure or typify each other to be fulfilled in later stories, even if there were differences between them, and to point to contrasting, complementary *meanings*.

These stories included more than use of objects, like tools used to till the soil. They concentrated on *presences* interacting with each other to build the ethos and institutions of their cultures. And, as in descriptions of *Korn*'s work, mutual aid, and mutual nurture (chapters 5, 6, and 7 above), all these ascending levels of interwoven fulfillments necessarily included relationships and meanings that could only mythopoetically be expressed. Biblical narrators, prophets, poets, sages, scribes, and Jesus constantly and necessarily used images, metaphors, and parables that point to truths and attitudes that could only be evoked by what stimulates one's apprehension.

An original connotation of *literal* included a freedom that allowed a hearer to *hear* what a speaker or text intended to convey, not just a limitation to what was the most obvious fact or reference. *Figuration* or *typology* "was a natural extension of literal interpretation."[6] It was *literalism* applied also to the entire sequence of stories woven into a single history with a coherent pattern of meaning. Prophecies and their fulfillment, passages complementing or challenging other passages, or testaments that fulfill an earlier one can be added to a coherently expanding larger story.

The larger story was traced by written or spoken *Ur* Testaments, Old Testaments, and New Testaments, to say nothing of apocryphal, pseudepigraphic, or traditional epics appearing in earlier or later eras. Those reading John's presentation of the discussion Pilate initiated with Jesus recognize that not all pilgrims in a long-evolving kingdom of heaven could have agreed that these testaments somehow told a single story.[7] Within each era of this story, there were those who protested that the "fulfillments" being proclaimed had betrayed earlier convictions. Though I believe that my reinterpretations of some significant Romans passages reinforce the reinterpretations of twentieth-century Paul scholars, some will disagree and I have to be willing to repent and correct what I may have misinterpreted.

---

6. Frei, *Narrative*, 2.
7. John 18:28—19:16.

The Third Element

Since this one story "was indeed the one and only real world, it must in principle embrace the experience of any present age and reader."[8] Readers who belong to this faith tradition are asked to figure themselves into its story and meaning. Each also becomes a type with a disposition, a pattern of actions and passions that shapes the lives of individuals and an era's events as figures of the storied world.

"In addition, *figuration* made sense of the general extra-biblical structure of human experience, and of one's own experience, as well as of general concepts of good and evil drawn from experience." These events and meanings must be "ranged figurally into the smaller as well as into the overarching story. Biblical interpretation became an imperative need, but its direction was that of incorporating extra-biblical thought, experience, and reality into the one real world detailed and made accessible by the biblical story—not the reverse."[9]

In his preface, Hans Frei lists the three sources that had most influenced his thoughts about interpreting important texts. The first had been Erich Auerbach's classic *Mimesis: The Representation of Reality in Western Literature*.[10] When Auerbach compared the epics of Homer to the Old Testament narratives, he insisted that these radically differed. Homer sought to make his readers forget their reality so that they could try to relive themselves into the heroic age he pictured. Somehow everything in their decayed post-heroic age had to mimic the old divine plan.[11]

When I describe Homer and Hesiod, I will agree that their worldview had been shaped into long cycles of an ordering of the cosmos that, after a golden heroic age, inevitably reversed into its disordering until all things and processes returned to the soupy immortal chaos that could eventually and eternally repeat long cycles.

Hans Frei insisted that the Old Testament writers had a strikingly different vision. Continuing disagreements, later oppression by enemies and even exiles, had to be fitted into their Creator's progressive grand plan. "In the process of interpretation, the story itself constantly adapted to new situations and ways of thinking, underwent ceaseless revision, but in steadily

---

8. Frei, *Narrative*, 3.
9. Frei, *Narrative*, 3.
10. Auerbach, *Mimesis*.
11. Frei, *Narrative*, 3.

PROF. FREI'S ANALYSIS OF A MAJOR MODERN SHIFT IN READING BIBLICAL NARRATIVES

Seventeenth-century radical interpreters had begun to give up the biblical vision, and, in the eighteenth century, the "outlook it represented broke down with increasing rapidity."[13] Even devout conservative Christian interpreters "signal a subtle transformation" by concentrating on typology "to locate the events of their day vis-à-vis the narrative framework of biblical story and history, and to locate by means of biblical sayings the present stage of the actual events we experience and predict future stages as well as the end of actual history."[14]

This new kind of prophecy sought also to interpret "mysterious signs and number schemes" from biblical texts to verify what had not yet come to pass. This concentration on present events as hidden *signs* verifying what would happen in fact detached

> the "real" historical world from its biblical description. The real events of history constitute an autonomous temporal framework of their own under God's providential design. Instead of rendering them accessible, the narratives heretofore indispensable as means of access to the events, now simply verify them, thus affirming their autonomy and the fact that they are in principle accessible through any kind of description that can manage to be accurate either predictively or after the event. It simply happens that again under God's providence, it is the Bible that contains the accurate descriptions. There is now a logical distinction and a reflective distance between the stories and the 'reality' they depict. The depicted biblical world and the real historical world began to be separated at once in thought and in sensibility, no matter whether the depiction was thought to agree with reality . . . or disagree with it.[15]

In other words, instead of fitting the present actions of the God-with-us into the evolving God story that includes our story, eighteenth-century interpreters sought hidden clues in the biblical narrative to predict the end

---

12. Frei, *Narrative*, 3–4.
13. Frei, *Narrative*, 4.
14. Frei, *Narrative*, 4.
15. Frei, *Narrative*, 4–5.

THE NEED TO QUESTION OUR READINGS 213

of this era and to depict a world to come. This called attention to the Bible account as *accurate* so that they could confidently depict the not-yet they hoped for. In principle, human attempts to understand what is happening to them "elevates" them from their contexts so that they can obtain an objective and even "divine" point of view. Instead of fitting their experiences into the *realistically* evolving biblical story, they were trying to fit the biblical story within a worldview ideally expressing their hope of heaven.

In addition to a heightened stress on the Bible's accuracy, eighteenth-century interpreters sought to bridge the gap between the apostolic grasp of reality and their eighteenth-century sense of reality by asking how their quest for meaning could be found in the Bible. Instead of reading it to discover their place in its meaningful story, they were again starting with themselves. Thus, Prof. Conyers Middleton then argued that "it didn't matter whether Gen 1–3 was allegory or fact, since its meaning was the same in either case."[16] God created the world, humans had fallen, and the biblical story revealed the saving truth even if its story wasn't entirely factual.

This reversal was one sign of the breakdown of the older literal-realistic interpretation. Another was the collapse of its figural-typological applications. "Figural interpretation became discredited both as a literary device and as a historical argument."[17] As a logical literary device, figurations offended against the new assumption that a propositional statement has only one meaning. "As a historical argument . . . it strained credulity beyond the breaking point."[18] This meant that sayings and events in a past era could not be predictions of persons or events in a future era.

> Furthermore, figural reading was no longer a persuasive instrument for unifying the canon. Literal reading came increasingly to mean . . . grammatical and lexical exactness in estimating what the original sense of a text was to its original audience, and the coincidence of the description with how the facts really occurred. Realistic reading came in effect to be identical with the latter; it consisted of matching the written description against the reconstruction of the probable historical sequence to which it referred. Increasingly, historical-critical reading became the heir of the older type of realistic reading . . . [but was no longer] concerned with the unity of the canon.[19]

---

16. Middleton, "Allegorical and Literal Interpretation," 131. Cited in Frei, *Narrative*, 5.
17. Frei, *Narrative*, 6.
18. Frei, *Narrative*, 6.
19. Frei, *Narrative*, 7.

In the long quotation above, Prof. Frei implied that instead of reading narrative biblical passages to learn how to interpret them realistically, as in the past, they were now reading its narratives to find what verified their own interpretation of what marked its consistency. He noted that this now made it important to stress that the canonic narratives were entirely accurate.

The heirs to earlier realistic readings were historical criticism and biblical theology. But these "were different enterprises and made for decidedly strained company."[20]

ACCIDENTAL, BUT REVELATORY, CONNECTIONS TO MY *KORN* HERITAGE

It now ironically amuses me that it is appropriate to tell a story that illustrates one of the complex consequences of cultural shifts like the one researched by Prof. Frei. After finishing the 1961–1962 school year at Corn Bible Academy teaching three English classes, I was asked to move to Hillsboro, Kansas, so that I could teach some sections of freshman English courses and to do one of the duties of a departing staff member.

Fortunately, I was able to rent a modest basement apartment in a home across the street of the Hillsboro City Park that bordered the Tabor College campus. Its owner was a retired Nebraska farmer. One of his two daughters was married to the third son of my father's sister Martha whose *Korn* husband had agreed that HR could live with them to attend Tabor. His other daughter, who was also intelligent and charming, was married to a wonderfully creative professor at Tabor whom I had met on my seven-month westward journey home from Saigon and whom I had visited while passing through Switzerland. (An aside to readers: I add these details to convince you of the benefits of an ethnic heritage.)

Clarence Hiebert had invited me to accompany him to a seminar that he attended weekly that met with Karl Barth to discuss theological issues— in English. Though I remember none of the topics discussed that evening, I was captivated by Barth's *presence* and have marveled that I had met one of the important twentieth-century shapers of Christian theology. I have also told this story in this chapter because in the preface of the book Prof. Frei wrote that I am here citing, he specifically credits Karl Barth, along with Erich Auerbach and the English philosopher Gilbert Ryle as the three "authors who have been particularly influential on my thought."[21]

---

20. Frei, *Narrative*, 8.
21. Frei, *Narrative*, vii.

While teaching at Tabor College, I rented a basement apartment from a retired Nebraska farmer who was the father-in-law of the Clarence Hiebert mentioned above. One afternoon I sat together with this farmer in his backyard, and he told me his interpretation of the beginnings of history. I was astounded that his story expressed so many of the ideas and patterns reflected in archaic mythic lore and that it had somehow reached rural Nebraska.

Since remembering and writing about Elder H. H. Flaming mentoring my father while wandering with him on late night walks, I wondered whether he had learned from someone like him about ancient interpretations of the human condition. But later, while still in Hillsboro, I thought it also likely that intelligent and thoughtful people aware of the patterns of natural powers, of the land, and of the *presences* also of plant and animal life forms might recover the Ur patterns of thought of primitive peoples.

I suppose that many are becoming so tired of hearing the concerns of present prophets asking us to continue wrestling with racial, sexual, gender, ecological, political, and other prejudices and presumptions that we suspect that all publicized wrestling matches are, like game shows, rigged to keep us expensively entertained instead of leading to satisfying solutions. I ask readers to accept (and even forgive) what may be my presumptive request that they listen to Hans Frei who discerns that even Christians protesting modernisms have so succumbed to the spirit of this era that they are losing the ability to hear what earlier seekers heard when listening to canonic texts.

Despite occasional doubts and a few wearying setbacks, my continued wrestling is increasingly motivated by the joy mysteriously experienced also by my elders who expressed with *Gottesfurcht* their awe that an ultimately creative *Presence* accompanied their pilgrimages.

There is a lurking paralysis that freezes those who doubt their ability to choose the most important evils, or the strength to defeat apparently stronger evildoers, or to ask others to enter with them into truly dangerous wrestling arenas. But like my *Korn* elders, I had been freed from the fear of being responsible for the consequences of battles with natural demonic forces. My *Korn* elders used *Gelassenheit* to point to the freedom to "let go and let God."

I ask others to pilgrimage with me because, though confident that I (and they) can recognize evil deeds and heresies, neither I nor they can judge the *hearts* of those who commit them or even our own hearts. I understand Rom 2:16 to say that only God can do that.

PROF. FREI DEFINES HIS THESIS AND HIS QUEST TO CLARIFY AND RECOVER BIBLICAL REALISM

Of course, the Bible's unity and reliability continued to be profoundly important to retain its authority. Prof. Frei insists that his focus is not primarily about historical criticism of the Bible and its history. Though he will frequently deal with that important topic, proper interpretation includes more than "the single meaning of a grammatically and logically sound propositional statement."[22] Indeed, all commentators agreed that this "something more" included "ideational meaning or religious significance."[23] The rest of his book concentrates on one segment of interpretation and, in particular, on "the eighteenth- and early nineteenth-century discussion about the proper rules and principles to guide interpretation of the history-like stories of the Old and New Testaments."[24] Even within those parameters, he concentrated "on how the older realistic and figural approaches to these stories broke down."[25]

The last half of his introductory chapter carefully describes the focus of his research, describes the unfortunate consequences of the shift he reports, and explains his conclusion that fundamentalist and evangelical Christians who vigorously fought aspects of this shift significantly succumbed to it.

I shorten a thesis that he somewhat discursively qualifies because of the complexity of its implications.

> A realistic or history-like (though not necessarily historical) element is a feature, as obvious as it is important, of many of the biblical narratives that went into the making of Christian belief. . . . But since the precritical analytical or interpretive procedure for isolating it had irretrievably broken down . . . the specifically realistic characteristic, though acknowledged by all hands to be there, finally came to be denied for lack of a "method" to isolate it. And this despite the common agreement that the specific feature was there![26]

Despite "a strong resurgence of serious realistic literature and criticism" in the eighteenth and early nineteenth centuries[27] in England,

---

22. Frei, *Narrative*, 9.
23. Frei, *Narrative*, 10.
24. Frei, *Narrative*, 10.
25. Frei, *Narrative*, 10.
26. Frei, *Narrative*, 10, 16.
27. Frei, *Narrative*, 16.

in effect, the realistic or history-like quality of biblical narratives, acknowledged by all, instead of being examined for the bearing it had in its own right on meaning and interpretation was immediately transposed into the quite different issue of whether or not the realistic narrative was historical.[28]

DOES A NARRATIVE THAT IS HISTORY-LIKE HAVE TO BE HISTORICALLY ACCURATE?

Though it is relatively easy to list the characteristics of realistic narratives, interpreters have been unable to agree which narratives were historical. The preceding quotations highlight the paradox. Prof. Frei noted that Erich Auerbach's masterful analysis of this genre of literature includes a conclusion that "in Western literature . . . [its] three historical high points" were the *Bible*, Dante's *Divine Comedy*,[29] and nineteenth-century novels.[30] Yet, large parts of the Bible are not historical narratives. Dante wrote allegorically and novels are fictional. Prof. Frei stressed that

> biblical commentators again and again emphasized the simplicity of style, the lifelikeness of depiction, the lack of artificiality or heroic elevation in theme in such stories as the first three chapters of Genesis, the story of Abraham's willingness to sacrifice Isaac, and the synoptic gospels.[31]

Prof. Frei also noted that earlier biblical interpreters assumed that "the realistic feature had naturally been identified with the literal sense which in turn was automatically identical with reference to historical truth."[32] But after the early modern era, "the 'literal sense' of the stories [was] logically subordinated to probable and language-neutral historical veracity."[33]

And then one would have had to allow the (new) literal sense to stand as the meaning, even if one believed that the story does not refer historically. But commentators,

> especially those influenced by historical criticism, virtually to a man failed to understand what they had seen when they had

28. Frei, *Narrative*, 16.
29. Dante, *Divine Comedy*.
30. Frei, *Narrative*, 15.
31. Frei, *Narrative*, 10.
32. Frei, *Narrative*, 11.
33. Frei, *Narrative*, 11.

recognized the realistic character of biblical narratives, because every time they acknowledged it they thought this was identical with affirming not only the history-likeness but also a degree of historical likelihood of the stories. Those who wanted to affirm their historical factuality used the realistic character of history-likeness as evidence in favor of this claim, while those who denied the factuality also finally denied that the history-likeness was a cutting feature—thus in effect denying that they had seen what they had seen because (once again) they thought history-likeness identical with at least potentially true history.[34]

After typing this long quotation, I started a next paragraph with "In other words" and then wondered how to say it clearly and simply. When I began to wonder how I could have explained it to my *Korn* elders had they asked me to do so, I realized I might need more words than he had used to convince them that so paradoxical a shift could have sneaked by them unnoticed.

I think I could have started by admitting that I was fortunate that before becoming their Mennonite Central Committee missionary to Vietnam, I had stumbled into becoming an English major learning to distinguish different literary genres (*types* of literature) and subtle stylistic nuances. It was also fortunate that I had chosen the monastic feel of the Yale Divinity School to recover from the culture shock of Vietnam.

I had not understood why an ecumenical statesman I had met in Indonesia and an admired missionary in India had recommended that I should attend Yale Divinity School, but it had occurred to me that after three years in Vietnam I had become critical of both Bible Belt religiosity and conservative Cold War politics. Granted my wariness, attendance at a seminary approved by Mennonite Brethren might edge me into greater heresy. Since seminaries like the one at Yale had been assumed to be "liberal," perhaps my heightened wariness would there edge me in a "right" direction.

I was exposed to challenging material and I gradually discovered that those who taught wanted us to understand what the church's most able theologians had taught and to want to emulate what its saints had most faithfully incarnated. I was also hearing from them, "Remember your leaders, those who spoke the word of God to you; consider the outcome of their way of life, and imitate their faith."[35] *Remember* and *imitate*, but not blindly. Place what they taught and did in the context of the consequences of their lives and of those who heard their words and imitated their faithfulness.

---

34. Frei, *Narrative*, 10–11.
35. Heb 13:7.

"Be strengthened by grace, not by regulations" (v. 9). Like Jesus, "go to him outside the camp.... For here we have no lasting city" (vv. 13–14)—to live with gratitude and joy.[36] After graduating from seminary, it had been appropriate for me to return to *Korn* to remember and to rethink the heritage of my elders in the light of the long history of other heritages.

---

36. Heb 13:5–17.

CHAPTER 12

My Haphazard Pilgrimage Home

Pilgrimage suggests a guided and protected journey to an enduring fulfillment. Looking back while nearing the end of a long pilgrimage, I knew I had a goal—going home—but I did not know the routes I would take. That made for a haphazard journey. I also confess a lifelong presumptuous eagerness to learn and experience much, though fearing that I would often fail to cope appropriately.

I remember moments in India when I chided myself for having been an almost apathetic observer of events that had perhaps been dangerous. "Delbert," I would muse to myself, "you might as well have been sitting in your favorite chair at home doing nothing." Phrases from a song about a sentimental journey played in my mind incessantly.

I had completed a three-year commitment to help resettle refugees in a newly divided Vietnam and to aid others under the auspices of the Mennonite Central Committee, in the name of Christ. Fellow MCC volunteers had wonderfully planned and carried out the medical program that had served tribal groups from a clinic and hospital a handful of miles from Ban Me Thuot in South Vietnam's high plateau area. They had also done most of the deliveries of food, clothes, and other supplies to the poor and displaced there and in other places.

During my last two years I also directed the relief efforts of The Church World Service program in South Vietnam that channeled the donations of many Protestant Christians in the United States. I had mostly handled logistics and governmental relationships from an office in Saigon and, for Church World Service, managed some other distributions and programs from Saigon, one of which collected mostly individual Protestant families from North Vietnam to settle along a small river in the mountains north of Saigon on a road leading farther up to the resort town of Dalat. Though apparently thriving when I left in mid-August 1957, this one had been especially difficult, and I was completely worn out.

Though ready to leave but not to come home, I asked the Maersk Line agent in Saigon if I could book a passenger cabin on one of their freighters moving through Asia. Unfortunately, since the Six-Day War in that area had closed the Suez Canal about a year earlier, Maersk had decided to no longer accept tourists in the small number of cabins on many of its freighters. The agent happily called a few days later to tell me that they were making me a "guest," though requesting a hundred dollars for incidental reasons. I was alone for a month or more except when eating with the captain, first mate, and engineer of the *SS Peter Maersk*, and leisurely sailing between extended stops in Bangkok, Singapore, Jakarta, and along Sumatra. I happily watched flocks of little flying fish from its decks and intermittingly read a World War II novel about, as I remember it, not being able to "go home again." In Colombo, Ceylon (now Sri Lanka), I unloaded my Italian motor scooter, toured a bit, and found a northern port where I could take a ferry to a south Indian port and drive to Madurai.

While disembarking and unloading the Italian motor scooter I had purchased in Saigon, the captain of the *SS Peter Maersk* presented a telegram waiting for me in Colombo. It was from a young diplomatic aide from New York who, with a few others, had organized a well-educated group of Vietnamese and other English-speaking friendship circle in Saigon. She had decided to extend her return home by touring India. Her telegram was an anxious plea that I meet her when she arrived in Madurai.

FROM MADURAI TO GADWAL, ANDRA PRADESH, INDIA

The timing was right—and fortunate. The railway hotel had failed to reserve the room she had ordered. I had been sleeping on a bench the YMCA had provided me along a dusty city street. She had, for a week or so, accompanied a group of actors whose director was filming a movie in North India. He later became the husband of Gina Lolabrigida, the famous Scandinavian actress. They had strictly warned her not to visit South India without an escort.

We could find no other appropriate hotel, and I suggested taking a bus to Kodaikanal where I had a "clan cousin," married to a teacher at one of India's most elite high schools. An older brother of Adam Ewert, one of our MCC Vietnam members, also taught there, as did the daughter of an MB missionary who had returned to teach at the attached grade school where she had also roomed and boarded. She had been a student at Tabor College the two years I attended. Two other young Mennonite ladies from central Canada had also become teachers there. Our arrival was entirely unexpected, but we were warmly welcomed. "Kodai" was situated several hours up the road at a beautiful high mountain resort northwest of Madurai.

A couple of days later Margie and I bussed back to Madurai where lodging for her with a female missionary had been arranged. For a day and a night we took a canal bus-boat west until she could take an airline flight to Mysore (now Mysuru) where she had planned to attend the famous yearly Dasara Festival of Lights. Quite late in the evening, Margie awakened me. We were moored to a dock and a handful of young males were leering at us. I had been sleeping on a raised platform along the edge of the boat and chattered amiably with them until, eventually, the canal boat edged away from the dock and resumed its journey. From Mysuru she continued to fly west while I scootered north past Bangalore and reached Kurnool.

In 1957 India's highways had so little traffic that my scariest encounters happened when I absentmindedly veered to the lane which, for English and Indian road rules, was the lane used by oncoming cars and trucks and I had to veer back quickly enough to get into what for me was the *wrong* lane. I also had interesting encounters when threading my way through packs of Brahma cows filling the road. Occasionally, the pack's bull would charge at me and I had to reach out to push the cows aside to squeeze past while yelling at them and blowing my horn. Fortunately, the bulls were also sufficiently blocked that I managed to get ahead of the herd and speed ahead of the bulls who may not have been anxious to tangle with a noisy motor scooter driven by someone whose smell wasn't familiar.

I had learned that the only bridge across the Krishna River that was at the southern border of Andra Pradesh, the province within which the MB mission field was located. I had known some of these missionaries and their children who attended Tabor College. I had intended to spend a couple of weeks visiting "our field." I came to the train station in the early afternoon and asked an agent when a passenger train that could also accept my scooter would come so I could take a relatively short trip to Gadwal, where the most southern mission compound was located. The agent told me that the next passenger train would get me to Gadwal after midnight. The missionary there would have known of my father but had probably never heard of me. Even if I could find him, I should not startle him in the middle of the night.

"Is there any other way I could get across this river?" He suggested that I could push the scooter across the almost mile-long railway bridge on a walking path used by locals. "What happens if a train comes?" He agreed that could be bad, and I asked when the next one would come. He replied, "Goods trains can come at any time. Only passenger trains have schedules." I was annoyed but desperate and I asked, "What would you do?" He shrugged, adding that I could try.

I pushed the scooter up an embankment to the tracks and discovered that the path for peasant and other local hikers lay between the narrow-gauge rails used by some trains and the standard-gauge tracks for large trains. It consisted of approximately foot-wide strips of corrugated metal roofing whose valleys were too narrow to cradle my scooter tires, which were not broad enough to safely span two ridges. I would have to walk carefully along the edges of the ties that extended a bit beyond the right standard-gauge track.

This meant that my scooter tilted toward me across two rails. The small suitcase attached to a rack above the rear wheel of the scooter also had roped to it my tightly rolled-up sleeping pad and its thin insulating "mattress." The scooter's unbalanced angle and weight quickly tired me and I could not use the opposite side of the ties to vary the strain on my muscles since any stumble might tumble me through unshielded electric wires servicing villages and towns beyond this large river.

I moved forward as quickly as I could but realized that it might be safer to dare driving the scooter on that narrow path. Unfortunately, its wheels dangerously lurched me over the roofing's ridges and I went back to a long tedious trudge. When a peasant woman had caught up with me began speaking, I first ignored what I could not understand. When she urgently tugged on my shirt, I looked back to see an oncoming train.

I had become aware of a small platform cantilevered from the trestles some distance ahead, and we raced for it. A man already waiting on it helped me wrestle the scooter onto the platform with perhaps no more than a minute or two to spare, and the train rattled past. I was now fairly sure of having enough time to get to the other side before another train came. On the other side of the bridge, there was a narrow dirt path along the steeply sloping embankment on which I had to drive the scooter. That also was dangerous and tiring.

Eventually, I reached a dirt road that crossed the train tracks. A bus full of passengers was parked along the side of the road and I shut off the scooter's motor to get advice from the faces in an open window. A young man with an adequate command of English came to the window, and I asked how I could find my way to Gadwal. The road I was on would take me to a town about fifty miles north, from which I could turn onto another road angling south and a bit east about sixty miles to Gadwal.

I told him that I did not have enough petrol to drive so far north. After a lengthy discussion he returned to tell me that I could drive a few miles north to Ieej, turn right through the village and cross a creek. Though there was no road, I would find the tracks of Jeeps and other vehicles to follow through a longish stretch of wilderness until I came to a road that led south to Gadwal. Apparently, that was my best option. The narrow lane leading to Ieej led through deep mud puddles, and a Jeep was parked at the second one. Though the two men in it had some kind of "official" duties, their English was so poor that I learned almost nothing. They did stress that I should stay in the village that night and not go past it until the morning. I should have heeded that, but they could not explain their reasons. Children yelled while chasing me, and men staring at me from doorways made me so uneasy that I decided to keep driving.

By then the sun had set and sometimes I had to move from side to side to find tracks to follow. For a while I amused myself calculating the odds that I was choosing the right trail when the one I was on diverged into two. It finally became apparent that at least most of these were detours through rough stretches. It had recently rained and I encountered two wide patches of water. Much of the time I had to use the scooter's lower gears, and, after having had to switch to the tiny auxiliary gas tank, I more carefully tried to avoid wasting my meager supply.

When I came to the second "lake" in front of me, I turned off the engine and stared at it until I became aware that three young men were standing behind me. They were strangely and scantily dressed and had long strands of what resembled costume jewelry.

I had lived long enough in southeast Asia that an appeal for advice or help might best assure my safety. I greeted them, but they did not respond. I did the only thing I could think of. I smiled a plea while gesturing at the back of my scooter. They uttered quiet "whoops" and pushed me through the water.

Having crossed it, I thanked them but remained uneasy, started the engine, and moved away from them speedily enough to discourage them from chasing me. After several miles, I noticed a mud wall on the right side of the ruts I was following. Beyond the corner of the wall was a road and I turned south on it. A hundred feet or so later I saw that the wall of the village had a gap and that more than a dozen were rising from their mats on the ground in an open space. I hoped that they would welcome me to sleep with them.

I had seen a young boy run from the group and assumed that he was fetching someone I could speak English with. He quickly reappeared with Timothy, a young man who approached me warily. I greeted him and asked if the road behind me led to Gadwal. He only agreed that it did, and I wearily wondered whether I should keep moving. I explained that I did not have enough petrol to get there and asked whether a man with oxen and a trailer could take me. He said that oxen had to rest to help with the work in the fields. I told him I would pay the driver. When he asked if I could pay three rupees (less than an American dollar), I quickly offered four.

The boy again ran off and I assumed he was looking for someone to bring me to Gadwal. I told Timothy that when someone with an oxcart comes, tell him to take me to the mission compound in Gadwal. He became animated. "What caste are you?" he asked. I had become accustomed to this question since having become sufficiently tanned and wearing clothing disheveled by long hours on the road that they assumed I was a native, and I usually said that I was an American.

Recognizing that I was near the southern edge of the MB mission field, I responded that I had no caste and was a Christian. The young man raised his hands and exclaimed, "I Christian too." When I added, "I Mennonite Christian," his arms shot up and he shouted, "I Mennonite too!" No oxcart had appeared and it was clear that he would be my host.

I learned that Timothy had been an orphan who had been allowed to grow up on the Gadwal mission compound where he had been helped to become the owner of a foot-treadle sewing machine and that he had recently brought his young bride to this village, whose tailor he had become, and to which he was sent to be an evangelist. His small home had been well-built and furnished and was close to the break in the wall where we were standing.

Timothy took me there and hesitantly asked whether I was hungry. I was, but I was sure that I would have to admit having eaten that day. If my memory can be trusted, I had been so anxious to get across the river that I had eaten only what I had found in the scooter's small compartment, some dry bread, a small chunk of stale cheese, part of a cucumber, and, I think, an orange. His wife prepared some coffee and I gladly accepted that. He took his small cot to the opening where the other residents had been sleeping on mats to escape the heat of their houses.

I wanted to decline the use of his cot because it was several inches shorter than I, but realized that I had to accept it. Villagers discreetly arranged themselves and a dog or two around me and I lay on my sleeping bag marveling at a full moon so bright that I thought I could have read a book since it was nearly midnight and it hovered above us. Though several months of difficult travel lay ahead, I knew that I was already experiencing a wonderful, unanticipated "coming home."

After breakfast, two single missionary ladies appeared in a van. One was a nurse, who once a week, conducted a clinic for ailing people in that area and the other was a Bible teacher who presented illustrated Bible stories to eager children. Though they knew of my father, who had become a loved MB conference leader, I had to relay a lot of down home "gossip" to convince them that I was not an Anglo-Indian con-man preying on their converts.

I enjoyed experiencing their graced competence and, after thanking Timothy and his spouse, my scooter was loaded in their van and I arrived in Gadwal and became the guest of the missionary. He asked how I had so oddly appeared. When I got to the events of the previous day, he visibly paled. "Those passing at night through that wilderness are often found with their necks cut."

The next day he asked me to accompany him to a wedding ceremony in another nearby village. After the ceremony, we were seated on the ground and large leaves stitched together with twigs were placed before us. Onto them curries and other spicy foods were ladled. I was still hungry after several days of driving to Gadwal, and I was happy to accept a generous second helping. When the missionary suspected that I wanted a third helping, he leaned over. "Delbert, the reason the curries are so hot is that these poor people hope the guests won't eat a lot." I have told this story to a few residents in the independent care residence in which I have retired because it helps to explain why I bring small bottles of spicy condiments to the dining room.

FROM GADWAL TO KARACHI, WEST PAKISTAN

From this southern edge of Andra Pradesh, I drove north, stopping to visit several MB missionaries in their compounds and found that in Vietnam I had experienced the dilemmas then often confronting missionaries encountering the need to indigenize maturing churches. Perhaps especially in countries that, since World War II, had been freed from colonizing Western regimes, it had become important to decolonize those whom pioneer missionaries had Christianized.

In the next two years, a mostly Hindu India was separated from a Muslim West Pakistan and to the east (the latter later became Bangladesh). Indeed, Hyderabad had become fully part of India only after expelling a Muslim ruler in 1948. When later visiting the central Sikh temple in Amritsar in Punjab, I could still view bullet holes in its walls left from the battles that *followed* liberation from England. My four-and-a-half-month tour of India and West Pakistan ended January 1, 1958.

Even Christian evangelists had to reinforce the Western superiority of the *natives* whom they exploited. India had been freed from English political domination in 1946. As one elderly and thoughtful missionary admitted, he had become very uncomfortable in the almost-mansion that an earlier missionary had been "encouraged" by a local maharajah to build as a condition for entering his area.

He had also remained deeply troubled from a recent visit by the MB Foreign Mission Board's administrator and two others, one of whom had been a former Corn pastor, when they had come announcing a bold policy for turning over the management of MB mission churches to leaders its members would select. He understood the need for that, but sweeping policy changes wouldn't fit all situations equally well and many would be greatly troubled. Since that administrator had been both bold and wise, he resigned several years later and arranged that my father should succeed him because he would complete what needed to be done, and he also had the gift of reconciling and comforting opposed partisans.

Visiting in the homes of some I had met while growing up was a welcome adventure after what was becoming the "ordinary" routine of haphazard events. An endless "vacation" was turning out to contradict the intention of the term. When the lack of ordinary rhythms and tasks becomes one's routine, experiencing an ethnic clan member's home in India became a welcome "vacation." It was also true that this anticipation of home was undergoing different forms of a "modernizing" that had been changing my *Korn* elders.

I was housed for an enjoyable week or two in Shamshabad, near Hyderabad, where a seminary and other MB institutions were centered. Nearly four decades later, in 1997, I lived there in a guest bungalow while my wife, Marjorie J. Gerbrandt, MD, for a month was a visiting doctor living in Jadcherla where a missionary doctor had founded a hospital. Our son, John, then an MCC volunteer serving in Bangladesh, met us and we also attended a Mennonite World Conference in Calcutta (Kolkatha).

From there, John, Marj, and I visited Saigon and toured major sites at Angkor Wat in Cambodia. Marj and I also attended a fiftieth anniversary celebration of the Mennonite Central Committee and Church World Service programs in Vietnam in 2004. A large banquet in Hanoi, which I could now enter for the first time, featured an address by a vice president of a reunified Vietnam.

In late fall 1957, I toured from Shamshabad north to Siliguri where I parked the Lambretta and was driven to Darjeeling to meet three young lady teachers and the retired piano teacher from Reedley whom a different "Marjie" and I had met in Kodaikanal. They had invited me to accompany them on a trek to view Mt. Kanchenjunga. On a walk to the grand market so that I could buy a warm shirt, we met Tenzing Norkay walking past us and chatted briefly with him. He was the famous Sherpa guide who, with Sir Edmund Hillary, had been the first to climb Mt. Everest. I do not know how often Mt. Kanchenjunga has been climbed, and my source, published almost fifty years ago, listed only a single ascent by an English expedition led by Charles Evans that stopped a few yards short of its summit in deference to the scruples of Sikkimese authorities.

From Darjeeling, we were driven north along the Nepal border trail that led east for thirty-five miles over three or more ridges that, if my memory holds, began at about twelve thousand feet and, after several longer ascents than the following descents, led to a vantage point allowing an unencumbered view of Kangchenjunga. Virtually its entire glacial whiteness rose from its base many thousands of feet below us. The highest of its peaks towered to just over 28,200 feet.

It is the third highest mountain in the world, and since it does not, like Everest, rise from the long High Himalayan Ridge, it is one of the largest mountains in the world. I have read that an almost equally massive volcanic mountain rises from a trench in the southwest Pacific Ocean, but its crest peaks a thousand or so feet below the surface of that ocean. This mountain's *presence* can perhaps be best appreciated when comparing it to Mt. Kilimanjaro in Africa and Mt. Denali in Alaska that are almost nine and eight thousand feet lower. To more accurately compare these three, one would need to know the level of the plains from which they rise.

I was so deeply affected by its massive frigid glare that I have never been tempted to prove my virility, courage, and determination over so great a death threat. What would that have proved? But I wondered if such climbs could become an addiction. After all, a few years after such a triumph, I might only need again to prove that I hadn't degenerated.

I had become convinced that the disciplines and attitudes I learned in *Korn* were helping me to recover from the culture shock I experienced in Vietnam. These meditations about coming home, again, is partly motivated by my conviction that future generations need to recapitulate, in part and probably differently, what my elders had modeled and taught me. I hope that many who read it will think how to model and to make it possible for our postmodern heirs to reexperience what I and many of my peers had inherited.

After returning to Siliguri, I retrieved my scooter and visited wonderful Indian cultural and religious sites like the Taj Mahal, Buddha's birthplace, temples, and museums. The day I arrived in Delhi the MCC director and his wife probably reluctantly agreed that I could stay with them though they were that evening expecting to host the Church World Service director with his wife and two preschool boys, who were driving from their home in Karachi. He had formerly been a MCC volunteer with significant foreign experience.

We waited for them. Perhaps around nine p.m., the phone rang and the Church World Service director's wife tremulously told us that they were in a village hospital about fifty miles north of Delhi, that her husband was the most seriously injured, and that they needed to be helped. The three of us arrived an hour or so before midnight. They were in a large, very bare, stand-alone room being attended by, I think, a night watchman.

The Delhi director and his wife had, within the year, lost their eight-year-old daughter to an illness and were quite shaken, and they let me try to cope. We dismissed the night watchman. The husband was in bad shape and would need hospitalization in Delhi. I convinced the couple I had driven with to take the slightly injured boys to Delhi for the night, while I tended their parents and they should return the next morning prepared to transfer all of us to Delhi. I spent that night moving between the wounded couple. She had deep cuts on her neck and face, and the hospital's doctors had ably sewn her cut and bandaged her, but he needed to be watched and she needed to be constantly reassured.

Specialists in a large Delhi hospital made adjustments and, in less than a week, I told them I would drive north to Amritsar, turn west to Lahore, West Pakistan, and then south to Karachi and continue to help them in their own home. I don't remember Christmas, but, by January 1, he was able to drive me to the port and I joined about four hundred oil field workers, Muslims on pilgrimage to Mecca, and others traveling deck class on a British-India freighter which, on the upper decks, also had a large number of berths for passengers. My original haphazard plan had been to drive farther north and cross the Kyber Pass into and across Iran. Winter had come and, in those years, it might always have been too dangerous.

Most all the deck-class passengers brought their own food supplies, including live chickens to be butchered and cooked on charcoal pots. I purchased lower-class passenger meals. The only other deck-class white male was a young Frenchman with a very young infant. A couple spotted them from an upper deck and offered to take the infant up to their room. The father soon became ill and was taken to the ship's infirmary. I had loaned him twenty dollars for his trip to Beirut. He was sending his wife there from South Africa when their effort to settle failed. Weeks later, I found him in Beirut and was repaid.

TO COME HOME AGAIN TO *KORN*

To help the heirs of the still premodern elders who stoutly resisted "modernist heresies" to understand that many of *them* had begun to succumb to the "spirit of our modern age," I suggest that we think about what they were experiencing. They confronted the consequences of many thousands of years during which primitive hunters and gatherers learned to cope with the natural forces of deserts, forests, and savannas and, beyond "gardens of Eden," learning to cultivate the plants, seeds, and fruits of their gardens and fields.

Having progressed to the primary and secondary social groupings that made significant cultures and large civilizations possible, they also confronted the "principalities and powers" that ruled the institutions that enhanced their opportunities while, too often, subordinating them to the tyranny of tyrants. To escape what oppressed them and to enhance their pleasures, some did succumb to addictions. It is also true that sages and saints and those with ordinary common sense were gifted with versions of *Gottesfurcht* and *Gelassenheit*.

Prof. Prigogine has clearly shown that for more than two thousand years the Western world has wrestled with "sciences" implying that if the natural forces that govern nature are rational, then all is determined to be what must be. We have also been told that if the cosmos has been shaped by the accidents of arbitrary chance, then entropy and chaos is endemic. And, since Abraham, a Creator who accompanies his children has offered a narrow but radical path to a fulfilled kingdom of God.

Recently, Dr. Prigogine and other scientists have been suggesting a "new physics" with a "narrow path" between determinism and chaos.[1] In Homer's *Odyssey*, the Greco-Roman world had learned that "between Scylla and Charybdis" symbolized narrow passages between equally ominous disasters. The ship-wrecked Odysseus had to pass between a sea monster and a vortex.

My *Korn* elders resisted Scylla, that I here identify with deterministic itness, the immortal and irresistible sea-monster with six heads with three rows of teeth in each head. She normally grabbed and ate fish but could also scoop up and eat six sailors at a time passing by her on a ship beneath her cage. They could not accept a "bottom-up" version of evolution that said their very distant forebears had come out of the ocean to shed their scales for skin. Perhaps I could not have convinced many of them that scientific theories would continue to evolve, but I do expect many of their heirs to

---

1. Prigogine, *End of Certainty*, 187.

acknowledge that the consequences of the expanding technologies that science makes possible are wonderful gifts that might suck us into dangerous vortexes, which I identify with the endless consequences of chaotic options.

My elders succumbed partially but dangerously into Charybdis, the vortex opposite Scylla in the narrow channel through which Odysseus had to pass after having been cast into the sea while trying for twenty years to return home. He climbed into a tree growing above Charybdis until able to drop into the sea before the vortex re-occurred. We now say that we are "between a rock and a hard place" or have to choose "a frying pan or the fire."

I suggest our version of Charybdis was the technology that could not wholly be resisted. I suspect that the Amish resisted more wisely than did we. They, at least, waited to accept more efficient farming and business technologies until they had reasonably well adapted them to serve some of their needs in ways that did not egregiously change their faithfulness. They could place telephone kiosks at the end of their driveways to avoid interrupting their interactions during meals, but I wonder whether they have tamed computers.

Of course, the tools that wonderfully extended the strength and reach of my elder's hands and the speed and power of their legs tempted them to exalt their self-sufficiency and pride, but that temptation had always existed and most of them had learned to resist it.

The more dangerous seductive power of this Charybdis lay in its alien *itness*. These mostly metallic tools shifted their attention to the *material* objects that obviously had to be manipulated. Unlike the oxen and horses that pulled their plows, tractors did not exude a subjective *presence* that had to be coddled or even respected. Tractors were soulless slaves. Even their maintenance demanded only that moving parts be oiled, belts tightened, gasoline be poured into tanks, and interconnected points be aligned to avoid unnecessary wear and tear. With the addition of many machines, to say nothing of chemical fertilizers and insecticides, their attention was increasingly focused on the It-world rather than the Thou-world of responsible responses to personal *presences*. Their worldview was being altered.

I return to *The Eclipse of Biblical Narrative* to explain the effects of farm machinery on how we read canonic texts. Even a simple harrow that can be pulled by a team of horses had come with a manual detailing its proper use, maintenance, and repair, and all technical manuals use an I-It rhetoric. It is profoundly ironic to remember that the twentieth-century Hebrew prophet, Martin Buber, whose *I and Thou* masterfully contrasted the *Thou* world and the *It* world and did so using a mythopoetic rhetoric.

Since the modern meanings of "literal" and "realistic" were constantly reinforced by the reading of technical manuals, many of my *Korn* elders, like

Bible-Belt fundamentalists, were unconsciously sucked into "modernist" interpretations that got built into "evangelical" descriptions of the "inspiration of the Bible." In short, Prof. Frei was urging that those who affirm "literal" readings of the Bible were becoming "modernists." Instead of using the images, metaphors, and parables that point beyond factual details to reveal the deeper truths of inter-relational initiatives and their dialogical responses that also stimulated continuing counter-responses that maintained their wrestling with the larger *presences* and the *Presence* of the Spirit of Truth and of "Our Father," they increasingly demanded that the Bible live "up" to the spirit of factual discourse and of ideological certainties instead of into the realistic and expanding biblical narrative.

Thus, I recognize that it was appropriate for the precocious Jewish boy, Ilya Prigogine, to mention archaeology along with other early fascinations before seriously studying chemistry and physics. And fortunately, history, philosophy, and other humane passions continued to motivate him until he, too, could fully understand that even the so-called "hard sciences" lead to wonders and mysteries so great that especially the investigation of the frontiers of the knowledge of the tiniest of the basic elements, like the vast outer reaches of an expanding Big-Bang, inspires the awe and wonder that returns truth-seekers to the childlikeness that allows them to enter the kingdom of Heaven.

A RESPONSE, A CONFESSION, AND A RESOLVE

In this book I have meditated on my pilgrimage to recover my heritage. I have also confessed my attempts to speak prophetically when I sensed that our churches were too easily succumbing to what seemed to be evangelistically or politically popular, whether or not it authentically reflected our historic testimony.

I have also eagerly sought to be "ecumenical" and to learn from other Christ-followers what would increase our faithfulness. Perhaps in the light of my attempts to reread Hans Frei's *Eclipse of Biblical Narrative*, it has occurred to me that I too may have departed from the realistic tradition that celebrated God's guidance by concentrating on the critical analysis of what I thought to be misguided attempts to grow God's kingdom or to be implicitly heretical. For example, even though 90 percent of the "letters to the editor" of our denominational magazine thanked me for having clarified what had also been troubling them, I realized that many did not write thoughtful responses to my long and critical "New Wineskins for Old Wine"; many readers assumed that I had a "dangerous mind." I had to accept that I had failed to be winsome.

    I have tried in this book to applaud what I have gained from my elders. However, in my late chapters I have again been critical of much of what has changed us. I have meditated on biblical passages that can liberate us from judgmentalism toward others or the fear that God is angry with us. Whether or not I become charming, I resolve to be welcoming.

A Glossary of Words for Which I Stipulate "Technical" Meanings

***Abstract* and *Concrete*.** The master metaphors that shape this book are *abstract* and *concrete*. The Latin noun *concretio* was used of organisms that mature and flourish. Its prefix implied the process of the growing together of its parts to form a unity larger than the sum of its parts. It secondarily was used of material that thickens, condenses, congeals. When a tooth is pulled out (extracted), it dies. When a young person acquires a spouse, the former "grown together" unity of the original nuclear family is disturbed, but an extended family can integrate individuals into clans, and into ethnic communities, cultures, and civilizations. Individual identities can be integrated into nexuses of relationships enhancing larger socio-political identities.

I trace the progressive growth or loss of order in cultures and civilizations by describing three sorts of abstraction. *Persons were abstracted—to specialize in functional abstractions—that became abstractly rationalized.* I recognize that polytheistic cultures tended to assume the endless cycling of ordering and disordering of very long cosmic epochs. Since the ancient Hebrews encountered a Creator with the loving patience of an ideal father, their canonic texts radically pictured an eschatologically fulfilled "new heaven and a new earth."

City*.** See ***Village*, *Town*, and *City.

***Congregare*.** As in *concretio* (see above), this Latin word combined a "together" with a noun. I had intended an ironic comparison with this word's use for herds of animals and flocks of birds. Fortunately, the continued use of *congregation*, perhaps especially in Catholic use of that term for holy orders, etc., led me away from stressing that chirping birds appropriately illustrated the stages of abstraction inherent in city *worship centers* as I note in chapter 9. *Church* had appropriately been derived from the Greek word for "the Lord," *Kyrios*.

Concrete. See **Abstract** and **Concrete**.

Corn and *Korn*. The later English word that became the name for the larger community was the German word for *grain*. Chapter 1 puzzles at length over its confused early history, and that chapter's excursus offers an interpretation of the confused history of its use of these names. I use the German *Korn* for the larger community that included a handful of churches affiliated with two closely related Mennonite denominations and Corn for its central village.

***Englisha* and gentiles.** Our ethnic community's colloquial Germanic expression for all the *them* who did not share our presumption of privileged *Usness*. I add that I have been so convinced that Hebrew rabbinical literature produced a loanword from the Greek word for *race, stock,* that it became the word for the many *them* that are "over against" each *Us*. To highlight this irony, I often spell *Gentile* with a lower case "g."

***Geist*.** I use this German word for *spirit, mind, soul* to emphasize the experienced *presence* of *Korn*'s "personality." Having grown up experiencing *Korn*'s patterns and attitudes, each of us reflected individualized versions of its identity along with its "common sense."

***Gottesfurcht* and *Gelassenheit*.** These German words profoundly expressed my elders' sense of their freedom to wrestle freely with the Creator who told Adam and Eve that they and all their heirs were to imitate God (Gen 1:26–28). They had learned that though expulsions from temporary "gardens of Eden" were painful, God's creative *Presence* continued with exiles. *Gelassenheit*, "let go and let God," expressed their faith that God was the sufficient condition who fulfilled what could never be fully *realized* on earth because their best efforts, though necessary, could never guarantee their success or even survival. The combination of these two words freed them to continue a "calling" that would otherwise have been so daunting that they would have been paralyzed. Instead, the cooperative energy of large work animals, of their neighbors, and of the natural and God-given energies of light, earth, air, and water often raised the labor of their bodies into the ecstasies of a dance expressing grateful praise.

Hairesis. The Greek verb from which this is derived meant *to take* or *to choose*. In the New Testament those who accepted the partial group of insights from which a particular theology was formed was called a *hairesis*. Pharisees, Sadducees, and early Christ-followers are examples of first-century *haireses*. Since each of these uses important truths, they can influence many to choose among them. The English word *heresies* now specifies ideologies deemed to be unorthodox.

Halig. As Joseph T. Shipley noted, *wealth* had emerged from the Anglo-Saxon *wela*, as had *well*. Similarly, *health* and *heal* had emerged from the Anglo-Saxon *hal*, as had *holy*. In each case, the meaning of the original root or roots must have been *wellbeing* (as in *commonwealth* and, by the fifteenth century, *wholesome*). I infer from this very long history that the original sense of what is wholly good eventually divided into what is material wealth, physical health, and spiritual holiness. To fix this in one's memory, I suggest that *hal-i* (holy) *-butt* (an Anglo-Saxon word for a flat or thick outside, as in *butt*ocks) names the holy flounder that was often favored for eating on Fridays when other meat was forbidden.[1]

Hof. This was our German word for *farmyards*, which I claimed in chapter 3 evoked the aura of its family and of the larger spirit or soul of *Korn*.

Korn. See **Corn and *Korn***.

Logos. The columns devoted to this entry in Bauer's *A Greek-English Lexicon of the New Testament and Other Early Christian Literature*[2] explain the complexity of this Greek word. The Gospel of John's prologue profoundly and poetically explores its theological importance. I begin with its first sentence, "In the beginning was the Word, and the Word was with God, and the Word was God." The creative power of God's *speaking* in Gen 1 implied also the wisdom, motives, plan, and workings that theologians, sages, poets, prophets and all the rest of us who continue to seek "enlightenment" and wholeness seek. John's prologue ended by proclaiming the personification of this "Word" in the world.

Mutuus. From this Latin word several words and concepts are derived that are basic for centering the chapters of my attempt to evoke the character and the meaning of *Korn*. Chapter 4 concentrates on the significant places and *times* that shaped *Korn*'s concrete identity. Chapters 5, 6, and 7 describe their mutual interactions with their ecology, with the mutual aid that sustained them, and the mutual nurture that inspired them to become grateful for a "promised land" nestled under the aura of God's canopy. Though few of them were likely to use two other words derived from *mutuus*, they recognized the creaturely limitations inherent in the constant changes, of a *mutable* world that inevitably produces *mutants*.

1. Shipley, *Dictionary of Word Origins*, 811.
2. Bauer, *Greek-English Lexicon*, 478–80.

Mythos. The Greek word for a story. Later enlightened Greek sages and philosophers understood that the stories chanted by bards like Homer pointed *truthfully* to what had been experienced from the primordial age when properly interpreted. Canonic *mythoi* clarified important truths about relationships with the supernatural, natural, human, and subhuman *presences* that shape lives and histories.

Presence, presences. See also *Hof*, where I noted that significant places, like concrete persons, project the influence and character of those who inhabit and shape them. So, also, the institutions and practices of cultures and nations and of civilizations project their *Geist* and the impress of their ethos so powerfully that New Testament passages personalize their *daimonic* powers in the expression "principalities and powers," whether or not living and concrete supernatural demons were thought to be literally influencing their rulers and "diseased" individuals needing to be healed, exorcized.

For example, a literal translation of the Greek phrase that is translated "the wiles of the devil" in Eph 6:11 speaks of the "*methodeias* [of the] *diabolou*." These *methods* are regularly described unfavorably and translators use "wiles" or "craftiness." *Diabolos* was the Greek word for *slander*, and with the article, *one who slanders*. But New Testament texts with the word often omit the article. John 6:70 and 13:2 speak of the one who betrayed Jesus as a *diabolos*, and John 13:27 says, though using the article, that *satan* entered him.

The Hebrew word *satan* named an adversary with a preceding article that was sometimes translated, "the adversary," the devil, though *demon* could also be used. However, Mark 8:33 reports Jesus saying to Peter, "Go behind me *satanas*" without using the article. Is the *human spirit* of slander and of antagonism being named? In his discussion of the word *satan*, Joseph T. Shipley says that this Hebrew word "refers to human adversaries; when it refers to the (fallen) angelic tempter, it is always The Adversary. This is usually translated *diabolus* (see devil) in the Vulgate, but in the New Testament Greek the usual form is *satanas* which is also used in the Vulgate and in English by Wyclif."[3] The gospel writer is saying that Peter's "satanic" thoughts are human thoughts. When he had responded to Jesus asking, "Who do you think that I am?" Peter had responded, "You are the Christ, the Son of the living God." In Matthew's longer response to his declaration than is given in Mark 8 or Luke 16, Jesus blessed Simon Peter, "For flesh and blood has not revealed this to you, but my Father who is in heaven." These Gospel texts insist that the concrete Creator can inspire Peter's truthful thoughts, but that this "satanic" thought had been human.

---

3. Shipley, *Dictionary of Word Origins*, 811.

I add that the Lord's Prayer given in Matthew ends with "but deliver us from evil" (Matt 6:7–13). The Greek phrase used in Matt 6:13 had been, "Deliver us from *tou diabolou*, using the genitive case with its appropriate article, which allows it to be translated either as "from the evil one" or with "from evil." Footnotes in study Bibles note this ambiguity and Matt 6:13 ends the Lord's Prayer with, "But deliver us from evil." Matthew's phrase also used the genitive case, but uses a more common New Testament word for wickedness so that it reads *tou ponērou*.

I used *daimonic* because this anglicizes the Greek word *daimōn* that meant *demon* or *evil spirit*. In the ancient polytheistic age, most peoples, *gentiles*, supposed that the realm of the demons was an intermediate level between high heavens (the Divine) and the earth. Like the *Korn* elders I admired, I too resist becoming fully acclimatized to the spirit of "this age," but I am reasonably content to join those who demythologize pagan myths.

Shalom. The Hebrew word for peace, which implies the concrete fulfillment of *presences* and of communities.

Theopoetic. This recently coined word refers to the kind of rhetoric that is appropriate for God, lesser gods, and other divine *presences*. It combines *theo*, God, with the English word *poetic*, which derives from the Greek word *poieō*, to make, to form. Since ancient Greeks assumed the basic physical elements that combine to form the cosmos were fire, air, water, and earth, these elements had been immortal, and they had no word for their creation. In early Christian literature, *poiēma* was formed to speak of the creation described in Gen 1. The rhetoric that allusively and symbolically points to the truth about significant relationships cannot be the factual or mathematical rhetoric that is appropriate to objective *its*. Martin Buber profoundly and poetically describes in *I and Thou* the "poetics" that expresses the music and message of our deep relationships.

Town. See **Village, Town, City**.

Ur. When acknowledging the importance of foundational texts in chapter two, I realized that preceding them there had been a long history of oral *mythoi* and legends that were distilled into what became *canonic*. The Old and New Testaments of the Bible were cherished by my elders, the great majority of whom had little or no awareness of this history. I quite arbitrarily decided to call them Ur Testaments. *Pretexts* might be more literally appropriate, but that coinage has unfortunate connotations.

The ancient Middle Eastern canonic *Enuma Elish*, that Gen 1 partly reedits and radically reinterprets, can help more of us to take more seriously the Ur texts of others. The heirs of the Hebraic-Christian tradition who have learned that God has always accompanied his children from all mythical "gardens of Eden" should want to trace the lessons of their pilgrimages to better discern our own.

Village, Town, City. The first glossary entry says that *concrete* and *abstract* were the metaphors guiding my meditations about *Korn*. My penultimate entry admits that *village*, *town*, and *city* became the metaphors that shaped my attempts to understand the concrete basic communities whose common sense and more or less *Halig Geist* guided many groups of elders to dream of building a lasting city. The trajectory of their histories led through the towns to which the first level of abstraction took them and where their heirs could systematically learn the arts and skills of the second levels of abstractions that produced the prosperity that gave them the means and the aspiration to explore the world. In time, the cities and civilizations they built inspired the vehicles that explore our solar system and the even more powerful telescopes, rockets, and energy receptors that allow us to contemplate the nature of outer spaces.

Indeed, humans had always explored the "heavens" hidden in their minds and souls. May we pay attention to build even in our world what *realizes* that for which we dream, that *faiths* that for which we hope, and that *lovingly embraces* all of the "fellow travelers" we encounter.

Yisra-el. My stubbornly Germanic, gentile, early twentieth-century elders identified themselves with ancient Israelites. But with whom and what did Hebrew heirs identify? After wrestling all night with a strange *presence*, the Jacob who was the son of Isaac who was the son of Abraham was renamed Israel. In Hebrew *Yisra* meant "to wrestle," *El* named the Creator God who in Genesis was called *Elohim* using the plural form that identified the divine father with all the heirs who continue to wrestle with God. I don't know whether any of my *Korn* elders had heard any of these Hebrew etymologies, but their sometimes clumsy actions spoke more eloquently than did their words.

For gentile, polytheistic, neighbors of Christ-followers after the Roman general Constantine had dragged his army through a pond and Christianized the Roman empire, it had been natural to conceive of demons, and to rely on a wrathful God to oppose a personalized devil named Satan. But neither the New Testament texts I explored in the glossary to this point nor the New Testament passages that refer to "rulers and authorities" or in the phrase translated "principalities and powers" do I find an important angel of light named Lucifer who had at some point become a fallen "Satan."

I urge readers to read carefully the classic New Testament passages that describe *presences* or *quasi-presences* responsible for a world created good but corrupted. These are Rom 8:36–39; Eph 1:11–14; 3:7–13; Col 1:15–20; 2:8–15; and Titus 3:1–10. For a full scholarly exegesis, I recommend Walter Wink's three-volume masterpiece: *Naming the Powers*, *Unmasking the Powers*, and *Confronting the Powers*. His later book, *The Powers that Be*, summarizes the trilogy.

Bibliography

Achtemeier, Paul J., ed. *Harper's Bible Dictionary*. San Francisco: Harper and Row, 1985.

Allen, Rosie, et al. "Long-Term Mental Health Impacts of the Covid-19 Pandemic on University Students in the UK: A Longitudinal Analysis over 12 Months." *British Journal of Educational Studies* 71:6 (2023): 585–608. https://doi.org/10.1080/00071005.2023.2215857.

Arndt, William E., and F. Wilbur Gingrich. *A Greek-English Lexicon of the New Testament and Other Early Christian Literature*. Chicago: University of Chicago Press, 1978.

Auerbach, E. *Mimesis: The Representation of Reality in Western Literature*. Princeton: Princeton University Press, 1953.

Bauer, Walter. *A Greek-English Lexicon of the New Testament and Other Early Christian Literature*. University of Chicago Press, 2000.

Bergson, Henri. *An Introduction to Metaphysics*. Indianapolis: Hackett, 1999.

Berry, Wendell. "Renewing Husbandry." *Orion*, Sept. 2, 2005. https://orionmagazine.org/article/renewing-husbandry/.

Bloom, Allan, and Adam Kirsch. *The Republic of Plato*. Vol. 2. New York: Basic Books, 1968.

Buber, Martin. *I and Thou*. New York: Scribners, 1970.

Cary, M., et al. *Oxford Classical Dictionary*. Oxford: Clarendon, 1949.

Cruden, Alexander. *Cruden's Complete Concordance to the Old and New Testaments*. Grand Rapids: Zondervan, 1967.

Dante, and John D. Sinclair. *The Divine Comedy of Dante Alighieri*. Translated by John D. Sinclair. New York: Oxford University Press, 1961.

Dueck, Alvin C., and Kevin Reimer. *A Peaceable Psychology: Christian Therapy in a World of Many Cultures*. Grand Rapids: Brazos, 2009.

England, Jeremy L. "Statistical Physics of Self-Replication." *The Journal of Chemical Physics* 139:12 (2013). https://pubs.aip.org/aip/jcp/article/139/12/121923/74793.

Fiala, Andrew. "The Past Seems So Much Better Than Today: But Nostalgia is like a Fading Sunset." *Fresno Bee*, June 25, 2023. https://ground.news/article/the-past-seems-so-much-better-than-today-but-nostalgia-is-like-a-fading-sunset?utm_source=headline-link&utm_medium=share.

Finkelstein, Israel, and Neil Asher Silberman. *The Bible Unearthed: Archaeology's New Vision of Ancient Israel and the Origin of Sacred Texts*. New York: Simon and Schuster, 2002.

Frei, Hans. *Eclipse of Biblical Narrative: A Study in Eighteenth and Nineteenth Century Hermeneutics*. New Haven: Yale University Press, 1974.

Friesen, Abraham. *In Defense of Privilege: Russian Mennonites and the State Before and During World War I.* Winnipeg: Kindred, 2006.

Friesen, John Stanley. *Missionary Responses to Tribal Religions at Edinburgh, 1910.* Vol. 1. New York: Peter Lang, 1996.

Gillette, Ned. "Trekking around the Continent's Highest Peak." *National Geographic,* 156:1, July 1979.

Goertz, Jack R. *Sophie's Story.* Bremerton, WA: Self-published, 2004.

Graduate School of Education and Human Development at George Washington University. "History and Evolution of Public Education in the US." Center on Education Policy. 2020. https://files.eric.ed.gov/fulltext/ED606970.pdf.

Hawking, Stephen. *A Brief History of Time: From Big Bang to Black Holes.* New York: Random House, 2009.

Homer. *The Odyssey.* Translated by Emily Wilson. New York: Norton. 2018.

Hunter, James Davison. *The Death of Character: Moral Education in an Age without Good or Evil.* New York: Basic Books, 2008.

———. "The Denial of the Moral as Lived Experience." *The Hedgehog Review,* May 2024.

James, William. "The Dilemma of Determinism." In *The Will to Believe and Other Essays in Popular Philosophy,* 145–83. Boston: Harvard University Press, 1956.

Johnston, W. Marshall, and Daniel J. Crosby, eds. *A Dangerous Mind: The Ideas and Influence of Delbert L. Wiens.* Eugene, OR: Wipf & Stock, 2015.

Joy, Charles R. *Harper's Topical Concordance.* New York: Harper and Row, 1976.

King, Leonard W., ed. *Enuma Elish: The Seven Tablets of Creation; The Babylonian and Assyrian Legends Concerning the Creation.* San Diego: Book Tree, 1999.

Klaassen, Martin. *Geschichte der wehrlosen Taufgesinnten Gemeinden von den Zeiten der Apostel bis auf die Gegenwart.* Danzig: Groening, 1873.

Klaassen, Walter. *Anabaptist: Neither Catholic nor Protestant.* Waterloo, ON: Conrad Grebel, 1973.

Kline, D. *Great Possessions: An Amish Farmer's Journal.* San Francisco: North Point, 1990.

Krahn, Cornelius, and Richard D. Thiessen. "Klaassen, Michael (1860-1934)." *Global Anabaptist Mennonite Encyclopedia Online.* Updated Feb. 2007. https://gameo.org/index.php?title=Klaassen,_Michael_(1860-1934)&oldid=92309.

Leontiev, D. A. "Ilya Prigogine and the Psychology of XXI Century." *Psikhologicheskii zhurnal* 39:3 (2018) 5–14. https://doi.org/10.7868/S0205959218030017.

Liddell, H. G., and R. Scott. *Greek-English Lexicon.* Oxford: Clarendon, 1968.

Loewen, Jacob. "A Personal Reaction to 'New Wineskins for Old Wine.'" *Christian Leader,* 1966, 4–6.

MacIntyre, Alasdair. *After Virtue.* Edinburgh: A&C Black, 2013.

Mastroianni, Adam M., and Daniel T. Gilbert. "The Illusion of Moral Decline." *Nature* 618 (2023): 782–789. https://www.nature.com/articles/s41586-023-06137-x.

McLuhan, Marshall. "The Medium Is the Message (1964)." In *Crime and Media,* 20-31. Routledge, 2019.

Middleton, Conyers. "An Essay on the Allegorical and Literal Interpretation of the Creation and Fall of Man." In *The Miscellaneous Works of the Late Reverend and Learned Conyers Middleton,* [121–131]. London: Manby and Cox, 1752.

Needham, Joseph. "Science and Society in East and West." *Science & Society* 28:4 (Fall 1964) 385–408.

Niebuhr, H. Richard. *The Responsible Self: An Essay in Christian Moral Philosophy*. New York: Harper and Row, 1978.

Penner, Lloyd Chester. "The Mennonites on the Washita River: The Culmination of Four Centuries of Migrations." EdD diss., Oklahoma State University, 1976.

Popper, Karl R. *The Open Universe: An Argument for Indeterminism*. Vol. 2. London: Psychology Press, 1988.

Potok, Chaim. *My Name Is Asher Lev*. Milwaukee, WI: Anchor, 1972.

Prigogine, Ilya. *The End of Certainty: Time, Chaos, and the New Laws of Nature*. New York: Free Press, 1997.

Quiring, Horst, and Richard D. Thiessen. "Klaassen, Martin (1820-1881)." *Global Anabaptist Mennonite Encyclopedia Online*. Updated Feb. 2007. https://gameo.org/index.php?title=Klaassen,_Martin_(1820-1881)&oldid=145573.

Race Forward. "Historical Timeline of Public Education in the US." Reports: Education. Accessed June 14, 2024. https://www.raceforward.org/reports/education/historical-timeline-public-education-us.

Rauschenbusch, Walter, and Ira Sankey. *Evangeliums Lieder (Gospel Songs)*. New York: Biglow and Main, 1897.

Rose, Herbert Jennings. "Household." In *The Oxford Classical Dictionary*, edited by M. Cary et al., 960–1. Oxford: Oxford University Press, 1949.

———. "Worship." In *The Oxford Classical Dictionary*, edited by M. Cary et al., 960. Oxford: Oxford University Press, 1949.

Shipley, Joseph T. *Dictionary of Word Origins*. 2nd ed. New York: Philosophical Library, 1945.

Simpson, D. F. *Cassell's New Latin – English Dictionary*. New York: Funk and Wagnalls, 1959.

Snow, Charles Percy. *The Two Cultures*. Cambridge: Cambridge University Press, 2012.

Strong, James. *The Exhaustive Concordance of the Bible: Showing Every Word of the Text of the Common English Version of the Canonical Books, and Every Occurrence of Each Word In Regular Order; Together with a Comparative Concordance of the Authorized and Revised Versions, Including the American Variations; also Brief Dictionaries of the Hebrew and Greek Words of the Original, with References to the English Words*. Vol. 1. New York: Abingdon, 1890.

Swartley, Willard, and Donald B. Kraybill. *Building Communities of Compassion*. Scottdale, PA: Herald, 1998.

Toews, Paul. "New Wineskins for Old Wine: A Fifty-Year Retrospective." In *A Dangerous Mind: The Ideas and Influence of Delbert L. Wiens*, edited by W. Marshall Johnston and Daniel J. Crosby, 36–59. Eugene, OR: Wipf & Stock, 2015.

Walzer, Michael. *Thick and Thin: Moral Argument at Home and Abroad*. Notre Dame, IN: University of Notre Dame Press, 1994.

Webster, Noah. *Webster's New Universal Unabridged Dictionary*. Deluxe 2nd ed. New York: Simon and Schuster, 1979.

Weisberg, David B. "Cyrus II." In *Harper's Bible Dictionary*, edited by Paul J. Achtemeier, 3–17. San Francisco: Harper and Row, 1985.

Whitehead, Alfred North. *Process and Reality*. New York: Simon and Schuster, 2010.

Wiebe, Vernon. *Come Let's Stand United: A History of Corn Academy 1902-1977*. Hillsboro, KS: Mennonite Heritage, 1977.

———. *Corn Is Born: An Incomplete History of Dutch-German Settlement in Western Oklahoma*. Self-Published. 1993.

Wiens, Delbert. "From the Village to the City: A Grammar for the Languages We Are." *Direction* 2:4 (1973) 98–149.

———. "The Making of Sages, Philosophers, and Theologians." In *The Seminary Story: Twenty Years of Education in Ministry, 1955–1975*, edited by A. J. Klassen, 99–102. Fresno, CA: Mennonite Brethren Biblical Seminary, 1975.

———. "New Wineskins for Old Wine: A Study of the Mennonite Brethren Church." *The Christian Leader* (October, 1965) 3–24. https://www.academia.edu/8957101/New_Wineskins_for_Old_Wine.

Wink, Walter. *Engaging the Powers*. Vol. 3. Minneapolis: Fortress, 2017.

———. *Naming the Powers: The Language of Power in the New Testament*. Vol. 1. Philadelphia: Fortress, 1984.

———. *The Powers That Be: Theology for a New Millennium*. San Jose, CA: Harmony, 2010.

———. *Unmasking the Powers: The Invisible Forces That Determine Human Existence*. Vol. 2. Philadelphia: Fortress, 1984.

Wolchover, N. "First Support for a Physics Theory of Life." *Quanta Magazine*, 2017. https://www.quantamagazine.org/first-support-for-a-physics-theory-of-life-20170726/.#

www.ingramcontent.com/pod-product-compliance
Lightning Source LLC
Chambersburg PA
CBHW062008220426
43662CB00010B/1268